THE MESSENGER IN THE ANCIENT SEMITIC WORLD

HARVARD SEMITIC MUSEUM

HARVARD SEMITIC MONOGRAPHS

edited by
Frank Moore Cross

Number 45
The Messenger in the Ancient Semitic World

by
Samuel A. Meier

Samuel A. Meier

THE MESSENGER IN THE ANCIENT SEMITIC WORLD

Scholars Press
Atlanta, Georgia

The Messenger in the Ancient Semitic World

by
Samuel A. Meier

The author gratefully acknowledges the financial support of the following in the publication of his work:

Melton Center for Jewish Studies,
The Ohio State University

College of Humanities,
The Ohio State University

Office of Research and Graduate Study,
The Ohio State University

Library of Congress Cataloging in Publication Data

Meier, Sam.
The messenger in the ancient Semitic world / by Sam Meier.
p. cm. --(Harvard Semitic monographs ; no. 45)
Bibliography: p.
Includes index.
ISBN 1-555-40289-5 (alk. paper)
1. Messengers--Assyria. 2. Messengers--Iraq--Babylonia--History.
3. Messengers--Iraq--History--Sources. I. Title. II. Series.
HE9756.I72M45 1989
383'.145--dc19 88-31164

Printed in the United States of America
on acid-free paper

To my parents

Contents

Preface

The research represented here originally resulted in a dissertation presented to the faculty of Harvard University in 1986. Much of it has since been reworked, and additional data have been incorporated.

I am grateful to Prof. Frank Moore Cross, Jr. for his invitation to publish this work in the Harvard Semitic Monograph Series. My tutelage under his guidance, as well as under Professors William L. Moran, Paul Hanson, Thomas O. Lambdin, Michael Coogan and Piotr Steinkeller, was far too brief, and I am grateful for the horizons which they opened for me. Their influence can be seen throughout the present work, but its shortcomings must be seen as slips of my pen.

I extend my thanks to the Melton Center for Jewish Studies and the College of Humanities at the Ohio State University for their financial support in assisting with the publication of this book.

ABBREVIATIONS

The versification of the Massoretic text has been emloyed throughout. Abbreviations are essentially those found in the "Instructions for Contributors," *Journal of Biblical Literature* 95 (1976) 331-346, or in R. Borger, *Handbuch der Keilschrift-literatur*, Vol. 2 (Berlin: Walter de Gruyter, 1975) xi-xxxii. In addition, the following abbreviations also appear:

AASOR XVI	R.H. Pfeiffer and E.A. Speiser, *One Hundred New Selected Nuzi Texts*. *AASOR* 16. New Haven: 1936.
Apla.	G. Dossin, "Aplahanda, roi de Carchemish," *RA* 35 (1938) 115-121.
Anzu	B. Hruška, *Der Mythenadler Anzu in Literatur und Vorstellung des alten Mesopotamien*. Budapest: 1975.
Asmar	R. Whiting, *Old Babylonian Letters from Tell Asmar*. *AS* 22. Chicago: Oriental Institute, 1987.
CTH	E. Laroche, *Catalogue des textes hittites*. Paris: Éditions Klincksieck, 1971.
DN	Divine name
DS 28	Fragment 28 in H. Güterbock, "The Deeds of Šuppiluliuma as Told by His Son, Muršili II," *JCS* 10 (1956) 75-130.
EA 24	English translation courtesy of W. Moran, who was provided with a German translation courtesy of C. Wilhelm.
EE	*Enuma Elish*

ELA T. Jacobsen, "Enmerkar and the Lord of Aratta," *The Harps that Once . . .: Sumerian Poetry in Translation* (New Haven: Yale, 1987) 280-319. Sumerian cited from S. Cohen, *Enmerkar and the Lord of Aratta* (Unpublished Ph.D. dissertation, University of Pennsylvania, 1973).

Emar D. Arnaud, *Emar - Textes sumériens et accadiens*. 3 Volumes. Paris: Recherche sur les Civilizations, 1985-1986.

EnEn A. Berlin, *Enmerkar and Ensuhkešdanna*. Philadelphia: University Museum, 1979.

GN Geographical Name

Halaf J. Friedrich, G. R. Meyer, A. Ungnad, E. F. Weidner, *Die Inschriften vom Tell Halaf. AfO Beiheft 6*. Berlin: 1940.

Hermopolis J. C. L. Gibson, *Textbook of Syrian Semitic Inscriptions II - Aramaic Inscriptions*. Oxford: Clarendon, 1975. Pp.125-143.

IE G. Farber-Flügge, *Der Mythos "Inanna und Enki" unter besonderer Berücksichtigung der Liste der ME. Studia Pohl* 10. Rome: Biblical Institute, 1973.

KTU M. Dietrich, O. Loretz, and J. Sanmartín, *Die Keilalphabetischen Texte aus Ugarit. AOAT* 24/1. Neukirchen-Vluyn: Neukirchener, 1976.

Lex. Aeg. Wolfgang Helck & Eberhard Otto, eds., *Lexikon der Ägyptologie*. Wiesbaden: Harrasowitz, 1972-.

Lugal-e J. van Dijk, *LUGAL UD ME-LÁM-bi NIR-GÁL*. Vol.1. Leiden: E. J. Brill, 1983.

Lú-dingir-ra	M. Civil, "The 'Message of Lú-dingir-ra to His Mother' and a Group of Akkado-Hittite 'Proverbs'," *JNES* 23 (1964) 1-11; M. Çiğ & S. N. Kramer, "The Ideal Mother: A Sumerian Portrait," *Belleten* 40 (1976) 413-421.
M.A.R.I.	*Mari Annales de Recherches Interdisciplinaires*.
MB	Middle Babylonian
MBLETU	O. R. Gurney, *The Middle Babylonian Legal and Economic Texts from Ur*. Oxford: Alden, 1983.
Nabop.	Nabopolassar
NA	Neo-Assyrian
NB	E. Ebeling, *Neubabylonische Briefe*. *ABAW* 30: 1949.
NBU	E. Ebeling, *Neubabylonische Briefe aus Uruk*. *Beiträge zur Keilschriftforschung und Religionsgeschichte des Vorderen Orients* 3 (1930-1934).
OAss	Old Assyrian
OB	Old Babylonian
OBTIV	S. Greengus, *Studies in Old Babylonian Texts from Ischali and Vicinity*. *Bibliotheca Mesopotamica* 19; Malibu, Undena, 1986.
PDK	E. Weidner, *Politische Dokumente aus Kleinasien*. *Boghazkoi Studien* 8,9. Leipzig: J.C. Hinrichs, 1923.
PN	Personal Name

ROMCT — G. J. P McEwen, *The Late Babylonian Tablets in the Royal Ontario Museum. ROM Cuneiform Texts* II. Toronto, Canada: Royal Ontario Museum, 1982.

SANE — *Sources from the Ancient Near East.* Malibu: Undena.

SLA — R. Pfeiffer, *State Letters of Assyria. AOS 6.* New Haven: American Oriental Society, 1935.

STT 28 — O. R. Gurney, "The Sultantepe Tablets," *AnSt* 10 (1960) 105-131.

Sud — M. Civil, "Enlil and Ninlil: The Marriage of Sud," *JAOS* 103 (1983) 43-66.

Shulgi A — J. Klein, *Three Shulgi Hymns*. Ramat-Gan, Israel: Bar-Ilan University, 1981

Shulgi B & C — G. R. Castellino, *Two Šulgi Hymns. Studi Semitici* 42. Rome: Istituto di studi del vicino Oriente, 1972.

Streck — Maximilian Streck, *Assurbanipal und die letzten assyrischen Könige bis zum Untergang Ninevehs. VAB* VII. Leipzig: 1916.

SV — J. Friedrich, *Staatsverträge des Hatti-Reiches in hethitischer Sprache. MVAG* 31 (1926); 34 (1934).

TCAE — J. Postgate, *Taxation and Conscription in the Assyrian Empire. Studia Pohl Series Maior* 3. Rome: Biblical Institute, 1974.

TFS — S. Dalley & J. N. Postgate, *The Tablets from Fort Shalmaneser*. Oxford: Alden, 1984.

TR S. Dalley, C. B. Walker, J. D. Hawkins, *The Old Babylonian Tablets from Tell Al Rimah*. London: British School of Archaeology in Iraq, 1976.

UL *Utukki Lemnuti* - R. C. Thompson, *The Devils and Evil Spirits of Babylonia*. London: Luzac & Co., 1903-4.

Wenamun Translation of H. Goedicke, *The Report of Wenamun*. Baltimore and London: Johns Hopkins University, 1975.

INTRODUCTION

This study is intended as a format to collect and sift a part of the considerable data available from the ancient Near East with regard to messenger activity. Such a pursuit is facilitated by anthropological data in the field of communication and diplomacy in primitive societies,[1] and by the availability of landmarks penned by Valloggia for Egypt[2] and, a bit further afield, Mosley for Greece.[3] For the Semitic world, only a few brief articles[4] and a dissertation[5] have dedicated themselves to the subject. This is a

[1] R. Numelin, *The Beginnings of Diplomacy*, (Copenhagen: Ejnar Munksgaard, 1950).

[2] M. Valloggia, *Recherche sur les "messagers" (wpwtyw) dans les sources égyptiennes profanes* (II Hautes Études Orientales 6; Genève-Paris: Librairie Droz, 1976).

[3] D. Mosley, *Envoys and Diplomacy in Ancient Greece* (Wiesbaden: Franz Steiner, 1973). The results of this study were incorporated in a broader formulation in F. Adcock and D. Mosley, *Diplomacy in Ancient Greece* (London: Thames and Hudson, 1975).

[4] J. Munn-Rankin, "Diplomacy in Western Asia in the Early Second Millennium B.C.," *Iraq* 18 (1956) 68-110; R. Follet, "Deuxième bureau et information diplomatique dans l'Assyrie des Sargonids - quelques notes," *RSO* 32 (1957) 61-81; V. Korošec, "Relations internationales d'après les lettres de Mari," *La Civilization de Mari* (XVe Rencontre Assyriologique Internationale; Paris: Société d'Édition "Belles Lettres", 1967) 139-149; A. Crown, "Tidings and Instructions: How News Travelled in the Ancient Near East," *JESHO* 17 (1974) 244-271; Y. Holmes, "The Messengers of the Amarna Letters," *JAOS* 75 (1975) 376-381.

[5] J. Greene, *The Old Testament Prophet as Messenger in the Light of Ancient Near Eastern Messengers and Messages* (Unpublished Ph.D. dissertation, Boston University, 1980). This work's shortcoming

remarkable phenomenon in so far as one of the crucial sources which are available to us is the vast corpus of letters testifying to a vigorous communication network. The study of letters is intense, while those who carried them are relatively neglected.

This work is not intended as a thorough analysis of all messengers[6] but is confined only to the *mal'āk* of the West Semitic world and the *mār šipri* of Akkadian (down to the Persian period[7]). We do not deny that there is considerable overlap among various messenger figures, and at times we will make reference to other messenger types for illustrative purposes and to suggest alternatives when other direct evidence fails. But for the sake of stabilizing this study with clearly defined boundaries, we limit our

---

lies in failing to work from original sources and in treating too briefly its major focus: only five pages are devoted to Sumerian messengers, four pages to Babylonian, five to Assyrian, four to Hittite, three to Ugaritan, eighteen to Egyptian - the entire Sumero-Hamito-Semitic-Indo-European complexion of Near Eastern messengers is analyzed in the space of some forty pages.

[6] The diversity of messenger figures attested in Mesopotamian sources - *lāsimu*, *ṣubāru*, *šipru*, *rakbu*, *qurbūtu*, *āliku*, *allāku*, *ālikānu*, *sukkalu*, *našparu*, *mubassiru*, *nāgiru* - necessitates an analysis of each figure in its right. We have chosen the most generalized and long-lived term from Mesopotamia to correspond with the equally generalized Hebrew term. The translation of both is equally problematic, and ultimately context-sensitive: "envoy", "messenger", "representative", "ambassador", "agent" all may comfortably apply depending on the situation. The equivalency of the two terms will become clear in the discussion to follow. The simultaneous discussion of the two terms is motivated by the complementary nature of the data supplied by each, as well as the desire to envigorate biblical studies with significant data which as yet remains unsifted.

[7] This is a boundary set by the biblical material, as well as being the period in which occur the penultimate appearances of the *mār šipri* in Semitic sources. Post-Persian attestations of the *mār šipri* are poorly documented; note G. McEwan, *Priest and Temple in Hellenistic Babylonia* (*Freiburger Altorientalische Studien* 4; Wiesbaden: Franz Steiner, 1981) 63-66.

primary discussion only to these two figures.[8] A corollary of this specific investigation is that there may be many messenger figures who bore the designation *mār šipri* who will slip between our fingers simply because they are not so designated in our source material.[9]

Although the messenger can be documented in a spectrum of activities,[10] we propose to investigate in detail the messenger as he fulfills one aspect of his duties as a *mār šipri* or *mal'āk*, namely his role as a mediator of communication. The *mār šipri* functions in a variety of environments (the data and sources for the *mal'āk* in this regard being by contrast limited). He is not only a bearer of messages, for he transports goods and is active in the market place. In addition to being identified as a *mār šipri*

---

[8] We have also excluded the *šipru* as a specific target of research. This is a designation which, although occurring elsewhere, is attested primarily in the Old Assyrian material. We do not deny the clear connection between the *mār šipri* and the *šipru* (see below), but our preliminary investigation of the sizable body of Old Assyrian evidence has revealed too many peculiarities and distinctives which would prompt an independent analysis. The small portion of the Kultepe material which has been published further inhibits any attempt at thoroughness in this regard.

[9] For example, it is clear that the OB Mari administration, although frequently identifying foreign envoys as *mārī šipri*, characteristically designated its own messengers from Mari as servants (*wardū*) of the king, less frequently calling them *mārī šipri* (e.g. *ARM* VI 79; XIV 126). But not every *wardu* is a messenger. Mari also preserves texts where men from various locales are simply called "man (*lú*) from GN" while others in these same lists are explicitly called *mār šipri* (e.g. *ARM* XXII.151,274). But other texts employ the epithet *mār šipri* as a comprehensive term encompassing all types of foreign visitors (*ARM* XXIII.243).

[10] "Le *mal'āk* est le transmetteur de messages, l'espion, l'auteur d'actions aussi disparates que la destruction d'une armée, le fait d'amener une femme ou de tirer quelqu'un d'une citerne" (J.-L. Cunchillos, "*La'ika*, *mal'āk* et *mĕlā'kāh* en semitique nord-occidental," *Rivista di Studi Fenici* 10 [1982] 160).

when serving as a witness to legal transactions,[11] he may be found in court itself as a part of the legal process,[12] appearing there in order to defend those whom he represents[13] or even his own activity as a messenger outside the court.[14]

---

[11] *MDP* XXII 162.34 163.24; *MDP* XXIII 174.23 175.22 176.22 323.8; *ARM* VIII 67.10'; *VS* VI 43.31; *ROMCT* 34.16-17; *YOS* VI 145.23.

[12] In 1436 B.C., Dayyan-Marduk's messenger, Ili-iddina, is involved in settling a court dispute (H. Petschow, *Mittelbabylonische Rechts- und Wirtschaftsurkunden der Hilprecht-Sammlung Jena* [*ASAW* 64/4; Leipzig: 1974] 13). He is not a claimant or litigator but functions with the judge in overturning a ruling regarding witnesses. Is his status as a messenger significant for his role in court? The one whom he serves as a messenger has no discernible involvement in the case. Note the "messenger of the judges" apparently representing the judges who arbitrated an earlier case regarding borrowed grain (*VS* VI 43.31). A poorly preserved judicial decree in Akkadian found at Ugarit records the seals of two Hittite messengers, one of whom is well-known as an international envoy (*PRU* IV 106; for Tiliteshub, see *CTH* 158,163 *KBo* XXVIII 8,14 and the Karnak treaty introduction discussed in E. Edel, "Die Teilnehmer der ägyptisch-hethitischen Friedengesandschaft im 21. Jahr Ramses' II," [*Or* 38 (1969) 177-186] 181-182).

[13] At Nuzi, Hutiya, son of Kushiya, is identified as a royal *mār šipri* (*HSS* XIII 363.66,81). He appears more than once in court representing the palace, and even though he is never identified there as a *mār šipri*, the designation may nevertheless have been appropriate: "In place of Shilwateshub the prince, he has sent me (*ištapranni*) to plead his case" (*HSS* IX 8.2-3 12.3-4). When Hutiya wins the case, it is the prince who despatched him who benefits: "Hutiya won the case and the judges made PN pay 33 yokes and one ox to Shilwateshub" (*HSS* 8.32-35 12.37-40).

[14] In thirteenth century B.C. Ur, a messenger is taken to court by one who claims that he gave a live ox to the messenger for delivery but that the messenger disposed of the ox *en route*; the messenger claims that he never received the ox (*MBLETU* 9). Compare the later messenger held guiltless (as far as the preserved document is concerned) when his prisoner escapes while the person who captured the runaway is guilty when he escapes the second time (*YOS* VII 146).

The profile of our source material is responsible for much of this diversity. We intend to employ all epigraphic and literary data available, being aware that various genres may skew the portrait which emerges. The investigation of administrative, pedagogical, epistolary, or literary texts requires sensitivity to cultural, geographical and functional variables. For example, the weight of data from royal archives tips the scale toward a view of messenger activity on the highest social level. And even here there is diversity in points of view now available to us. The royal archives of Bogazkoy and Amarna in the latter half of the second millennium B.C. preserve the correspondence of kings and queens themselves, with messengers rubbing shoulders with royalty, intimately involved in negotiations which change the course of history. Judging by personal names in these contexts, the messengers in one's employ are generally natives of one's own country, although it is not unknown (though still rare) for one bearing a foreign name to be despatched as envoy to the land where the name he bears is indigenous.[15]

From Old Babylonian Mari, information about individual messengers comes primarily from texts generated within the administration of one kingdom. These letters and administrative texts describe a phenomenon similar to that known at Amarna and Bogazkoy, but do so as outsiders not involved in the inner circle. Where we can see the king's pleasure or wrath exhibited toward individual messengers in the Middle Babylonian material, these OB texts preserve for the most part the external routines which comprise the messenger's world outside the presence of the monarch. To a degree unparalleled in MB material, the OB texts show us the messenger on the road.

---

[15] Hattushili's Hittite messenger, Riamashi, bears a transparent Egyptian name (E. Edel, "Neue keilschriftliche Umschreibungen ägyptischer Namen aus den Boǧazköytexten," *JNES* 7 [1948] 17-19). From the beginning of the first millennium B.C., a Canaanite messenger commemorated by an Egyptian inscription bears an Egyptian name although his father bore a Canaanite name (Valloggia, *Recherche*, 188-189).

The archives at Nuzi[16] in the Hurrian sphere present yet another perspective of messenger activity as seen in the lives of specific messengers: messengers in the royal service do not walk with international stature but are themselves an essential component of the internal bureaucracy of the kingdom. In particular, messengers are involved in the transfer of movable properties, many in the queen's service where they are responsible for grain transfers from the royal inventory to other individuals and cities.[17] These individuals are messengers "of the palace" (*ša ekalli*[18]), unlike the OB and MB designations, "messenger of my brother/sister" or "messenger of (the man/king of) GN". It is less common when a perspective emerges in the second millennium B.C. which is untouched by the hand of royalty. Even evidence of identifiable non-royal messengers may be recorded in royal contexts (e.g. the king receives gifts from them[19] or adjudicates cases in which they are involved).[20]

All three of these second millennium contexts picture the possibility of a messenger serving for extended periods of time in this capacity, whether it be within a kingdom's bureaucracy or on the international level. Furthermore, the data on the international level indicate that a messenger to major powers tended to be country-specific. Although the possibility exists of ambassadors at large, the individuals investigated did not dilute their abilities or rapport in a specific culture by travelling officially to several major powers. Indeed, both MB and OB (to a lesser extent) material testify that even a messenger's escort from his host country would accompany him on several trips, enhancing this bond.

---

[16] For an introduction to individuals explicitly identified as *mārī šipri* at Nuzi, see W. Mayer, *Nuzi-Studien* (*AOAT* 205/1; Neukirchen: Neukirchener, 1978) 161-164.

[17] *HSS* XIV 129.7 130.9 134.9 139.4-9 150.7-8 159.9 161.9.

[18] *HSS* XIII 54.9; XIV 129.7 159.9. If the transcription of *HSS* XIII 363 can be trusted, enough of the sign was legible to apply the title *mār šipri ša šarri*(?) to the messenger Hutiya (cf. 1.66,81).

[19] E. F. Weidner, "Aus den Tagen eines assyrischen Schattenkönigs," *AfO* 10 (1935-1936) 37.

[20] *MBLETU* 9.

Identifiable Neo-Assyrian messengers appear in contexts very much like that of Mari, where the data stem from the internal administration of empire. Unlike Mari, however, Assyrian archives seem to have preserved texts[21] not only of arriving and forwarded messengers but of Assyrian messengers available for employment by the palace.[22]

In the first millennium, the nature of the source material allows us to meet large numbers of individual messengers outside of a specifically royal environment. The status of those who employ them is not always certain, but one now finds many messengers in the service of temple officials or independent entrepreneurs. No longer do royal perspectives dominate (although still present) as economic texts convey an impression of messengers as primarily agents and representatives with veritable power of attorney. Two parties may be represented by two messengers who themselves are responsible for an economic transaction messenger to messenger.[23] Messengers could have their own independent status within the bureaucracy at the

[21] *ABL* 627 preserves the names of five messengers bearing Babylonian names and is unusual on several counts: it explicitly names the messengers in a group, records a large number of messengers in one context, identifies patronymics for most of the messengers, and gives no reference to their origin (no suffix such as *mārī šiprīšu/šunu*). Is this a document authenticating messengers or an administrative tablet (no total is given)?

[22] A fragmentary eighth century Nimrud list mentions *mārū šipri utrū* ("reserve"(?); B. Parker, "Administrative Tablets from the North-west Palace, Nimrud," [*Iraq* 23 (1961) 15-67] 15). Only four of the original seven names remain, all of which are good Assyrian names and consequently represent messengers of the Assyrian administration, in contrast to Mari which recorded lists of visiting messengers. The fact that such a list existed in which individuals within the administration were identified as messengers suggests a clearly defined pool of men who could fulfill this role.

[23] *YOS* VI 22.

highest levels,[24] as those who send other messengers are also despatched as messengers themselves.[25]

In focusing upon the messenger as he performs his task as a message-bearer, our intention is to follow the messenger chronologically from beginning to end: from the time he is selected for the task up to the time he is sent back to the one who originally despatched him. We are specifically interested in the messenger himself - his behavior, what others expect of him, how he is treated, what he expects of others. Consequently, our objective is not to treat all aspects of long distance communication,[26] but only those which bear specifically upon the messenger in his performance of this one task.[27]

This work is thus not an exhaustive study of the *mal'āk* or the *mār šipri* in general. The boundaries which we have established exclude angelology and divine messengers as specific targets of research. Assuming that there is a correlation between human institutions and metaphors for the divine realm, insights

---

[24] For example, messengers are also identified as *sēpiru* (Nabon. 478.12; *AnOr* 8 61.11), *šatammû* (*AnOr* 8 61.8), *rēš šarri bēl piqitti* (*AnOr* 8 61.10).

[25] The governor of Babylon sends Nabu-mukin-apli, the *šatammû* of Eanna, as his messenger (*AnOr* 8 61). Nabu-mukin-apli also is attested as sending messengers himself (*YOS* VII 84,146; *AnOr* 8 62).

[26] For example, the full dimensions of international protocol among royalty is beyond the scope of this work, e.g. sending greetings (*šulma šâlu*), the exchanging of oaths, international marriages, or exchanging gifts (this one aspect alone has been admirably treated by C. Zaccagnini, *Lo Scambio dei Doni nel Vicino Oriente durante i Secoli XV-XIII* [Rome: Centro per le Antichità e la Storia dell'Arte del Vicino Orient, 1973]). The scribal role in the composition of letters is by definition beyond the boundaries set for this work, as is the relative speed of communication by different types of messengers (e.g. notifications of anticipated arrivals of messengers imply at least a two-tiered messenger network).

[27] We do not mean to imply that the bearing of gifts or the escorting of brides was not an essential part of communication. But analysis compels dissection of wholes, and we are placing the magnifying glass specifically upon the messenger himself.

from theological speculation and mythology will be employed only as it gives immediate insight into perceptions of messenger activity among humans.[28] The perception of the prophet as a messenger sent from God (Hag 1:13) is a subject which can also benefit from this study but is not appropriate as a primary source for this investigation. We wish to remain precise and deal with messengers *per se* and not with possible permutations of the social reality as employed by the prophets who may have used the notion as a metaphor for their social status and message.

In our attempt to flesh out these two designations, we will at times employ data from beyond the Semitic world. The studies noted earlier on classical Greece and Egypt prove invaluable as references for contrast and comparison, and it would be a serious loss not to integrate the data which they provide. But where does one draw the boundary? It is likely that the Egyptian *wpwty* is the counterpart to the *mār šipri*,[29] the Hurrian *mār šipri* Keliya is known elsewhere as a *paššitḫi* in his own tongue (*EA* 24 IV.36), lexical lists identify the Sumerian *kin-gi₄-a* as a *mār šipri*, and the *ḫalugatalla* is the Hittite counterpart to the Akkadian *mār šipri* - should not these equations be pursued?

Undoubtedly yes. But as one moves into starkly new cultural contexts, changing social dynamics come into play. We will follow the wisdom of Valloggia and Mosley in setting cultural boundaries for our study. We feel it necessary to limit the investigation to individuals identified as *mār šipri* or *mal'āk* in Semitic sources

---

[28] See H. Röttger, *Mal'āk Jahwe - Bote von Gott* (Frankfurt am Main: Peter Lang, 1978). Excluding the *mal'āk YHWH* is not a serious omission in the light of observations made by D. Irvin, *Mytharion* (*AOAT* 32; Neukirchen-Vluyn: Neukirchener, 1978) 91f., for it is often not clear to what degree the divine *mal'āk* is an interpolation in the text, a hypostasis of deity, or an independent figure in his own right (cf. S. Talmon, "Synonymous Readings in the Old Testament," *Studies in Bible* [*Scripta Hierosolymitan* 8; ed. C. Rabin; Jerusalem: Magnes, 1981; 335-383] 368-369). The figure is too problematic to form the foundation for our study. Rather, research into the *mal'āk YHWH* may benefit from this study.

[29] *uput(i)* in *EA* 151.20 152.56; note the hesitation in M. Valloggia, *Recherche*, 4-5.

(which in this case means texts written in Akkadian, Ugaritic, Aramaic and Hebrew). This will mean, of course, that many non-Semites who are identified as *mār šipri* will be included. Furthermore, it will include sources in which the effective authors may be non-Semitic even though they employ a Semitic language. However, the fact that a Semitic language is adopted as the medium of communication by a non-Semite suggests a disposition toward Semitic culture with regard to the process of communication.[30]

Although much valuable material will eventually be available from Ebla, unresolved issues of syllabary, lexicon, language and social structure make any applications of the material to the study at hand highly tentative and premature. We are largely omitting Sumerian data for the simple fact that the data are too profuse and require a separate treatment of their own.[31] There is no doubt a considerable continuum between the Sumerian institution and its later Semitic counterpart, but bridging that gap is best attempted when one knows where to put the two ends of the bridge. On the other hand, we have felt free to employ Sumerian literary texts in our investigation, for they continued to be copied in the Semitic world, attaining a canonical status in the scribal traditions and often supplemented with an Akkadian translation which preserves valuable bits of information.

[30] On occasion, texts in non-Semitic languages illuminating international messenger activity will be employed when it is apparent that the context is precisely the context in which Semitic messengers function (e.g. Egyptian accounts of messengers in the Levant, the Hurrian *EA* 24 or the Hittite *DS* 28). The fact the the forum is international implies that in spite of regional peculiarities, there exists some mutual perception of how messengers (should) behave.

[31] In addition to numerous appearances of the *kin-gi$_4$-a* in legal and economic texts in general, note the special problems posed by the so-called "messenger texts," which are certainly misnamed. For bibliography, see R. McNeil, *The 'Messenger Texts' of the Third Ur Dynasty* (unpublished Ph.D. dissertation, University of Pennsylvania, 1970).

With regard to the actual terms, some feel that the root *l'k* is not indigenous to Hebrew since the verb form is absent.[32] The form is acceptable Hebrew, although the preservation of the initial *a* vowel instead of *a* > *i* is curious.[33] A source for the borrowing is obscure if it is not a Canaanite root,[34] and Hebrew is a Canaanite language. Not only is the noun omnipresent in west Semitic (Ugaritic, Aramaic, Hebrew, Phoenician), but the verb appears in Ugaritic, and within Hebrew the root was at one time generative (*l'k* > *mal'āk*, *mĕlā'kāh*). The lack of a cognate verb in Hebrew is noteworthy but not stunning, indicating merely that the root *šlḥ* extended its meaning and eventually replaced the verb *l'k* in Hebrew (unlike Ugaritic). The process is clear elsewhere, for in early Aramaic *ml'k* was the word for messenger (at Sefire where it is the object of the verb *šlḥ*) while in later Aramaic it disappears from the language when replaced by the passive participle of *šlḥ* (*šĕlīaḥ*).[35]

Turning to Akkadian, it is significant that both the west and east Semitic roots, though different, developed semantically in a similar fashion.[36] Where *l'k* and *špr* both signify as verbs "send

---

[32] W. Eichrodt, *Theology of the Old Testament* (Philadelphia: Westminster, 1967) II 23; P. Boneschi, "Is '*malak*' an Arabic Word?" *JAOS* 65 (1945) 108 n.4.

[33] Boneschi (*Ibid.*) considers the vocalization regular, but the examples he cites are all roots with first guttural.

[34] Without ignoring the pervasiveness of the root in south Semitic (Ethiopic *la'aka* "to send", Old South Arabic "send > dedicate(?)" [J. Biella, *Dictionary of Old South Arabic* (Chico, CA: Scholars Press, 1982) 256], Arabic *la'aka* IV "send as a messenger"), this is an unlikely source for a borrowing which must have occurred by the beginning of the second millennium in the light of Ugaritic.

[35] *Mal'āk* "(human) messenger" is known in Aramaic so far only at Sefire (*KAI* 221-224). The only other occurrences of the noun (from a later period: e.g. Dan 3:28 6:23 and incantation texts) refer to angels.

[36] If one is to translate the *hapax* in *AbB* II 152.19 as "messenger" (as does *CAD* M [1] 159: "I hereby send you PN my messenger(?)," *PN ma-la-ki aṭṭardakku*), its appearance is surprising in a language where the root *l'k* is to our knowledge non-existent.

with a message,"[37] each root has also developed a nominal form (*mĕlā'kāh*, *šipru*) signifying "task, work."[38]

The Akkadian *mār šipri* is often misconstrued as literally signifying "son of a message."[39] Since Old Assyrian and Old Akkadian preserve *šipru* with the meaning "messenger",[40] it is more likely that the *mār šipri* is an occupational designation (on the order of the *mār tamkārim* or *mār ummānim*) which arose in the OB period.[41] The *pirs* form in this case is likely a passive participle formation employed as an abstract noun (either someone or something sent, hence *šiprum* = "message" or "messenger").[42]

[37] J.-L. Cunchillos, "*La'ika, mal'āk* et *mĕlā'kāh*," 153-162.

[38] J.-L. Cunchillos, *Ibid.*, 157-158. See also E. Greenstein, "Trans-Semitic Idiomatic Equivalency and the Derivation of Hebrew *ml'kh*," *UF* 11 (1979) 329-336.

[39] *TWAT* IV, 889. Note how the syntax of the construct was misunderstood on occasion and the phrase treated as a single word in peripheral texts: *mār šipra* (accusative singular, *CTH* 173.r6; also in *PDK* 102.32, 108.35,38), *mār šipru* (nominative singular, *AASOR XVI* 7.2).

[40] Rare in Old Babylonian; cf. F. R. Kraus, *Vom Mesopotamischen Menschen der altbabylonischen Zeit und seiner Welt* (*MKNAW* 36/6, 1973) 72.

[41] See already R. Zehnpfund, "Babylonische Weberrechnungen," *Beiträge zur Assyriologie* 1 (1890) 535.

[42] *MAD* II^2, 156, a reference which I owe to the courtesy of W. Moran.

1

PREPARATION FOR THE MISSION

1.1 SELECTING THE MESSENGER

When a messenger was required for a specific task, the immediate crucial decision was whom to send. It would be convenient if the choice always had some divine initiative, as uniquely appears in the Sumerian story of Enmerkar and Aratta. There, Inanna tells Enmerkar (*ELA* 69-74; cf.105-109):

> Come here, Enmerkar, let me instruct you, and may you take my advice,
> Let me say a word to you, and may you listen!
> When you have chosen from out of the troops a word-wise envoy having (sturdy) thighs,
> Whither should he take the great message for word-wise Inanna?
> May he go up into the Zubi ranges,
> May he come down with it from the Zubi ranges.

Since this episode is exceptional, one must turn to the more mundane for hard data. In the palace bureaucracy reflected in 2 Kgs 9:17 (discussed below), one finds that in some cases it does not matter to the king who the messenger is. The selection is left up to lesser officials. The same lack of concern is suggested in documents which vaguely refer to "the bearer of this letter" without identifying who that bearer is.[1] Only in incantation texts does one find the query, "Whom shall I send?" (*mannu/a lu/ašpur*).[2]

But it is clear from the activities of messengers identifiable by name that some messengers were so efficient in performing their task and so adept at their diplomatic skills that they made a name for themselves in this regard. An Old Babylonian omen anticipated the arrival of "a well-known messenger,"[3] and there were often specific messengers who were in demand. Burnaburiash of Babylon requests that Amenhotep IV despatch Haya to him - "send no other noble."[4] Such a request is not unique, recurring when Tushratta of Mitanni makes a similar demand of the same pharaoh, but requesting a different messenger (*EA* 29.167).[5] Indeed, Tushratta's request for the messenger Mane is found in two different letters and several times within the same letter!

> And now may my brother despatch Mane, my brother's envoy. . . May my brother despatch Mane. . . And may my brother send Mane along and may he be on his way together with my envoys. Any other envoy may my brother not send, may he send only Mane. If my

---

[1] E.g. "the one who bears the tablet to you" (*ša ṭuppam ubbalakkim* in *AbB* VI 2.16-17; *ša kunukkam ubbalakkum* in *AbB* IV 145.36) or "the envoy who bears this document to you" (*mār šipri ša egirtu ubbalakkanni*, *TFS* 84:3-5).

[2] *Maqlû* I.53 (sent to Belet-ṣeri) and several texts presented by B. Landsberger and T. Jacobsen (sent to Anu's daughters) who observe, "we are intentionally kept in the dark about who speaks the liberating '*manna lušpur*' formula" ("An Old Babylonian Charm Against *Merḫu*," *JNES* 14 [1955] 14-21).

[3] *mār šip*[*r*]*im wēdûm iṭeḫḫiam*, "a well-known messenger will arrive" (*YOS* X.21.4). B. Landsberger ("Brief des Bischofs von Esagila an König Asarhaddon," [*MKNAW* 28/6; 1965] 42 n.64) discusses the adjective in detail, translating as "berühmt".

[4] [*rab*]*â šanâmma lā tašappara* (*EA* 11.15r). Contrast the request of Hattushili to "send quickly another messenger" (*CTH* 172.11r) when he is displeased with a Babylonian messenger's behavior.

[5] *EA* 29.167.

> brother does not send Mane and sends someone else, I do not want him, and my brother should know it. No, may my brother send Mane![6]

The Mitannian king's request for a specific messenger was reciprocated by the Egyptian king who insisted that the Mitannian messenger Keliya should come to him. Since Tushratta was unable to accommodate this request, he felt compelled to explain that Keliya's substitute was an acceptable alternative (*EA* 29.156-157):

> Mazipatli, my messenger, Keliya's uncle, [I now send] to [my broth]er. And I send him to my brother so he might rejoice, so may my brother not complain that I did not se[nd] Keliya.

In this framework, then, it is not remarkable when King David makes a special request of his general that he send Uriah to bear news of the battle. A king's request for a particular individual to bear a message need not arouse great curiosity, and the narrative gives no hint to the contrary (2 Sam 11:6-7):

> Then David sent word to Joab, "Send me Uriah the Hittite." So Joab sent Uriah to David. When Uriah came to him, David asked how Joab was doing, and how the people fared, and how the war prospered.

It becomes apparent that some envoys were so frequently in demand that they made a career of the commission in the royal service. Where messengers are identified by personal names, the evidence clearly points to many individuals who appear specifically as envoys over periods of up to several years. But it is also true that messengers could be sent only on specific tasks, as will be seen below.[7]

---

[6] *EA* 24.II.57-58,86 IV.52-57.

[7] In classical Greece, custom varied in this regard. "A man who was elected as envoy was elected solely for the duration of his mission. According to the degree of his political involvement and esteem he

There were no limitations with respect to candidates who could serve as messenger. The pool of candidates who could bear the title *mār šipri* or *mal'āk* seems boundless: male or female, rich or poor, stranger or relative, king or slave. Males clearly dominated in the role of messenger. Females could bear the title *mārat šipri*, a designation which unambiguously marks the gender of the envoy and which is attested in both the second and first millennium B.C. Ana-makanišu in the sixth century B.C. is identified by this title as a female messenger (*MÍ.DUMU šip-ri*; *Cyr*. 177.14). The choice of a female in this case was dictated by the sex of the sender, for a woman sends a woman to represent her and speak her words of approval for an economic transaction between men, of whom one party was her son.

In the OB period, a woman (Hannabnatum) records in a letter her dismay at having no female messenger to send (*DUMU.SAL ši-ip-ri*; *OBTIV* 11.12). She specifically cites in connection with this problem her inability to send wood to her father, presumably a task which she would entrust to female messengers if she had them. The context of the letter also makes it clear that the females whom Hannabnatum sends as messengers had the status of slaves (*amātum*; *OBTIV* 11.7,9). Again, women employed as messengers are found in the service of other women.[8]

One finds women sent on missions which imply messenger activity even though the description *mārat šipri* does not appear. Erishti-Shamash is accustomed to send her maid on missions if one can judge from the advice of a man to whom the maid is sent, "Don't send your maid again" (*ṣ[uḫ]ārtaki lā tatūrīma lā*

---

could be elected to few or many embassies" (F. Adcock and D. J. Mosley, *Diplomacy,* 156). Among those with distinguished careers as envoys were Demosthenes (at least seven years), Callias (fifteen years), Antalcidas (over two decades), Philocharidas (fifteen years). Sparta apparently preferred to maximize continuity of representation, unlike Athens (*Ibid*., 156-157).

[8] The circumstances may parallel the phenomenon of female scribes, attested for example in conjunction with the queen's estate (*TFS* 39.3-4 40.2-3).

tašapparī,[9] *AbB* VII 25.8-10). The feminine correspondence at Mari confirms the role of women as messengers for women, although no such woman is yet identified in our sources as *mārat šipri*. Kirum, the princess, sends to the king a woman whose name is not preserved, stating (*ARM* X 34.r2'-8'):

> PN I now send you (*aṭṭar*[*dakkum*]). May my Star, my father and my lord pay careful attention to her message, and that information tell to no one!

The confidence placed in this woman is equal to that of any other male envoy known. Indeed, the confidence of the princess in an intimate of her own sex makes the choice of female messenger quite appropriate, even though women are known to send males as well (e.g. the queens of Egypt and Hatti in the fourteenth and thirteenth centuries).[10] In addition to poetic metaphors describing female envoys (Pr 9:3; Isa 40:9), biblical narrative also pictures females bearing messages (2 Sam 17:17).

It is often important to choose a messenger with his or her own independent social standing. Between corresponding monarchs, it is a gesture of honor toward the recipient to send a messenger who is a noble.[11] Not only is this made explicit in biblical literature (Num 22:15), but elsewhere kings are scorned for the low characters which they are accused of sending in place of nobility.[12]

---

[9] In Old Babylonian, *ṭarādu* is the generalized verb meaning "to send" while *šapāru* signifies specifically "to send with a message".

[10] Yanana says that she sent (*ašpur*) another woman named Kukkihhiya to another locale, but en route she was abducted (*ARM* X 100.5); she consistently calls Kukkihhiya "my maid" (*ṣuḫārtī* 1.13,21,27; cf. 1.23).

[11] In the Neo-Assyrian period, a writer notes that since he is sick, in his place he is sending "my brother and ten nobles (*mārī banûti*) of Nippur to greet the king" (*SLA* 123.5-11).

[12] *EA* 1.15-19,32-34; see F. Pintore, "*Kamiru* o *kabtu* in *EA* 1?" *OrAn* 11 (1972) 37-38. Note the inscribed Persian period incense burner which once belonged to Iyyosh the *ml'*[*k*] (restoration by F. M. Cross, "Two Notes on Palestinian Inscriptions of the Persian Age,"

> When did you send an important person (*tašpura kabta*) who knew your sister to speak with her?... These are the people you send - a numbskull [ ] of Zaqara, an ass-herder [?].... Why don't you send an important person (*tašappara kabta*) who will tell you the truth?

Ramses II's care to specify the high rank and title of three messengers whom he sends as a delegation to the Hittite court must be seen as a calculated enhancement of the importance of their mission and their stature as messengers.[13]

Where one noble is a preferred messenger, a king will request that no other is to be sent.[14] Nobles also function as envoys between monarchs in the first millennium when Teumman the Elamite sends two *rubê* to Ashurbanipal,[15] to whom also Rusas of Urartu sends *rubê*.[16] Other identifiable nobles include Keliya (Hurrian *talmi* in *EA* 24.IV.37), Hattusha-ziti (*DS* 28) and Haya[17] (*EA* 11.r13).

[*BASOR* 193 (1969) 21-24]), whose condition led Albright to deduce that he represented a poor family and "can scarcely have been paid very well" ("The Lachish Cosmetic Burner and Esther 2:12," *A Light unto My Path*: Old Testament Studies in Honor of Jacob M. Myers [eds. H. N. Bream, R. D. Heim, Cary A. Moore; Philadelphia: Temple University, 1974] 25-32).

[13] *CTH* 165.1.11'-16'. For the reconstruction and translation, see W. F. Albright, "Cuneiform Material for Egyptian Prosopography 1500-1200 B.C.," (*JNES* 5 [1946] 7-25) 21; A. Goetze, "A New Letter from Ramesses to Hattusilis," (*JCS* 1 [1947] 241-251) 250 n.7; E. Edel, "Neue keilschriftliche Umschreibungen ägyptischer Namen aus den Boğazköytexten," (*JNES* 7 [1948] 11-24) 12.

[14] "Haya your noble whom you sent . . . send no other noble," *Ḫaya rabâka ša tašpura. . . [rab]â šanâmma lā tašappara* (*EA* 11r.13-15).

[15] E. Weidner, "Assyrische Beschreibungen der Kriegs-Reliefs Assurbanaplis," *AfO* 8 (1932) 181.

[16] *Ibid.*, 188; *rabêšu* in Streck 318.5f.

[17] It is likely that this figure is the same illustrious vizier known from Egyptian sources as "the royal messenger to every land" (M.

Consequently, in a complex narrative such as Numbers 22, diverse descriptions of Balak's delegation to Balaam as messengers (v.5), elders (v.7), princes (*śārîm* - v.13-15,21,35,40) and servants of Balak (v.19) need not be ascribed to different sources. Indeed, all of these citations are traditionally attributed to J.

But nobles do not top the social scale of individuals identified as messengers. Even a king could bear the title *mār šipri* when sent as the representative of the Great King to whom he was a vassal. Ehli-sharruma, king of Ishuwa, is such a delegate representing his king to another vassal in the second millennium (*CTH* 179.1).[18]

The sending of one's son as a messenger is also well-attested in both the first and second millennium. It is enshrined in second millennium treaties as a matter of course in international good will for the vassal to send his son as a messenger to the Great King,[19] and it is a sign of submission to later Assyrian monarchs.[20] If the

---

Valloggia, *Recherche*, 51-52) and the recipient of correspondence in the Amarna archives (W. F. Albright, "Cuneiform Material," 12-13).

[18] Who sent Ehli-sharruma is not immediately apparent. H. Klengel hesitantly notes that the king of Assyria despatches him, arguing that the third singular suffix on *mār šiprīšu* would be second singular (*-ka*, "your messenger") if he were the envoy of the Hittite king ("Zum Brief eines Königs von Hanigalbat," *Or* 32 [1963] 280-291). However, the most recent antecedent is the Hittite king spoken of in the third person: "My father (i.e. the Hittite king) heard. I was staying in GN, and he sent Ehli-sharruma his messenger to me" (l.14-17). Furthermore, the location of Ishuwa, Ehli-sharruma's city-state, in the upper Euphrates area, places him between Hatti and Hanigalbat, an unlikely position to be in the service of the Assyrian king.

[19] "If Šunaššura sends either his heir or his messenger (*lū apilšu lū mār šiprašu* <*išappar*>) before the Sun. . . , the Sun shall do them no harm" (*PDK* 103.31-33); cf. *PDK* 101.67-68 135.18 for the son's role as a representative. Note also the treaty between Kizzuwatna and Hatti: "whether he sends his son or his servant" (*lū mārašu lū ardašu . . . išappar*; *CTH* 26.11).

[20] "To save his life he (Ualli) spread forth his hands, besought my lordship. Erisinni, his heir apparent, he sent to Nineveh (*mār*

relative status between noble and king's son is indicated by priority of occurrence in lists, there is no absolute: the son may be mentioned before (*PRU* IV 83) or after (*PDK* 135.18) the noble. When they function as messengers, they maintain the social status due their rank and don as an extra privilege the role of messenger (*PRU* IV 83):

> If a prince (*mār šarri*) or a noble (*amīlu ellu*) goes as a messenger (*ina mār šipri(m?)*) from Hatti to Ugarit and it pleases the king to give gifts . . . .

The Hittite Hishmi-sharruma is one such prince who may have made several trips to Egypt. Though he is not identified as a *mār šipri*, he moves in the company of messengers when he travels between Egypt and Hatti (*CTH* 165.1.18-20), and Ramses requests that Hishmi-sharruma again make the trip to his court (*CTH* 165.1.r15-16). Toi, king of Hamath, sent his son Joram (Hadoram according to 1 Chr 18:10) with many gifts to acknowledge David's victories over Hadad-ezer (2 Sam 8:10). For a vassal, the presence of his son in the sovereign's court is an acceptable alternative to the vassal's appearance in person in order to confirm allegiance (*EA* 162.48,53), while for those seeking the mercy of a conquering king, there is the hope that the sending of one's sons will mollify the sovereign's wrath.[21]

In spite of the stature of such a messenger, a monarch's son could be abused as any other messenger. Rib-Addi laments that he had sent his own son to pharaoh, but four months had passed and the prince had not yet been able to meet with pharaoh (*EA* 138.75-78). The Egyptian court appears to have been insensitive in this regard, for a letter from Tunip, complaining of a twenty-year detention of their messengers, in particular points out that the son of their king should have returned long before (*EA* 59.13-20).

In the private sector, one might also send one's own son as a messenger. Presumably one's son will have greater reason to

---

ridūtīšu. . . išpuram) and kissed my feet. I took pity on him and dispatched my messenger of peace to him" (*AS* 5 54-55).

[21] *Asb.* 105.18-27.

champion the cause of his father. As one OB writer notes, "You sent (*tašpur*) a *ṣuḫāru*, your son, and I offered five minas wool to him - he didn't take it from me!" (*AbB* VII 23.5-10). A greater freedom of action may have accompanied the son who served as his father's messenger.

Merchants dominate the international sphere as messengers of monarchs, and bearers of news in general.[22] The kings of the Amarna period identify such men as both "my merchants" and "my messengers" (*EA* 39.10-16). The overlap of activities identified with messengers and merchants may account for the economic transaction of an Elamite messenger in Babylon during the reign of Samsuditana: Ishmekarrab-dayyan is called a *mār šipri* in a document which obligates him to repay within two months a loan of one-half mina of silver (*VS* XXII 34).

Scribes are known on occasion to function as messengers.[23] The fact that the scribal profession is noted in addition to their role as messenger confirms that messengers did not have to be literate, or at least they did not require training in the reading and writing of documents. The most illuminating narrative account of a scribal messenger appears in the tale of Wenamun's travels when the latter requests of his Byblian host, "Let your scribe be brought to me, that I may send him to Smendes and Tanetamun. . . and I will send him to them saying. . ." (*Wenamun* 2.34-36). Without a break, the next event is recorded as follows: "And he put my letter in the hand of his messenger" (2.37).

The variety of individuals who are sent on missions as messengers is thus enormous. One can also include individuals of lesser stature, such as a Habiru warrior, singled out as a messenger among his fellows.[24] Servants and subordinates functioned as messengers, their relative social status depending

---

[22] See the extensive bibliography on this subject cited in C. Zaccagnini, "The Merchant at Nuzi," *Iraq* 39 (1977) 172 n.11.

[23] Akapurhe in *HSS* XIII 175.4,11; Asali in *EA* 24.IV.36-37; Balaṭu in *GCCI* I 327.5 [cf. *YOS* VI 22.12]; Sin-nadin-zer in *AnOr* 8 61.11.

[24] A *mār šipri* in a list of *29* [ ] *māru ṣābu SA.GAZ AL.Šarkuḫe.KI*, *ATT*/8/211 l.28; see J. Bottéro, *Le Problème des Habiru*, (IVe Rencontre Assyriologique Internationale; Paris: Imprimerie Nationale, 1954) 183.

upon the position of their master or mistress. The *ṣuḫāru* is one such figure commonly found in contexts of delivering messages.[25]

It therefore seems clear that there are no precise limitations on who could serve as a messenger. In a royal context, a monarch would select the most dignified representatives if he wished to impress his royal peers, while lesser figures could be utilized where an assertion of prestige was either inconsequential or already well-established. In both the royal and private domain, an individual would be sent as a messenger who was the most directly involved and conversant with the issues in view, if negotiations were considered.[26]

But social position alone was not always the central issue in selecting a messenger. Certain qualities were desirable in a messenger. For significant royal embassies, one may presume that the oriental esteem for age no doubt excluded younger men from such service.[27] On the other hand, youth and its accompanying speed could be desirable and hence acceptable among extra-royal envoys or between kings where speed was of greater moment than making impressions.

In the case of Mane and Keliya we are told that it is their reputation for speaking the truth which makes them desirable as messengers (*EA* 24.IV.19-29):

---

[25] For bibliography on this broad subject, see J. MacDonald, "The Supreme Warrior Caste in the Ancient Near East," *Oriental Studies Presented to Benedikt S. J. Isserlin* (ed. R. Ebied and M. Young; Leiden: E. J. Brill, 1980) 39-71.

[26] The marriage embassies of Amarna and Bogazkoy find the same names reappearing on multiple trips. The Egyptian messenger, Wenamun, was the "elder of the portal", a senior administrator. "It becomes clear why Wenamun was selected for the mission to Byblos: he was familiar with the administration of the estate of Amun" (Goedicke, *Wenamun*, 17-19).

[27] In Classical Greece, thirty years was generally a minimum age to serve as herald. Special delegations might have higher limits, such as the Athenian envoys to Perdiccas who each had to be over fifty years old. Note the Chalcis law that no one over fifty could serve as herald. For details see F. Adcock and D. J. Mosley, *Diplomacy in Ancient Greece*, 157.

> May my brother not hear those words, if Mane and Keliya do not say them. But the words that Mane and Keliya say about me (or) about my land, they are true and right, and may my brother hear them. That again, which anyone might express to me about my brother (or) about his land, those words I will not hear, if Keliya and Mane do not say them. But what Keliya and Mane will say about my brother (or) about his land, they (i.e. the words) are true and right, and I will hear them.

This faithfulness/truthfulness as a desirable quality in a messenger is mentioned several times.[28] In Egyptian wisdom literature, one may find in more explicit detail the context in which the Egyptian and Mitannian kings are speaking. Note, for example, the instructions of Ptahhotep:

> If you are a man of trust, sent by one great man to another, adhere to the nature of him who sent you. Give his message as he said it. Guard against reviling speech, which embroils one great man with another; keep to the truth, don't exceed it, but an outburst should not be repeated. Do not malign anyone, great or small, the *ka* abhors it.[29]

There is nowhere else such a list of qualities which make a desirable messenger as this list which is found in Ptahhotep. But

---

[28] This quality must be evident to both sender and recipient. Similar to Mane and Kaliya, Thrason and Thrasybulus in fourth century Athens "were especially trusted in Thebes and consequently sent there often," just as Themistocles or Nicias, held in high regard by Spartans, were sent to Sparta (F. Adcock and D. J. Mosley, *Diplomacy in Ancient Greece*, 157). Note also the praise accorded by Athens (the host city state) to the envoys of Macedonia and Mytilene (*Ibid.* 165).

[29] M. Lichtheim, *Ancient Egyptian Literature*, Vol.1 *The Old and Middle Kingdoms*, (Berkeley and Los Angeles: University of California, 1973) 65.

the biblical Proverbs ratifies the desirability of faithfulness with the picturesque simile, "Like the cold of snow in the time of harvest is a faithful messenger to those who send him."[30] The Sumerian tale of *Inanna and Enki* includes an address by Inanna to her attendant Ninshubur, "Come, oh messenger of faithful words."[31]

Faithfulness is extolled not only in literature but in Mesopotamian letters as well, from both the first and second millennia. On some occasions, one writer will request that a trustworthy (*taklum*) individual be sent on a mission as a messenger.[32] More rarely the term *kayyamānu* is employed for this quality.[33] The third millennium complaint by Shulgi reflects the same concern: "The man whom you sent as a messenger (*lú in-ši-gi*$_4$*-na-zu*) is not dependable, he does not follow your instruction."[34] The fact that many messengers did not live up to the expectations of their senders in this regard will be seen later when discussing the actual delivery of the message.

---

[30] *ṣîr ne'emān* (Pr 25:13). Snow in harvest is actually a calamity, and the apparent gloss, "he refreshes the spirit of his masters," is no doubt intended to explicate this difficulty; however, it is the coolness of snow to a laborer and not its falling from the sky which is in view here (W. McKane, *Proverbs*, [London: SCM, 1970] 585-586).

[31] *ra-gaba-e-ne-èm-ge-en-ge-na-mu* "meine Botin des beständigen Wortes" (*IE* 34,35).

[32] *ina wardūtīšu 1 taklam lišpuramma*, "Let him send from among his servants one who is trustworthy" (*ARM* X 32.r17-18); *ištēn taklam šupramma*, "Send one trustworthy individual" (*AbB* VI 57.5-6); *1 awīlam taklam šupur*, "Send one trustworthy man" (*AbB* VI 154.10); [*šarru*] *bēlī liprus* [*lišpur*]*a PN-ma qurbūtu awīlu taklu umuru šu šutuma lillika*, "In fact, the king, my lord, should (now) decide what to do (with these ceremonies) and send word (about it). The *qurbūtu* PN is a trustworthy (and) reliable man. He should go!" (*LAS* 190.r11-15).

[33] *ina qātē manma kayyamānu ša kapdu inaššû inamdaššu u gabarušu inašša* "He will give it to someone trustworthy who can bring it quickly, and he will bring his answer" (*NB* 141.9-14).

[34] F. A. Ali, *Sumerian Letters*, (unpublished Ph.D. dissertation; University of Pennsylvania, 1964) 39.

In spite of Ptahhotep's lengthy and detailed admonition noted above, he omits one quality which recurs persistently in the Semitic world. Indeed, a reference to a messenger's speed occurs more frequently at Mari than any other quality. Several times, a writer requests that swift (*qallu*) individuals be sent as messengers.[35] The same root is later used in a biblical text to epitomize messengers: ***mal'ākîm qallîm*** (Isa 18:2).[36] The juxtaposition of speed with faithfulness is noted on occasion,[37] and in narrative accounts, messengers are despatched with instructions to go quickly, which they obey.[38]

Beyond these two qualities of faithfulness and speed, other desirable features of a messenger occur sporadically. An ability to speak articulately or diplomatically best summarizes the semantic field of one such quality. The messenger whom Enmerkar despatches to the Lord of Aratta is described as ***kin-gi₄-a inim-zu***

---

[35] *2 awīlī qallūtim ana ṣēr PN/aḫīka šupram*, "Send two swift men to PN/your brother" (*ARM* I 39.17'r.; II 10.4'r); [ ] *qallūtum liblūšunūti. . . 2 qallūtum ṭuppam. . . libl[ūnim]*, "Let swift ones carry them (i.e. tablets). . . let two swift men bring the tablet" (*ARM* I 93.11-17). In particular, it is the *ṣuḫāru* who is singled out as swift. *2 ṣuḫārūka qallūtim* (sic!) *ṭuppātīk[a] li[l]qû*, "Let two of your swift lads take your tablets" (*ARM* I 97.16,17); [*2 ṣuḫārū*]*ka qallūtu*[*m li*]*lqûšūma. . .* [*l*]*ibl*[*ūnim*], "Let your swift lads take it (i.e. the tablet) and. . . bring it," (*ARM* I 105.9-13); *ṣuḫārīka qallūtim* [*šū*]*bil*, "Let your swift lads carry (the tablets)" (*ARM* IV 31.13-14).

[36] In the first millennium, the self-praise by Nabonidus focuses upon the *našparu*'s speed: "I am the quick messenger (*našparu ḫanṭu*) of the great gods" (*VAB* IV 252, I.8).

[37] *ina mārī tamkarī taklūtim 2 šina idiššunūšimma liḫmuṭū* "Give (the letter) to two merchants who are trustworthy and let them hurry" (*AbB* VIII 15.34-36).

[38] In Ugaritic: "Don't delay! . . . They did not delay" ([*al tṯb*] . . . *lyṯb*; *CTA* 2 1.13,19) is superior to assuming the root *ṯwb* (J.C. de Moor, *The Seasonal Pattern in the Ugaritic Myth of Ba'lu According to the Version of Ilimilku*, *AOAT* 16, (Neukirchen-Vluyn: Neukirchener, 1971) 128. Note the Sumerian text *Sud* 28-30,43-45.

"a messenger eloquent of speech."[39] When Kakka is sent by Anshar, he is extolled as one who is "nimble in speech" (*tiṣburu tele''i*).[40]

In one instance where a message is specifically designated as an oral report that is not to be written down, the man who is to be the messenger (*kallûm*) must be one *ša awātim ina pîm iṣabbatu* "seizes words in his mouth,"[41] that is, he has a good memory. The messenger who does not easily tire (*lā aniḫu*) is also desirable, so much so that it becomes a noble epithet which kings claim for themselves when describing themselves as *našparu*.[42] Otherwise, the colorless *damqu* "good, fine" is used to describe an acceptable messenger.[43]

A memorandum from Mari (*ARM* XXIII 100) provides a candid glimpse into the bureaucratic machinery required for despatching a messenger who in this case appears to be

---

[39] This is S. Cohen's translation; cf. T. Jacobsen's "word-wise envoy" (*ELA* 71,106). For the Akkadian equivalents *lamādu ša awati* and *mudê amati*, see S. Cohen, *Enmerkar and the Lord of Aratta*, 175. In the light of the plot development where the message eventually becomes so cumbersome that even this best of messengers can no longer repeat it, one might expect that *inim-zu* indicates one who has a good memory. The desirability of a good memory does seem to recur elsewhere (see below), but Inanna in this text is also described as *inim-zu* (l.107), as are the elders of Aratta (l.373).

[40] For the semantic range of *ṣabāru*, see *CAD* Ṣ 2-4.

[41] *ARM* I 76.27. The original editor preferred the notion of articulate speech for this idiom ("qui puisse bien parler des choses"), but *CAD* Ṣ 25 clarifies the semantic field of *awatu* used in conjunction with *ṣabātu*.

[42] Samsuiluna is *našparī dannam lā āniḫam* (Samsuiluna C 32; *BAL* 48); Nabonidus is *našpar lā āneḫi* (*VAB* IV 234,I.9). Such a messenger is one who "completes every mission" (*mušallim kal šipri*; *VAB* IV 252,I.8).

[43] *Mār šipri damqa* (*EA* 147.17,31). Note also: "Mane, your envoy, is very good; there does not exist a man(!) like [him] in all the world" (*EA* 24.II.95,96).

functioning as an escort to another individual[44] travelling to Eshnunna. In this written recommendation, Ahunata is preferred for two explicit reasons: 1) he is experienced or well-informed (*ḫukkum*) and 2) his father had made the same trip five or six times. The second quality suggests the possibility that family connections were instrumental in procuring a commission as messenger. That such was the case not only in the OB period but also in the MB period and the Israelite monarchy appears in the specific cases of Keliya's relatives,[45] Ahimaaz,[46] and king Zedekiah's messengers to Nebuchadnezzar (Jer 29:3).[47] The fact that a son customarily carried on his father's occupation in the OB period may account for the origin of the term *mār šipri* (<*šipru* "messenger"), if it is not simply an occupational designation referring to membership in a class or "guild" (see Introduction).

On the other hand, these qualities which might recommend a messenger to repeated service were not the only factors involved in selecting a messenger to convey a given message. Often, the exigencies of a situation did not allow the sender much freedom of choice. It appears that at times the messenger himself may have had some say in determining whether or not he would go. One

---

[44] An Awil-Addu is so far known elsewhere only as a Babylonian (*ARM* XVIII 59.18). The text under discussion may also be interpreted to mean that Awil-Addu was the first individual who was recommended to travel, but an objection is raised by one who prefers Ahunata (the text simply states *lillik*, not *ittīšu lillik*). Furthermore, it is quite possible that the text does not deal with messengers at all, since the rubric reads *aššum. . . alākim tašpuram* and not *aššum. . . šapārim/ṭarādim tašpuram*.

[45] Keliya's uncle and brother are sent as messengers, even though the Egyptian king wants Keliya (*EA* 29.156-162).

[46] Although his father, Zadok (2 Sam 15:36), is a priest and not a messenger, he is at the heart of the royal administration. The choice of Ahimaaz as a messenger in 2 Sam 15-17 is more than expedience, for he appears elsewhere in this role (2 Sam 18).

[47] Elasah and Gemariah are the sons of a royal scribe and of the high priest respectively, whose fathers also function together (2 Kgs 22:3-14).

OB writer laments a lack of communication: "You sent no one to me - the road is long and so no one wants to come to me."[48] Such reluctant messengers stand in contrast to Ahimaaz who volunteers for a mission. In fact, Ahimaaz even succeeds in convincing the sender, Joab, against his better judgment that he should be sent on the mission (2 Sam 18:19-23).

However, when the king sent a messenger, there could be no bargaining. In the Neo-Assyrian empire, some men were certainly conscripted to serve as messengers for the palace bureaucracy and military, although we know very few details.[49] An illustration of such conscription may come from the introduction of the so-called "Dialogue of Pessimism" (*BWL* 144,145):

> ["Slave, listen to me."] "Here I am, sir, here [I am."]
> ["Quickly, fetch me the] chariot and hitch it up so that I can drive to the palace."
> ["Drive, sir, drive . . .]. . . . will be for you;
> [ ] will pardon you."
> ["No, slave, I] will by no means drive to the palace."
> ["Do not drive,] sir, do not drive.
> [ ]. . . he will send you (*išapparka*) [ ]
> "And will make you take a [route] (*ušaṣbatka*) that you do not know;
> "He will make you suffer agony [day and] night."

The text implies that a man with a chariot in close proximity to the palace is in danger of being conscripted into the king's service as a messenger. This notion is echoed in the *Poor Man of Nippur*, for after hiring a chariot, the "poor man" is greeted with the query, "Who are you?" to which he replies, "The king, your lord, sent me (*išpuranni*) to [ ]."[50]

A further source for messenger-personnel attested in the OB period is the prisoner of war (*asīru*). When the deaths of certain

---

[48] *mamman ul tašpuram girrum rūqma mamman ana alākim ul imaggaranni* (*AbB* VII 144.4'-7').

[49] *TCAE* 228.

[50] *STT* 38.89-90 (O. R. Gurney, "The Sultantepe Tablets," *AnSt* 6 [1956] 145-164).

asīru are reported, it is noted that these men were in the custody of a merchant and under the orders of a messenger-supervisor (*ugula kin-gi₄-a*);[51] couriers (*rá.gab*) are among those who vouch for the report.[52] Food provisions are distributed to couriers (*rá.gab* and *kin-gi₄*-a) at the "prisoner compound" (*bīt asīrī*)[53] to individuals who are clearly described as "foreigners."[54] This "*asīru* office"[55] is also clearly responsible for provisions for incoming messengers, giving in one case 3 *sutu* of flour to three messengers (*kin-gi₄-a*) of Rim-Sin, one *sutu* to two more of his messengers, and one *sutu* to the "court-barber who with a chariot had come from Larsa."[56]

Leemans raises the obvious question: how would it be possible to trust these types of messengers? Presumably, such messengers could not be expected to make a round-trip unless they were under bond, and so a one-way trip to their homeland is more likely. Conceivably, merchants from the *asīru*'s home could employ such men to relay messages for them.[57] The status of the *asīru* is often a peculiar one with dynamics beyond the scope of this discussion as a type of individual known throughout the Near East in the second millennium B.C. in the employ of the government.[58]

The conscription of individuals to serve the king's need for messengers is evident in second millennium B.C. Ugarit. One document records how the King of Ugarit made several grants to the merchant Sinaranu, among them the exemption from serving as a messenger for the king.[59] This particular case assumes the

---

[51] W. F. Leemans, "The *Asīru*," *RA* 55 (1961) 58-59.

[52] *Ibid.*, 59.

[53] *CAD* A (2) 332.

[54] W. F. Leemans, "The *Asīru*," 67-68.

[55] *Ibid.*, 71.

[56] *Ibid.*, 68.

[57] As Leemans notes, *Ibid.*, 64.

[58] *Ibid.*, 74-76.

[59] Nougayrol makes it appear as if the merchant supplied messengers: "Des messagers du roi il n'aura pas à fournir" (*ina mārī šipri šarri(?) lā illak*; *PRU* III 107.54). The translation proposed by Bottéro is

practice of customarily employing merchants as an extension of one's communication network noted above.

The type of message also determined the selection of the messenger. Joab, for example, declines to accept the request of Ahimaaz to serve as a messenger, observing that he could run on another day but not on a day of tragic news; he then sends the Cushite to relay the bad news.[60] Furthermore, because of the poor treatment of messengers between hostile powers (to be discussed below), it is likely that dispensable envoys were sent for declarations of war. It is probable that good news was carried by one's best representatives, while bad news was left to the less fortunate.

1.2 OCCASIONS FOR SENDING

The occasions on which one sends a messenger can not be classified in their entirety: one sends a messenger when one wishes to communicate, and such communications span the spectrum of human experience.[61] Nevertheless, certain occasions can be singled out as peculiar contexts for messenger activity between those who are on speaking terms.[62] Such contexts can

---

preferable: "Il n'accomplira point le service des messagers royaux(?)" (J. Bottéro, *Le problème des Habiru*, 121).

[60] We will discuss in section 3.1 the reactions of individuals on seeing approaching messengers, but it is worth noting at this point how a good man is associated with good news in biblical literature (2 Sam 18:27; 1 Kgs 1:42).

[61] Among the more curious examples, one might note the messenger delegated by a prisoner to supervise legal transactions while he is incarcerated (*ROMCT* 2 50-51).

[62] Messengers between inimical parties were exceptional, apart from declarations of war or attempts to become allies. We will discuss elsewhere the international code by which messengers of non-allied powers were repulsed, but the following succinct statement presents the ancient perspective: "[As for those who are] hostile (*nakru*), their messengers do not travel back and forth (*ittanallakū*); so why have you

be recognized by at least two features: 1) an individual is defensive and makes excuses as to why a messenger is not sent, or 2) one makes accusations or inquiries as to the failure of another to send a messenger.

In general these two responses tend to surface when an individual experiences (what are perceived to be) major turning points in one's life. The great traumas and tragedies of life stimulate messenger activity. Illness, perceived as having one foot in the grave, was not taken lightly:

> You wrote to me as follows: "Why didn't you write me about your illness? It is customary that one write to his brother about his illness." I'll send good news, namely, I was sick, but now I have recovered![63]

---

stopped your [messengers]?" (*CTH* 172.53-54). Indeed, it is a bad omen when "the city-dweller will correspond vigorously (*ištanappar*) with the enemy" (J. Nougayrol, "'Oiseau' ou oiseau?" *RA* 61 [1967] 25 l.10). Consequently, a cessation of messengers could provoke consternation, prompting fears that perhaps former friends were no longer so amicable. After one OB king complains, "Why does your lord (Zimri-Lim) always write ([*i*]*štanappar*) to Adalshenni but he didn't write to me?" (B.590 in A. Finet, "Adalšenni, roi de Burundum," *RA* 60 [1966] 24-26, l.10-12), this neglect becomes sufficient cause to refuse in turn delivery of a huge shipment of grain and wool to Zimri-Lim (cf. *SH* 827.50-54). A cessation of messenger traffic was particularly threatening when one was a vassal of the king who stopped writing (*EA* 47.14-20), and one greets a new king with the hope that "my messenger may yearly come [before you] and your messenger may yearly come before me" (*EA* 33.27-32).

[63] *ARM* X 169.6-17. Where the quoted letter ends is, as often, not clear. One may translate *ibaššīma* less loosely by redividing: "'Why did you not write?' Is it only about his illness that one writes to his brother? I'll write good news, namely, . . ." In either case, the assumption of the correspondence is that illness and recovery is worth writing about. Note the Aramaic correspondence from the middle of the first millennium: "And what is this, that you have not sent a letter to me? As for me, a snake bit me and I was dying and you didn't send to see if I were alive or dead!" (Hermopolis 5.7-9).

Elsewhere, the king of Babylon expresses disappointment that pharaoh sent no condolences when he was sick (*EA* 7.14-32). But in the light of the excerpt just noted, the tact of the Egyptian messenger in the Babylonian court is admirable as he subtly observes, "The country is not near that your brother should hear and send you condolences; . . . who would tell him so that he could quickly send you condolences?" Diplomatically, the messenger may be implying that it is the Babylonian king's own fault for not informing pharaoh. In any case, both the Babylonian king[64] and the messenger[65] acknowledge that no illness is too trivial to initiate messenger activity between allies.

If illness, much more so is death an occasion for despatching one's messenger.[66] One writer explains why no messenger arrived to express condolences about the death of another (*NBU* 117.6-16):

> When I heard of the death of Rimanni-Marduk . . . and sent my messenger on his behalf (*mār šipri ana muḫḫīšu ašpuru*), my messenger didn't reach him. They led him away when he encountered an ox marked with a star.

The support of extended family relationships and maintenance of social stability in such times motivate such a custom. This is particularly true in international politics among allies where death requires a reaffirmation of loyalty. It is important in this regard to note that Hattushili wrote to Babylon after the death of Kadashman-Turgu but before the accession of his son Kadashman-Enlil, reaffirming his alliance with Babylon and especially his loyalty to the deceased (*CTH* 172.12-15):

---

[64] "Why did he not send his messenger to me and investigate?" (*EA* 7.18).

[65] "Would your brother hear that you are sick and not send to you his messenger?" (*EA* 7.24-25).

[66] On the international level, W. Moran ("The Ancient Near Eastern Background of the Love of God in Deuteronomy," *CBQ* 25 [1963] 80-81) cited several texts affirming mandatory embassies upon the death of a king and the enthronement of his successor.

> I wiped away my tears, and my messenger [I commissioned(?)] and to the nobles of Karduniash I sent as follows: "[If the son(?)] of my brother you do not keep as ruler, I shall become your enemy [ ] in Karduniash I shall conquer.

Such an embassy is concerned with the political ramifications attendant upon the ruler's death, employing pressure in order to maintain stability. It can be assumed that under normal conditions, the death of a ruler would be announced quickly to intimate allies in order to insure that the type of support promised by Hattushili would be available. Normal conditions would include the immediate accession to the throne of the king's heir, which in the case just noted happened to be a juvenile, and hence Hattushili's non-compromising posture in his own interests. A more customary transfer appears in 2 Sam 10:1-3, where an embassy expressing appropriate mourning[67] is sent to the successor.[68] The OB Amorite funeral attended by messengers (*šiprū*) is also set in a context of succession (Asmar 11).

---

[67] This is not a festive embassy, for they are sent to express consolation (*lĕnaḫămô*, *mĕnaḫămîm*) and to honor the deceased (*hamĕkabbēd dāwîd 'et 'ābîkā*).

[68] The regulations for receiving news about the death of a member of the royal family are in a different category (E. Weidner, "Hof- und Harems-Erlasse assyrischer Könige aus dem 2. Jahrtausend v. Chr.," *AfO* 17 [1954-1956] 270). These Middle Assyrian decrees regulate the palace bureaucracy with and without the king's immediate presence, and the fact that the subject was worthy of regulation underscores its import for the palace. If the king is less than two hours away, the news is to be immediately sent to the king; if he is further away, then they are to await the king's return but are to begin the mourning rites. It might be advisable to consider death-bed or condolence correspondence as a distinct type of communication. It vigorously reappears later in the Greco-Roman world (e.g. John L. White, *Light from Ancient Letters* [Philadelphia: Fortress, 1986) 184-185). The letters of consolation, which Stanley Stowers identifies as a distinct literary form in this later period, probably have their antecedent in this much earlier

Consolation and comfort in tragedy are complemented by messengers sent in order to share in the joy of great moments. The accession of a new ruler would be accompanied by an embassy which would acknowledge the new king with abundant gifts and pledges of continued loyalty, received no doubt amid considerable festivity and generosity by the new monarch. Such embassies are to be distinguished from the envoys sent to honor the deceased monarch (*CTH* 173.r5-10):[69]

> When I came to the throne, you sent me no messenger. But it is a rule for kings who come to the throne: other kings, his equals, send him fine gifts, a garment worthy of kingship, excellent oil for anointing. But you - as of this day you have done nothing.

The accession of a king[70] is only one of many central celebration-events which stimulated messenger traffic. Special festivals which were not accompanied by an ally's messenger could prompt an accusing finger: "Why did you not send your messenger to me?" (*EA* 34.9-10). The answer preserved does not challenge the custom in the least (l.11-18):

---

phenomenon in the ancient Near East (S. Stowers, *Letter Writing in Greco-Roman Antiquity* [Philadelphia: Westminster, 1986] 142-151).

[69] This is a distinction which seems to be observed in other cultures (R.Numelin, *Beginnings of Diplomacy*, 138-139). Mourning periods for the deceased, well-attested along with free and full expression of grief in the Semitic world, do not permit simultaneous expressions of joy. Furthermore, our sources as noted above make the distinction themselves between sending the messenger to celebrate an accession or to participate in the mourning. Note also the beginning of a Babylonian letter: "After your father's wife had been mourned, I sent Hua my messenger" (*EA* 11:5; cf. W. Moran, "Additions to the Amarna Lexicon," *Or* 53 [1984] 301). Note the distinction made in *EA* 29.55-64, and see the fragmentary *CTH* 178.

[70] Note also the king of Alashiya's greeting to the new pharaoh: "I have heard that you are sitting on the throne of your father!" (*EA* 33.9-11).

> I didn't hear that you were engaged in a sacrificial celebration, so don't be offended (*lā tišakkan mimma ina libbīka*). Since I have heard, I now send my messenger to you! And so I send to you through my messenger one hundred talents of copper.

The one celebrating the occasion had the obligation to inform his fellows and send out the invitations. The Cypriot in the preceding excerpt is less direct than Kadashman-Enlil who accuses the Egyptian ruler (*EA* 3.18-20):

> When you celebrated a festival, you didn't send your messenger to me, saying, "Come, [eat and dr]ink", nor did you [send] festive gifts.

The messenger as the conveyor of gifts and tokens to a monarch who cannot attend a festive occasion reappears in literature (*EA* 357.1-6). The ritual is further reflected in the first millennium celebration of Ashurnaṣirpal II, who, celebrating the completion of his building projects, specifically notes that he invited 5,000 foreign representatives (*ṣīrāni*) of twelve named lands to partake of the extravaganza.[71] One may presume that Solomon's dedication of the temple, described as a pan-Israelite celebration in 1 Kgs 8:65, was equally a cosmopolitan affair, hosting the embassies of Solomon's vassals and peers. After all, Israel had wanted a king who adhered to the customs of royalty.

A particular joyous occasion for the movement of messengers was provided by international marriages, entailing the transporting of the bride and reciprocal gifts.[72] Here, too, one finds the protest of failure to live up to the traditional standard

---

[71] D. J. Wiseman, "A New Stela of Aššur-naṣir-pal II," *Iraq* 14 (1952) 35 l.143-148.

[72] See C. Zaccagnini, *Lo Scambio dei Doni nel Vicino Oriente Durante i Secoli XV-XIII* (*Orientis Antiqui Collectio* 11; Rome: Centro per le Antichità e la Storia dell'Arte del Vicino Oriente, 1973), where the bulk of the material employed for his thesis derives from such contexts.

expected on such occasions when messengers are sent (*EA* 11.19-20,r13-14):

> Haya has five chariots - will they take her (the princess) to you with five chariots?! . . . With Haya, your noble whom you sent, are a meager number of chariots and people. Send a multitude of chariots and people so that Haya may bring the princess to you.

In all of the above instances, there was an unwritten code of behavior to which individuals appealed and none protested: messengers provided a reaffirmation of social stability and kinship in the dramatic moments of life, whether crisis or celebration. The messenger facilitated the extension of social bonds beyond the horizons of immediate awareness. The messenger was not simply a liaison for extended economic transactions in an urban and cosmopolitan setting, for he was a vehicle for the perpetuation of human values in what could be an increasingly impersonal world of expanding dimensions. As will be shown, the messenger can not be classed as a neutral or impersonal element in communication. Instead, the messenger's humanity and personal involvement in his task enhanced his role as a mediator of human relationships in a society which could easily subvert such relationships.

1.3 COMMISSIONING THE MESSENGER

Once the selection of the messenger was achieved, one proceeded to the actual commissioning of the messenger for his task. But this phase presents a problem in the light of our sources. Literature from the ancient Near East provides a considerable body of data in which the verbal commissioning of messengers is clearly described, but it is intriguing that these same literary sources do not stress written communication. Rarely are written documents the object of even an allusion when we have some form of verbal commissioning of a messenger in literary texts. On the other hand, the actual written documentation which the messengers carried makes few allusions to this role of the messenger as a communicator. This curious contrast in perspective between the sources necessitates a careful investigation in order to identify the precise relationship of the message to the messenger and precisely what task he was commissioned to perform.

1.3.1 BIBLICAL LITERATURE

In biblical literature, the text more often than not makes explicit the oral nature of the messenger's communication. The initial structure of the narratives dealing with the sending of messengers by Jacob (Gen 32) and later by Balak (Num 22) is largely parallel when they state (both J), "And he sent messengers to PN to GN saying":

wayyišlaḥ̮ . . . mal'ākîm . . . 'el 'Esāw . . . 'arṣāh Sē'īr . . . lē'mor
(Gen 32:4,5)
wayyišlaḥ̮ mal'ākîm . . . 'el Bil'ām . . . pĕtôrāh . . . lē'mor
(Num 22:5)

Immediately following this introductory description, the oral nature of the communication is underscored, for Jacob says in v.5, "Thus you shall say to my lord Esau, 'Thus says your servant Jacob . . . .'" No such explicit delineation of the sender's speech as opposed to the messengers' speech occurs in the case of Balak, for Balak's message immediately follows the statement above that messengers were sent. Nevertheless, the oral character of Balak's message is still emphasized, for unlike the case of Jacob's messengers who are next seen returning to Jacob, Balak's messengers actually are pictured departing and subsequently repeating the message: *waydabbĕrū 'ēlāyw dibrêy bālāq* (v.7).

In addition to these two commissioning scenes from the Pentateuch, seven commissioning scenes are also found in the books of Samuel. When Joab wishes to relay information about the status of the war in general and the death of Uriah in particular, the oral nature of the message is emphatic (2 Sam 11:19-21):

> And he instructed the messenger, "When you have finished telling all the news about the fighting to the king, then, if the king's anger rises, and if he says to you, 'Why . . . .', then you shall say, 'Your servant Uriah the Hittite is dead also.'"

The oral nature of the communication is unequivocal in this account, for the messenger is instructed to withhold that information until a critical point in the communication is reached. Indeed, the narrative presents the messenger with the option of withholding certain information entirely should the king not become angry.

In the same chapter, a similar commissioning recurs when David sends Joab's messenger back (2 Sam 11:25):

> David said to the messenger, "Thus you shall say to Joab, 'Do not let this matter trouble you . . .'" and so encourage him."

In this case, David's concluding remark to the messenger implies that the precise words are not necessary so long as the message achieves its aim of putting Joab's mind at rest. The message requires the personal assurances of the messenger to be given to the recipient of the message.

Joab must send another message to inform David of the defeat of Absalom (2 Sam 18:19f). We have already noted the unique request of Ahimaaz to be the bearer of that message, a request which Joab roundly denies,[73] a feature to which we will return later. Joab instead commissions "the Cushite"[74] in the

---

[73] "You are not to carry tidings today; you may carry tidings another day, but today you shall carry no tidings" (2 Sam 18:20). The three-fold repetition of *yôm* and the root *bśr*, the first and last of which echo with *lô'* is uncommonly verbose for biblical dialogue.

[74] Restore the definite article before the gentilic in v.21b; see S. R. Driver, *Notes on the Hebrew Text and the Topography of the Books of*

following manner: "Then Joab said to the Cushite, 'Go, tell the king what you have seen'" (v.21). A similar vagueness in delivering an oral commission is evident two verses later when finally Ahimaaz pesters Joab to the point where he also is commissioned in the following manner: "So he said to him, 'Run'" (v.23).

A fifth scene from the books of Samuel entails the commissioning of a group of messengers by a group of people. Otherwise, the features are not new (1 Sam 11:9):

> And they (the Israelites) said to the messengers (of Jabesh-Gilead) who had come, "Thus you shall say to the men of Jabesh-Gilead: 'Tomorrow . . . you will have deliverance.'"

1 Samuel 25:5-9 contains the sixth commissioning scene which describes the embassy to Nabal, one of the most extended in the Old Testament. The account begins similar to the J accounts in the Pentateuch ("and he sent"), but instead of *mal'ākîm* being the object of the verb, 10 youths (*nĕ'ārîm*) carry the message (v.5-7).

> And David said to the young men, "Ascend to Carmel and go to Nabal, then ask him in my behalf how he fares. You shall say the following to my brother,[75] 'Are you well, and is your house well, and is all else of yours well? Now I have heard . . . .'"

This group of messengers is addressed as a unified group in the second plural. The greetings which they are to offer to Nabal are explicated by David as he gives to them the precise words which

---

Samuel (Second edition; Oxford: Oxford University, 1912) 331. The traditional vocalization of v.21a represents this messenger as a well-known adjunct to David's staff, no doubt a regular messenger of the king.

[75] So the Vulgate, but the text still remains awkward. It is difficult to understand why David would address Nabal as an equal ("brother") in the light of David's outcast status and the nature of the request. No textual reconstructions are at present completely satisfying.

they are to use. But the message which they are to speak is to be delivered as though it were David speaking in the first person.

The seventh[76] such commissioning of messengers in Samuel is the occasion on which Saul seeks to kill David through a bizarre bridal payment: 100 Philistine foreskins (1 Sam 18:25-26). "Saul said, 'Thus you shall say to David, "The king. . ."' And the servants told David these words."

Three[77] further narratives containing commissioning scenes occur in the books of Kings. 1 Kings 20 presents an instructive narrative, for messengers are despatched an impressive total of six times within 12 verses (v.1-12). The passage is peculiarly informative in that each time that messengers relay a message, the mission is described with varying degrees of schematization. We may schematically summarize the relevant structural detail so:

1) Ben-Hadad sent messengers to Ahab, saying, "Thus says Ben-Hadad . . . ."
2) Ahab answered . . . .

3) The messengers came again, saying, "Thus says Ben-Hadad . . . ."
4) Ahab said to Ben-Hadad's messengers, "Tell Ben-Hadad . . . ." The messengers departed and brought him word again.

5) Ben-Hadad sent to Ahab, saying . . . .
6) Ahab answered, saying, "Tell him . . . ."

---

[76] 1 Sam 18:22-24 could be a further case: "Saul commanded his servants, 'Speak (*dabběrū*) to David secretly, saying, "Behold, the king likes you . . . ."'" However, the functional word is "secretly," which from the context means "do not let David know I sent you." The servants are successful, for David's incredulous response is directed to them only (2nd plural pronoun). These are messengers, but a very special category comparable to spies or a fifth column, whose commission includes concealing the fact that they have been commissioned at all.

[77] We do not include 1 Kgs 2:29f., for this is the commissioning of an assassin who pretends to be a messenger.

The variety points to a narrator who is interested in keeping the story moving, one who is not bound by the rigors of narrative formulas. This is helpful, for the freedom of the narrator allows the reader in this case six different perspectives from which to view the action, a stereographic guide to precision. In missions 1,2 and 5 above, the expressions are sufficiently ambiguous to prevent any deductions as to how the messengers were commissioned. Mission 3 uniquely of the six describes the delivery of the oral message, not its initiation. However, missions 4 and 6 clearly show Ahab sending Ben-Hadad's messengers back with an oral message. Even here the narrator's penchant for variety is displayed: *'imĕrū* (v.9) alongside *dabbĕrū* (v.11).

In 2 Kings 1, a sick Ahaziah soliciting a prognosis on his illness sent messengers to Ekron (v.2): "He sent messengers, telling them, 'Go, inquire . . . ." The king of Assyria commissions messengers to go to Hezekiah in 2 Kings 19:9-10 as follows:

> He sent messengers again to Hezekiah, saying, "Thus you shall speak to Hezekiah, king of Judah . . . ."

There is a thirteenth commissioning scene in 2 Kings 9:17 which departs radically from these previously discussed. King Joram hears of the rapid approach of an armed contingent and wishes to discern whether they come in peace or hostility. Instead of immediately dispatching a member from his council, Joram gives orders that a messenger be found and sent: "And Joram said, 'Take a horseman (*rakkāb*) and send (him) to meet them and let him say (*wĕyô'mar*), "Is it peace?"'" Consequently, in this case it is the bureaucrats in the administration who select, inform and despatch the messenger, even though the initiative comes from the king. Indeed, when the messenger speaks, he introduces the message, "Thus says the king, 'Is it peace?'", even though he did not receive the message from the king himself. A similar procedure is no doubt in view in letters which conclude, "I send this tablet at the king's order" (*[ṭup]pi annêm [in]a qabê šarrim ušābilakkim*, *ARM* X 176.22-24). It cannot be determined how many more royal letters without such a comment also originated in such a fashion.

In all thirteen commissioning scenes, the oral nature of the communication was evident. There was no hint of any type of written documentation. One might object that elsewhere in biblical literature we do know that written documents were used. Indeed, the citation above from 2 Kings 19 continues on to state in v.14 that Hezekiah received "the letter from the hands of the messengers."[78] That problem will be addressed when discussing the actual delivery of the message. We wish to stress at this point, however, that in commissioning scenes in the Bible there is no reference to written documents; rather, the evidence points overwhelmingly to oral communication.

1.3.2 UGARITIC LITERATURE

A similar situation holds true in the seven[79] clear commissioning scenes in Ugaritic literature. It is immediately apparent that the commissioning of the messenger receives much more emphasis than is found in the Bible. The fullest commissioning scene occurs when Yam sends his messengers to retrieve Baal. We have labelled discrete elements in this narration with alphabetic notation in order to facilitate comparison with comparable narratives (*CTA* 2.1.11-19):

> A) Yam sent messengers, [judge Nahar an embassy,
> saying,]
> [fragmentary]
> B) So, lads, depart, [don't delay]
> D) Set your [faces] toward the assembled Council

---

[78] 2 Sam 11:14f. also is a reminder of the presence of written communication nestled snugly against a narrative (v.18f.) which deals solely with oral communication. But again, v.14f. tells us nothing about the commissioning of Uriah as messenger.

[79] *CTA* 3.4.76f. and the parallel 1.3.17f. may contain a commissioning scene. Anat replies to Baal's messengers, "Go, go, divine messengers" (*lk lk 'nn ilm*), but she gives them no clear message, and the text itself is problematic.

Within the [Mount of El]
E) Do not fall down at the feet of El,
Nor bow to the assembled Council.
[Remain standing, speak]
F) And repeat your message
And speak to the Bull, the divine Father
[Repeat it to the] assembled Council:
"Message of Yam, your lord,
Judge Nahar your sovereign:
'Give up . . . .'"

Although this account contains numerous distinct features, it is not the longest commissioning scene at Ugarit. An even lengthier description appears when Baal sends Qadish-wa-Amraru to Kothar-wa-Hasis in *CTA* 3, including an additional element "C" which anticipates the messenger's journey (*CTA* 3.6.6-25).

C) Cross river and cross mountain
Cross hill and distant horizon
Head straight for the fisherman of Athirat
Come, Qadish-wa(!)-Amraru
D) Then set your face toward Egypt
<To Kothar-wa-Hasis>, god of it all,
To Crete, his princely throne,
Egypt, the land of his inheritance.
E) Over a thousand fields, ten thousand acres,
Bow before Kothar and fall,
Prostrate yourself and honor him.
F) And speak to Kothar-wa-Hasis,
Repeat to Hayyan, skilled of hand:
"Message of Mi[ghty Baal,]
Wo[rd of the one who overcomes warriors:"]

The distinction of being the lengthiest commission belongs to the 35 lines below which are abbreviated here by eliminating the parallelisms in order to relate the essential framework, and which include a feature unique to this account. We label the feature X since it seems to be context-specific and generated by this specific narrative of the descent into the underworld (*CTA* 4.8.1-35):

D) Then set your face toward Mount Trǵzz . . . .
C) Lift up the mountain . . .
And descend to the Underworld . . . .
D) Then set your face toward <Mot> . . . .
X) Do not approach the son of El, Mot,
Lest he pop you in his mouth like a lamb . . . .
E) Over a thousand fields, ten thousand acres,
Bow before Mot and fall,
Prostrate yourself and honor him
F) And say to the son of El, Mot,
Repeat to the beloved of El, the hero,
"Message of Mighty Baal,
Word of the one who overcomes warriors:
'Greetings! . . . .'"

Only two elements are found when Baal sends messengers to Mot (*CTA* 5.2.8-10):

B) Depart, speak to Mot, son of El,
F) Repeat to the Hero, beloved of El,
"Message of Mighty Baal,
The word of the one who overcomes warriors:
'Greetings . . . .'"[80]

Two elements are also found when Baal sends Gapnu and Ugaru to Anat, but they are not the same two elements, nor do the same elements occur when Pabil sends messengers to Kirta:

Like lads, enter.
E) Bow down before Anat,
And fall, you shall prostrate yourselves.
Honor her.
F) And speak to the Virgin Anat,

[80] *CTA* 5 begins in the middle of a commissioning scene; unfortunately, only the message and not the commissioning is preserved. For this text, see the discussion below on the actual delivery of the message.

Repeat to the Kinswoman of the People,
"Message of Mighty Baal,
The word of the one who overcomes warriors:
'On the earth . . . .'" (*CTA* 3.3.5-11)

D) [Then you shall] set your faces toward the noble
[Kirta]
F) and say [to noble Kirta],
"Message of [King Pabil]:
'Take....'" (*CTA* 14.5.245-250)

On the other hand, only one of the above elements occurs when El sends Anat to Shapshu, while a new element is introduced, G (*CTA* 6.3.22-24):

El cried out to the Virgin Anat,
G) "Hear, oh Virgin Anat!
F) Speak to the Luminary of the gods, Shapshu:
'The furrows . . . .'"

The only element which occurs in all accounts is element F, a statement that the message is to be given orally. This emphasis echoes that already found in biblical literature, for again there is no hint in any commissioning narrative of a written document accompanying the message. The fluidity of the remaining elements[81] in the commissioning scenes is marked nevertheless by some regularity. Impressive as formulas are elements D, E and F.[82] Although not all six elements recur in every scene, they are

---

[81] We may summarize the occurrence of the elements as follows:

A) "PN sent messengers" - *CTA* 2.
B) "Depart!" - *CTA* 2; 5 (the form *tbʿ* is used in both).
C) Imperative on how to travel - *CTA* 3.6; 4.
D) "Set face toward destination!" *CTA* 2; 3.6; 4; 14.
E) "(Don't) Bow!" - *CTA* 2; 3.3; 3.6; 4.
F) "Say!" - *CTA* 2; 3.3; 3.6; 4; 5; 6; 14.

[82] See further in sections 3.3.1 and 4.4.3 for discussion of aspects of formulas E and F.

normally found in the same sequence, a notable exception being *CTA* 4 where the command "Set your face toward GN" occurs twice.

			CTA #
[idk pnm] al ttn		*'m*	2.1.13-14
[id]k pn[m al ttn]		*'m*	14.5.245-246
idk	*al ttn pnm*	*'m*	4.8.1
idk	*al ttn pnm*	*tk*	3.6.12-13
idk	*al ttn pnm*	*tk*	4.8.10-11

1.3.3 AKKADIAN

Mesopotamian literature contains several commissioning scenes with features which are familiar from the above discussion. For example, from *Atrahasis* comes this example:[83]

> Enlil opened his mouth and addressed [vizier Nuska,]
> "Nuska, open your gate, take your weapons [ ] In the assembly of all the gods,
> Bow down, stand up, set forth our charge:
> 'Anu . . . .'"

There is apparently a second embassy in this epic according to a Neo-Assyrian fragment with slightly different wording (*Atr.* 54,55):

> Anu opened his mouth to speak, addressing [Nuska],
> "Nuska, open your gate, [take] your weapons []
> In the assembly of the great gods bow down, [stand up],
> Speak to them (*qibâššunuti*) [ ]:
> 'Anu . . . .'"

[83] *Atr.* 50-51 1.118-124. For deviations from Lambert and Millard's text, see the parallel narrative in 1.134-165 (read *pušur tēretni* in 1.123 with suggestion made by W. Moran).

At least three commissioning scenes can be discovered or reconstructed in the NA version of Nergal's descent to Ereshkigal, taking the following form:[84]

> PN_1 opened his/her mouth and said to PN_2,
> "PN_2, I shall send you to GN/PN_3 . . . thus you shall speak."

A fourth scene, largely reconstructed, occurs with a more extended dialogue:[85]

> [Ereshkigal opened her mouth and said to Namtar her vizier,]
> ["Go Namtar . . . .] set your face [towards the gate of] Anu, Enlil and Ea, [And say:] 'Since . . . .'"

The earlier version of the same myth tends to omit such commissioning scenes; instead the text simply reads "the gods/she sent a messenger" (*EA* 357.3,7). One exception occurs, unfortunately fragmentary (*EA* 357.23-28): "[?]"Go [] saying [ ]"; Namtar departed."

A very full scene occurs in the *Enuma Elish* (III.1-13):

> Anshar opened his mouth to speak to Kakka, his vizier,
> "Vizier Kakka, you who please me always,
> I shall send you to Lahmu and Lahamu.
> You are able to discern,[86] nimble in speech.
> Have the gods, my fathers, brought before me . . . .
> Depart, Kakka, stand before them;
> Whatever I say to you repeat (*šunnâ*) to them:
> 'Anshar . . . .'"

---

[84] *STT* 28 I.6'-9',51'-52' VI.43-48. "Thus you shall speak" is omitted in the second embassy where Ereshkigal's messenger is not sent with a message but instead goes to retrieve the food from the celestial banquet.

[85] *STT* 28 V.a'-1'.

[86] *CAD* Ṣ 3: "clever in stratagems."

In the second tablet of the *Anzu* myth, two commissioning scenes appear. Ninurta calls Adad and asks him to report to the gods how his battle with the monster is proceeding. When he delivers this report, he is asked to return to Ninurta with a reply (*Anzu* II.70-73,101-105).

> He called to Adad and gave him instructions,
> "Repeat (*šunnīšu*) to him, to Ea Ninigiku, the deeds
> which you have seen:
> 'Oh, lord, ...'"
> When Ea Ninigiku heard the word of his son,
> He called to Adad and gave him instructions,
> "Repeat (*šunnīšu*) to him, to thy lord, my instructions,
> Whatever I say, save (*uṣur*) for him:
> 'In battle . . . .'"

In the ten commissioning scenes from these four literary works, there was a consistent emphasis upon the oral communication of the message with no reference at any time to a written document. A further noteworthy feature, particularly so since a parallel was found at Ugarit, is the command in *Atrahasis* to bow and stand before the recipients of the message, faintly echoed in the *Enuma Elish* command to simply stand. It is possible, therefore, that one should reconstruct as follows in the NA account of Nergal and Ereshkigal a command for the messenger Kakka to perform such obeisance when he arrives at his destination (when he arrives this is exactly what he does):[87]

> Kakka, I shall send you to the land of no return.
> To Ereshkigal . . .
> Bow down, kiss the ground before her,
> Straighten up, stand and speak . . .
>
> *Kakka ana erṣet lā tāri lušpurka*

[87] Reconstructing the missing beginning of *STT* 28 on the basis of *STT* 28 I.28'-29',52' VI.45 (cf. Gurney's reconstruction of I.7'-8' in "The Sultantepe Tablets," *AnSt* 9 [1959] 108).

ana Ereškigal . . .
kimis išiq qaqqaru maḫrīša
išir izizma kīam taqabbī

Once in the Neo-Assyrian account of Nergal and Ereshkigal there is an echo of a formula found in the Ugaritic material, namely the command to the messenger to "set his face" toward his destination. Finally, in both *Enuma Elish* and the account of Nergal and Ereshkigal, the decision to send the messenger is articulated deliberately: *luš̌pur* "I shall send."

1.3.4 SUMERIAN LITERATURE

An entire Sumerian composition which became popular throughout the ancient Near East assumes the form of a commission to a messenger.[88] Immediately after a vocative,[89] a command to depart[90] and deliver the message[91] appears without specifying what the message is. The messenger is not told the contents of the despatch, and he is told not to inquire (l.6-7): "Messenger (*lú-DU-kaskal-e*), without inspecting my greetings, put into her hands the letter of greeting." The remainder of the 54-line composition is a paean of praise describing the recipient for the messenger's benefit, closing with the greeting to be offered (l.54): "Say to her, 'Your beloved son, Lú-dingir-ra, greets you!'"[92]

Sumerian literature contains several commissioning scenes in the context of narrative. The most extensive accounts are found in the tale *Enmerkar and the Lord of Aratta*, where a single

[88] *Lú-dingir-ra*. The text is known in a four-columned tablet from Ugarit containing normal Sumerian, phonetic Sumerian, Akkadian and Hittite versions (*Ugar*. V 310-319).

[89] "Royal courier!" *lú-kaš$_4$-e-lugal-la*, l.1.

[90] "Start on your way," l.1.

[91] "Give this message to Nippur, start the long journey," l.2-3.

[92] Or "he is in good health" (*PN dumu-ki-ag-zu silim-ma*); cf. M. Civil, "The 'Message of Lú-Dingir-Ra' and a Group of Akkado-Hittite 'Proverbs'," (*JNES* 23 [1964] 10).

messenger makes three round trips and a final one-way trip (as far as the text is preserved). The narrator feels no constraint to be economical in his description of such scenes, and he continually varies them. Enmerkar first sends the messenger off with these words describing the message he bears (*ELA* 108-114):

> May you go up into the Zubi ranges,
> May you come down with it out of the Zubi ranges, . . .
> Envoy, when you have spoken to the Lord of Aratta,
> and elaborated on it (say):

A curious break in the commissioning occurs where the lord addresses the messenger with further orders on how he should behave on his journey (*ELA* 156-159):

> Once again, the lord added a word
> to the envoy going to the mountains to Aratta:
> "Envoy, fall down at night like the rain,
> rise up by day like a rising storm."

When Enmerkar sends off his messenger on the second trip, the commission is succinct (*ELA* 339-346): "Envoy, when you have spoken to the Lord of Aratta, and elaborated thereon for him (say): 'The base of my scepter . . . .' say to him." The third despatch contains no commissioning speech; the fourth and climactic despatch by Enmerkar we will return to in a moment.

In discussing the lord of Aratta who returns Enmerkar's messenger, one must keep in mind that the messenger's behavior may be out of the ordinary. This is not an initiating despatch, for the messenger is being returned to the one who originally sent him. The first time that the lord of Aratta sends the messenger back to Enmerkar, he says simply, "Envoy, when you have spoken to your master, the lord of Kullab, and elaborated on it (say): 'Me, a lord, . . .' Tell him: 'There will be no bowing of Aratta to Uruk!'" (*ELA* 219-226). But the messenger will not leave until he is certain that the one who sends him recognizes that the message is inadequate. The messenger brazenly talks back to the lord of Aratta in a seven-line provocation which deeply troubles the lord (*ELA* 236-293):

Then did the heart burn in the lord, the throat
choked up,
no retort had he, kept seeking and seeking for a
retort.
At his own feet he was staring with sleepless eyes -
began finding a retort,
found the retort, let out a shout -
loudly like a bull he bellowed
the retort to the message at the envoy.
"[Envoy,] when to your [master,] the lord of Kullab,
[you have] spoken, and have enlarged upon
it for him (say:)
'The [great] mountain range . . . .' say unto him."

It should also be noted that within the lord's speech, he interrupts once in a somewhat fragmentary passage to directly address the messenger (*ELA* 262-267): "Once more, envoy, I speak to you. I on my part shall frame a [r]equest skillfully for you, may it get across to you intact, and in Eanna . . . report to your master, the lord of Kullab, (saying:)."

The messenger is less provocative the second time the lord of Aratta sends him back to Enmerkar. The lord simply says in l.397-411, "Envoy, when you have spoken to your master, and elaborated thereon, (say:) 'May the scepter . . . .' say to him." In slightly different words, the third and last despatch by Aratta is also quite straightforward (*ELA* 454-461):

The Lord of Aratta entrusted to the envoy
a great seal, as it were, on the matter:
"Envoy, when you have spoken to your master, the
Lord of Kullab, and elaborated thereon to
him, (say:)
'May the champion . . . .' say unto him."

This Sumerian tale incorporates features we have not yet seen elsewhere. Novel and erratic features indicate the relish with which the narrator tells the story, and they suggest a realism in portraiture, such as the commission to ascend and descend the mountains (l.108-109), how to behave during the trip (l.156-159), the messenger's rebuke with the lord of Aratta's roaring rebuttal (l.236-293), and the punctuation of a message with an aside to the messenger (l.262-267). But perhaps the most remarkable feature of this story lies in the final despatch by Enmerkar, to which we now turn (*ELA* 470-494).

> "Envoy, when you have spoken to the Lord of Aratta,
> when you have elaborated thereon for him,
> (say:)
> 'Let the clothes . . . .' say to him.
> Next, when you have spoken to him, and have elaborated thereon for him, (say:)
> 'Quickly . . . .'
> Thirdly, when you have spoken to him and elaborated thereon for him, (say:)
> 'May I . . . .'"

Although the total number of lines which the messenger is required to remember amounts to a mere 25 lines of text, the hammer-like blows of one-two-three messages is too much for the over-taxed herald. Enmerkar then invents the written message (*ELA* 500-506):

> That day the words of the lord [ ] . . .
> were difficult, their meaning not to fathom,
> and, his words being difficult, the envoy was unable to render them.
> Since the envoy - his words being difficult - was unable to render them,
> The lord of Kullab smoothed clay with the hand and set down the words on it in the manner of a tablet.
> While up to then there had been no one setting down words on clay,
> now, on that day, under that sun, thus it verily came to be;
> the lord of Kullab set down wo[rds on clay,] thus it verily came to be!

These few lines are of crucial import in affirming what has been discerned in all literary commissioning scenes up to this point: the message which is entrusted to the messenger is an exclusively oral phenomenon. This final account is an exception which proves the rule, for the tablet is explicitly introduced only when the herald is incapable of transmitting an oral message. Even though the story is an etiology with little historical reality, it provides a candid perspective on how one culture perceived the responsibilities of the messenger.

A further Sumerian account about Enmerkar and Ensuhkeshdanna, lord of Aratta, provides little that is informative (*EnEn* 24-39): "He said to the messenger: 'He . . . .' Thus to Enmerkar he sent word." There is a further remark about a tablet, but the comment follows a fragmentary section and seems to echo the tradition which was discussed in the previous Sumerian work (*EnEn* 77-114):

> He (Enmerkar) patted it in the manner of (shaping) [a
> tablet];
> He examined it in the manner of (examining) clay.
> "He may . . . ."
> The messenger of Enmerkar to Ensuhkeshdanna . . . .

More informative with some novel features is a narrative about Inanna and Enki. When Enki discovers that Inanna has departed in a boat with the *me*'s, the following dialogue results (*IE* II.1-7):

> Enki spoke to his vizier Isimu:
> "Oh Isimu, my vizier, my sweet name of heaven!"
> "Enki, my king, at your service!"
> "How far off is the divine boat?"
> "Quickly [it has reached] the . . . quay."
> "Go! The divine boat must be returned!"

Such a dialogue recurs six times, only varying in the location to which Inanna has travelled and the individuals who are sent with Isimu to get the boat. The dialogue of question and answer recurs elsewhere in this tale when a messenger task is not in view.[93]

A very full account of how Enlil sends off his messenger is reported in the *Marriage of Sud*. After Enlil meets Sud, he wishes to make wedding arrangements and so summons his *sukkal* Nuska. In addition to a vocative, there is an explicit statement of his intentions (articulated before the message itself) as well as an order to move fast (*Sud* 28-31):

> He (Enlil) said, "Quick, please, Nuska, I will give you instructions about this, I want to send (*ga-e-gi*$_4$)[94] you to Eresh, Nidaba's city, the city whose grounds are august. Do not tarry. Repeat to her what I am going to tell you: 'I am an unmarried man . . . .'"

But the commissioning is not over, for Enlil has further directions for Nuska as to exactly how he is to handle the delicate negotiations. Upon completion of the verbal message, Enlil again emphasizes that the task is to be completed quickly (*Sud* 41-43):

> When you get there, the luscious woman of my choice will stay close to her mother. Do not go to her empty-handed, take her a treasure with your left hand. Waste no time. Bring me back her answer speedily.

The specification of the left hand is a covert ploy by which the messenger will reveal to the bride the full extent of his commission only slowly. Only when the betrothal negotiations have reached a certain point is he at his discretion to present the appropriate gifts (which up to that point were hidden) and so seal the agreement.[95] This feature by which the messenger does not

---

[93] *IE* 19.13f., 27.1f.,14f.

[94] The Akkadian counterpart is lost; *lušpur(ka)* is likely to be restored.

[95] The impure implications of the left hand in offering a gift to a prostitute (M. Civil, "Enlil and Ninlil: The Marriage of Sud," *JAOS* 103 [1983] 46-47) or the fact that the left hand is less used and hence more available (W. G. Lambert, "Further Notes on 'Enlil and Ninlil: The

immediately lay all of his cards on the table was seen already in the commissioning of a messenger by Joab (see above on 2 Sam 11:18-25).[96]

A further bilingual in Sumerian and Akkadian records Marduk's sending of his vizier Nuska. An initial vocative introduces the speech which is simply a command to report to Ea what has happened; no specific message is given (*UL* 96-97).

> O my minister Nuska! Bear my message to the Apsu, tell Ea in the Apsu the tidings of my son Sin who has been grievously dimmed in the sky.

1.3.5 OUTSIDE LITERATURE

We now leave Sumerian literature and pass on to isolated examples of commissioning scenes which are unique and fit no patterns. First, there is the Hittite account of the deeds of Shuppiluliuma by his son Murshili II. In response to the Egyptian queen's request for a husband, the incredulous Shuppiluliuma reacts (*DS* 28 A.iii.20-25):

> So it happened that my father sent forth to Egypt Hattusha-ziti, the chamberlain, (with this order): Go and bring thou the true word back to me! Maybe they deceive me! Maybe in fact they do have a son of their lord! Bring thou the true word back to me!"

A further Hittite narrative in a very fragmentary condition preserves a dialogue with individuals sent on a mission: "Go and say to the ruler of Hassu: 'I ....'" (*CTH* 7). A more complete Hittite

---

Marriage of Sud'," *JAOS* 103 [1983] 66) may account for the reference to the left hand. Note the messenger context in Jud 3:15-23.

[96] The messenger's behavior in the text published by S. Lackenbacher ("Nouveaux documents d'Ugarit," *RA* 76 [1982] 141-156) is also surely due to a specific commission to so behave. See discussion on this text in section 4.3.

narrative (in Akkadian) preserves features which are reminiscent of the Sumerian texts discussed above in which the sender interrogates the messenger before he is given the message (*CTH* 7.24f):

> "Are you listening (*teštenemme*)?"
> "I listen."
> "Go and say to them, 'Whether . . . .'"

Further along in the same document the king remarks, "Go, ask them, 'If . . .'" (Rs.18f.).

An exceptional case is that of the woman in the royal Assyrian harem in the second millennium B.C. who sends a fellow on an errand.[97]

> If a woman of the palace, whose shoulders are bare and who is not covered with a *kindabaššu* garment, calls a courtier [saying . . .] "I shall send you" and he turns around and speaks with her, he will receive 100 lashes.

The occurrence of "I will send you" *lašpurka* (variant *lū* [*ašpurka*]) reminds one of the occasional appearance in literary texts of the introductory address *lušpur*. This reappears also in hymns as a stock phrase, where the petitioner despatches a mediating female deity to plead his case: "I will send you (*lušpurki*) to my angry god, to my angry goddess."[98] The offense in the text above does not lie in the means of soliciting a messenger. The woman calls (*tartugum*), apparently the normal manner to enlist a messenger. The offense lies in her dress, which should have warned any male that he should not linger. A further stipulation on harem despatches makes it clear that permission

---

[97] E.F. Weidner, "Hof- und Harems-Erlasse assyrischer Könige aus dem 2. Jahrtausend v. Chr.," *AfO* 17 (1954-1956) 287.105-106.

[98] *lušpurki ana ilīya zenî ištarīya zenīti*, *AGH* 56.18, 301.14, 461.81.

from a higher authority was necessary before messengers could be sent:[99]

> [If the king] resides in a *bīt lušme* or a *bīt nari* or in the palaces in the environs of Ashur, no woman of the palace shall send out (*tašapparamma*). On account of (different garments listed) without asking the king or the *rab ekallim*, she shall not send (*tašapparamma*), and from the palace they shall not make a dispatch (*ušeṣṣû*).

1.3.6 LITERARY SUMMARY

In concluding this survey of literary and related descriptions of the commissioning of messengers, we have found an overwhelming testimony to the oral nature of the message. When the written document was introduced in the Enmerkar stories, it was to fulfill the purposes of the story-teller's objective: provide an explanation for the origin of clay tablets. In the commission by Lú-dingir-ra, the courier is explicitly told that he is not to know the letter's contents. Vocatives addressed to the messenger occurred on occasion (*CTA* 2,6; *Atr*.; *EE*; *Sud*; *ELA*; *IE*; *UL*; *Lú-dingir-ra*). Direct address to the messenger often featured imperatives such as go (2 Sam 18; 2 Kgs 1; *CTA* 2,5; *STT* 28; *EE*; *IE*; *Lú-dingir-ra*; *CTH* 7; *DS* 28), run, set your face (*CTA* 2; 3.6; 4; 14; *STT* 28), speak (*CTA* 2; 3.6; 3.3; 4; 5; 6; 14; *Atr*.; *ELA*; *CTH* 7), say, tell, repeat, bring word, bow (*CTA* 2; 3.3; 3.6; 4; *STT* 28), rise, stand, and others, some of which attained a formulaic status. "Thus says PN" is characteristic of West Semitic literature (Gen 32; 1 Kgs 20; *CTA* 2; 3.3; 3.6; 4; 5; 14). Characteristic of Akkadian was the phrase "I will send you" (*STT* 28; *EE*; Harem laws; cf. *Sud*).

---

[99] Weidner, "Hof- und Harems-Erlasse" 274.42-45.

1.3.7 THE EVIDENCE OF THE LETTERS

What about the evidence of the clay tablets themselves? This primary source material presents an intriguingly different picture. When messages are described as being sent by the writers of clay tablets, the stress is rarely oral. Note the following cases where the tablet containing the message is given to the messenger:

> I entrusted a tablet to PN's hand (*ṭuppa ana qātīšu attadin*) whom my brother sent to me - may [my brother re]ad and hear his/its word. (*EA* 20.33-35)

> [To] all royal messengers you give your tablet (and) you send (*tašappar*), and you send as well your messenger to them. But to mine - [to] my messenger you give [no] tablet, nor do you send your messenger [to m]e.[100] (*EA* 47.14-20)

> Earlier I had a tablet inscribed (*ušaṭṭeramma*) and entrusted it to the hand of PN_1 & PN_2 (*addin*) and sent them. On route, they were seized. Now I begin again. I am having inscribed on a tablet the equivalent of the former and I now send it. (*ARM* X 166.2-8)

The last mentioned citation includes another feature of despatching messengers according to the letters themselves, namely a reference to the actual inscribing (*šaṭāru*) of the tablet:

> These things in a tablet you wrote (*tašṭuram*) and sent me (*tušābilam*). (*SH* 827)

---

[100] A new collation by W. Moran indicates that Knudtzon's "with them ... with him" (referring to messenger) is more likely [*it-ti-i*]*a* "to them ... to me" with reference to kings.

> Write down the good news about yourself (*šuṭeram*) and send it to me.[101]
>
> After the *rab kissati* had inscribed (*išṭuru*) a message (*šipirti*) [for me?], I had it sent to the palace. (*NB* 323.9-13)

On occasion, the reference includes a note to the effect that the message which is inscribed on a tablet was dictated:

> A letter should be dictated, written (and) sent to him (*lisqurū lišṭurūne lušēbilenešsu*). (*LAS* 214.r1'-2')
>
> Why do you neither write your tablet nor dictate your document (*ṭuppīki lā tašaṭṭirī giṭṭīki lā taqabbī*)? Or will people say "Is this the mistress of PN . . . ?" But you are merely his daughter-in-law. (*SLA* 152.3-5r)

It is important to note that there is no reference to the messenger receiving an oral message. In the light of these texts, the one who received the message was a scribe who wrote the message down for another to carry. There is little here that is reminiscent of the imperatives encountered in literature. Rather, it is closer to the commissioning which was seen in the Sumerian account of *Lú-dingir-ra*.

Such an emphasis upon the writing of the letter without any reference to an oral communication corresponds to the unique account in biblical literature where a messenger carries a written document of whose contents he is ignorant (2 Sam 11:14-15):

> In the morning, David wrote a letter to Joab and sent it by the hand of Uriah. In the letter he wrote, "Set Uriah in the forefront of the hardest fighting, and then draw back from him, that he may be struck down and die."

---

[101] S. Greengus, *Old Babylonian Tablets from Ischali and Vicinity* (Nederlands Historisch-Archaeologisch Instituut te Istanbul, 1979) 21.20-23.

This message is solely a written communication whose objective is achieved only if the messenger does not deliver it orally. The irony of a messenger unknowingly carrying his own death-warrant underscores the narrative art which permeates the entire Uriah account. This fact reminds us that not only are the circumstances unique, but the format does not conform to the norm in messenger-commissioning scenes in ancient Near Eastern literary texts.

The contrast between the data supplied by the letters themselves on the one hand and the literary texts on the other is striking. In the literary texts one discovers an entirely oral commissioning, while the letters underscore the written phenomenon associated with the despatching of a message. If one or the other source material were missing, we would have little reason to suspect an entirely different manner of commissioning messengers. While the literary texts assert the messenger's knowledge of the message he carries, the letters themselves communicate independently of the messenger's voice. We will return to this problem and the significance of the epistolary imperative "speak!" (*qibīma*) when we discuss the actual delivery of the message, for the form in which the message is delivered gives considerable insight into how it was originally despatched.

The actual written correspondence seems to have been deposited in a bag with a strap which was slung over the messenger's shoulder or around his neck. This is the implication of Amenhotep II's description of a Mitanni messenger whom he intercepted in the Sharon plain of Palestine, "with a clay tablet at his neck (*r ḫḫ-f*)."[102] One may compare the well-preserved leather-bag which contained the Aramaic correspondence of Arsames in the Persian period,[103] and the much earlier Old

[102] E. Edel, "Die Stelen Amenophis' II. aus Karnak und Memphis," *ZDPV* 69 (1953) 162 n.86.

[103] G. R. Driver, *Aramaic Documents of the Fifth Century B.C.*, (Oxford: Clarendon, 1957) 3.

Assyrian *tamalākum*, a container for documents. Otherwise, the document is simply said to be "in the hand" of the messenger.[104]

1.4 LAST-MINUTE DETAILS

Having selected the messenger and entrusted the message to him, is he ready to be sent on his way? Not quite, for his welfare on the journey must be guaranteed. To insure a safe passage, the will of the gods must be favorable for the undertaking. Hemerologies advised that "one should not travel" on Ab 4,[105] while on Tammuz 4, 8, 11, and Adar 29 one should not set out on a journey - loss will result.[106] On Teshrit 7, "one should not go on a trip - he will be robbed."[107] At Mari, messengers would not be sent if the omens were foreboding (*ARM* II 97.5-11):[108]

> I investigated the omens about the welfare of the messengers and they were unfavorable. I shall do them again. When the omens are favorable, I shall send them.

The Neo-Assyrian kings a thousand years later were still concerned about the divine perspective and left behind several inquiries about the welfare of the messengers which they sent. "Shamash, great lord, reply to my inquiry with a reliable answer" is

---

104 *m ḏrt.f* of Muwatalli's messenger at Qadeš sent to Ramses II (M. Valloggia, *Recherche*, 141).

105 *kaskal nu-un-gin*; R. Labat, "Un almanach babylonien," *RA* 38 (1941) 29.

106 *ḫarrānam lā uṣṣā ṣītu*; R. Labat, *Hémérologies et ménologies d'Assur* (Paris: Librairie d'Amérique et d'Orient, 1939) 91.

107 *ana ḫarrāni lā illak ḫabtūtu iḫabbatuš* (*Ibid.*, 175).

108 Perhaps *ARM* I 117.5-16 is relevant as well, when Yasmah-Addu speaks of investigating the omens when messengers wished to move on, but twice they were unfavorable (reading *iptaslā*, "they twisted themselves together," with W. von Soden, "Zu den politischen Korrespondenz des Archivs von Mari," *Or* 21 [1952] 82).

the typical introduction to these unfortunately fragmentary texts which may nevertheless be extensively reconstructed due to their predictable formulaity.[109] When Esarhaddon sends a messenger to Kashtarit, lord of Karkassu, he queries, "Will he slay [. . .] that messenger [on the advice of] his counselors?"[110]

Even when the omens pointed toward a prosperous journey, it is likely that prophylactic measures were taken to avoid mishaps. In a Sultantepe text is recorded an "incantation for seeing a sign when starting [on a journey]" as the subscript specifies. The petition which one is to address to the constellation Ursa Major runs as follows:[111]

> Without your permission, even a mortally ill man cannot die, and a well man cannot start on a journey. If I am to succeed in this journey on which I am about to start, let them give me something (in my dream); if I am to fail in this journey on which I am about to start, let them receive something from me (in my dream).

When travelling by chariot to a foreign land, a noble who wished to return safely after accomplishing his mission[112] would perform the appropriate ritual and prayer to ensure that his chariot did not break down en route. Whereas the NA petitions above were

---

[109] Due to the fragmentary nature of the texts, it is often difficult to decide whether these requests were made before the messenger was sent or while he was en route (*AGS* 3). The Mari text cited above suggests that taking an omen for prophylactic purposes is more reasonable, for once the messenger has left, it serves little practical purpose to discover that he will not complete his mission.

[110] *PRT* 3.6-7; cf. 12.5 "will they seize that me[sseng]er?". Note *AGS* 38 where the issue seems to be upon hostile peoples falling upon the messenger and robbing him. *AGS* 25, in inquiring of the messenger's fate, asks, "Will Esarhaddon grieve?"

[111] *STT* 73.73-75 in E. Reiner, "Fortune-Telling in Mesopotamia," *JNES* 19 (1960) 27,33.

[112] *rubû šuātu ašar illaku ṣibūssu ikaššadu u ina ḫarrān illaku šalmussu ana mātīšu iturra*; F. Thureau-Dangin, "Le rituel pour l'expédition en char," *RA* 21 (1924) 130 l.7-8.

addressed to Shamash, the prayer for one's chariot addressed not only Shamash but Nergal and the gods of the steppe.[113]

This last reference is noteworthy, for in seeking divine assurance of a safe journey, it appears that a particular god's benevolence might be sought, at least in Mesopotamia. Nergal may be the deity to whom the traveller turns for protection and safety while on the road.[114] We cite here the ritual for the chariot alluded to above:[115]

> To the great gods, to Nergal and the gods of the steppe he shall offer a sacrifice; the great gods, Nergal and the gods of the steppe will take pity on the noble riding the chariot.

Similarly, the fifteenth day of Kislev is a day of consecration to Nergal, which if observed will mean that a man "will be safe in his journeys or travels."[116] It thus may be no accident that when Nergal is enraged, it is the messenger (*kaš$_4$/lāsimu*) on the road who feels his wrath (*Lugal.e* l.96). It is striking that Nergal is even described as a messenger in a late text: "valiant messenger, quick of knees" *(mār šipri qardu lāsimu birkī)*.[117]

Thureau-Dangin observes that Nergal is specifically mentioned in the context of the traveller because he is the principal god of the steppe through which the traveller is passing.[118] Recent studies of Nergal have stressed this god's role

---

[113] *ilāni ṣēri* (*Ibid.*, 130-131 l.9-16,20-25).

[114] W. Moran pointed out to me that the reading "Nergal" for ^{d}*U.GUR* in G. Dossin, "Prières aux dieux de la nuit," (*RA* 32 [1935] 181) should be read *DINGIR-lam*, i.e. the personal god. See E. von Weiher, *Der babylonische Gott Nergal* (*AOAT* 11; Neukirchen-Vluyn; Neukirchener, 1971) 28.

[115] F. Thureau-Dangin, "Le rituel," 130 l.9-11.

[116] *RMA* 151.r4-6; cf. S. Langdon, *Babylonian Menologies and the Semitic Calendars*, (Oxford: Oxford University, 1935) 94, where a similar text is cited.

[117] An Achaemenid hymn; J. Nougayrol, "Textes et documents figurés," *RA* 41 (1947) 41. See *AGH* 118.

[118] Thureau-Dangin, "Le rituel," 133 n.1.

under three or more categories "als kriegerischer Held, als Gott der Seuchen and als Herr der Unterwelt,"[119] but his role as a protector of travellers may not bc insignificant. As such, one might postulate Nergal as the patron deity in general of Mesopotamian messengers.[120]

When the oracles were favorable, would the messenger be immediately sent on his way? A few texts remind us that rations for the trip would be provided for the messenger,[121] and sometimes he might be provided with a means of transportation.[122] A Neo-Babylonian messenger is provided with 50 shekels toward the purchase of a donkey for the road and flour for his trip to Tema to which he is sent (*šapra*).[123] But there is little further data specifically relating to such provisioning of a messenger before he leaves. We will discuss such provisioning and transportation issues under the discussion of the messenger on the road where more data is available.

---

[119] M. K. Schretter, *Alter Orient und Hellas* (Innsbruck: H. Kowatsch, 1974) 62. Von Weiher (*Der babylonische Gott Nergal*) adds also his role as divine judge (20f.), benefactor (22f.), god of light (73f.), astral deity (76f.) and fertility (87f.).

[120] It is not his exclusive domain, of course, for other deities exercise their will over the traveler (e.g. Shamash [*BWL* 131]). But Nergal, associated with the steppe, would not be an unlikely deity to appear frequently in this context: *Nergal ur.sag edin.na.ka* (*KAR* 91.35; see A. Tsukimoto, *Untersuchungen zur Totenpflege (*kispum*) im alten Mesopotamien* [*AOAT* 216; Neukirchen-Vluyn: Neukirchener, 1985] 179). Note the popularity of the cult of Nergal among the later merchants of Palmyra.

[121] "I send (*altappar*) PN to the Sealand but he doesn't know the way. Send a man of yours with him who knows the way. Give him provisions" (*ṣidīti* - *NBU* 211.5-15). "Through PN's messengers send it (the garment); meal for the journey give to his messengers" (*qēm harrāni* - *NBU* 206.5-18).

[122] "Horse and donkey I gave him for his journey" (*EA* 161.23-24). "The messenger of the king of Akko is honored more than my messenger since a horse is put under him" (*EA* 88.46-48).

[123] *GCCI* I 294. It is tempting to see this as the same Nabu-mušetiq-urra who is called a *mār šipri* a decade earlier (*GCCI* I 150).

The message to be delivered often would require written authorization or documentation. If the messenger carried a letter, then a scribe would be needed to write down the message (if the messenger were not himself a scribe). From such scribal activity, we learn that occasionally the day of the messenger's departure was of sufficient significance that the scribe would include that datum as part of the document and message dictated by the sender, e.g. "Month X, day Y, I sent this tablet to my lord,"[124] usually as the very last item on the tablet.

Such a note, however, is not common and no doubt due to the exigencies of the immediate situation: noting the date of the messenger's departure exonerates the sender of any accusation that he might be responding too late while simultaneously placing a constraint on the messenger to move at an acceptable speed to arrive quickly at a destination where the receivers will know how long his journey took. Further precision is recorded when a message is sent at the end of the day (underscoring that messengers travelled by night),[125] at mid-day,[126] late afternoon,[127] or in the morning (*ARM* XIV 119.20). Such scribal notes, presented as part of the message itself, are found not only in the second millennium. In eighth century Assyria, a provincial administrator records the date on which he forwards another kingdom's messenger to the king: "On the 29th of the month Shabat they are leaving."[128]

Apart from scribal notices, extenuating circumstances such as the presence of hostile forces might prompt messengers to leave

---

[124] Month X, day Y *ṭuppi/am annêm ana ṣēr bēlīya ušābilam*, *ARM* III 5.39; XIII 29.25; XIV 31.20; see also *ARM* I 16.29; 31.39; 39.24; 70.19; IV 14.5'; 78.35'; XIV 90.17; 101.18'.

[125] *ARM* I 5.46; 8.40; 10.24'; 19.5'; 37.42; 53.9'; 60.38; 65.9; 88.31; 74.44; 90.27; II 8.29; 10.16'; 44.47 IV 45.7' 59.15; 80.12; XIV 104.18'. Note Enmerkar's messenger who travells by night (*ELA* 158).

[126] *ARM* IV 35.5' as restored by A.L. Oppenheim, "The Archives of the Palace of Mari II," *JNES* 13 (1954) 143.

[127] *ARM* I 67.18 with A.L. Oppenheim, "The Archives of the Palace of Mari," *JNES* 11 (1952) 131-132.

[128] H. W. F. Saggs, "Nimrud Letters," *Iraq* 17 (1955) 132.

under cover of darkness (*EA* 108.52-56),[129] or a doctor's continual vigilance over an ill patient might require round-the-clock notification (even at midnight[130]) of relatives with regard to the patient's condition.[131]

[129] Cf. J. Eidem, "News from the Eastern Front: The Evidence from Tell Shemshara," *Iraq* 47 (1985) 100 n.84.

[130] *ištu mūšu mešēli ištu mār šiprīya ana muḫ bēlīya ašpura*, "since midnight, since I sent my messenger to my lord (the patient's condition is described as of morning)" (*BE* 17/I 47.5-7).

[131] *um 29 KAM ina Šamaš napā[ḫi] mār šiprīya ultēṣa . . . [in]a Šamaš napāḫi ašappara . . . [ina] Šamaš rabê a[ša]ppara*, "The twenty-ninth day, I hereby send my messenger at sunrise . . . at sunrise I'll write . . . at sunset I'll write" (*BE* 17/I 33.25-31).

2

THE MESSENGER ON THE ROAD

2.1 THE RIGORS OF THE ROAD

There is no piece of ancient Near Eastern literature which takes so much delight in describing the messenger *en route* as do two Sumerian works about Enmerkar and Aratta. The bards wax eloquent in their hyperbole and similes as they describe what other literatures will find of no interest. When discussing the preparation to send the messenger, it was observed that in the tale of *Enmerkar and the Lord of Aratta*, Enmerkar (and Inanna) anticipated the messenger as he would "go up into the Zubi ranges" and "come down with it out of the Zubi ranges" (*ELA* 108-109). But when the messenger actually sets out,[1] the description becomes as long as the journey itself (*ELA* 160-171):

[1] In which direction would the messenger go to reach Aratta? On the elusive geographical location, see H. Sauren, "Der Weg nach Aratta," *Wirtschaft und Gesellschaft im alten Vorderasien* (ed. J. Harmatta and G. Komoróczy; Budapest: Akadémiai Kiadó, 1976) 137-144; G. Komoróczy, "Die Beziehungen zwischen Mesopotamien und dem iranischen Hochland in der sumerischen Dichtung," *Mesopotamien und seine Nachbarn*, (XXVe Rencontre Assyriologique Internationale; Berlin: Dietrich Reimer, 1978) 93 n.11. H. L. J. Vanstiphout ("Problems in the Matter of Aratta, *Iraq* 45 [1983] 35-42) discusses the distinct genre of "a challenge-and-contest between rulers, effectuated by messengers . . ." (p.39).

> The envoy heeded the word of his master. By night he went just by the stars. By day he could go by heaven's sun divine. Whither did he take Inanna's great words in the reed canister[2] for her? He had to go up into the Zubi ranges, had to come down with it out of the Zubi ranges. . . . Five mountain ranges, six mountain ranges, seven mountain ranges, he crossed over, lifted up his eyes, he was approaching Aratta.

This idealized messenger never rests; he certainly does not use the dark as an excuse to sleep. In addition to the five, six and seven mountains which he crosses serving as a formulaic nicety of poetry,[3] this repetition also focuses upon the real effort required of a messenger. The same feature recurs in a later journey (*ELA* 507-510):

> The envoy, like a bird, was beating the wings, like a wolf closing in on a buck he was hurrying to the kill. Five mountain ranges, six mountain ranges, seven mountain ranges, he crossed over, lifted up the eyes, he was approaching Aratta.

The simile of a wolf chasing his prey clearly depicts the eagerness and speed with which the messenger makes his journey. It is important to note that in this messenger's seven trips, there is no repeated stereotype description beyond the just noted passage of the mountains. Each journey is described in a distinct fashion. Further similes are introduced in which he is compared to several

---

[2] T. Jacobsen understood ^{giš}*su*$_{11}$*-lum-ma* = *kūru* (communication by W. Moran). But is this a container or some type of device designed to assist the messenger's recall, such a device being commonly attested in primitive cultures (R. Numelin, *The Beginnings of Diplomacy*, 164-167)?

[3] Compare *Gilgamesh and the Land of the Living* where only the first and the seventh mountains are mentioned (S. N. Kramer, "Gilgamesh," *JCS* 1 [1947] 3-23). See also M. deJong Ellis, "Gilgamesh' Approach to Huwawa: A New Text," (*AfO* 28 [1981-1982] n.17,18).

other types of animals such as a wild bull (297), a bird (436), a sheep (416), a colt (413), a wild donkey (414), a serpent seeking its prey (351), and a fish (437). All of these descriptions are spread out over several trips. This bewildering jungle of animals, however, is thrown altogether in one exuberant description in a kindred work, Enmerkar and Ensuhkeshdannna (*EnEn* 40-49):

> The messenger runs like a wild ram, flies like a falcon, at dawn he goes forth; at evening he . . . , like a swarm at dawn, over the open country he goes straightaway, like a swarm at midnight, he fills the interior of the mountains, like a throw-stick, he stands at the side, like a wild-donkey of Shakan he runs over the mountains, like a large powerful donkey, he races(?), a slender donkey eager to run, he rushes forth, a lion in the field at dawn . . . he goes, like a wolf seizing a lamb, he runs quickly.

Singleness of purpose in the speed with which he fulfills his task explicitly characterizes the animals enumerated. This corresponds literarily to the explicit desire for speed which was noted earlier when analyzing the qualities which make a good messenger. Returning to *Enmerkar and the Lord of Aratta*, the messenger's journey is depicted with graphic brush-strokes beyond the use of animal similes: he "kept lifting his nose into the wind" (*ELA* 415) and "plunged his foot into the dust of the road, sent rattling the little stones of the mountain ranges" (*ELA* 349-350).

The picture extensively painted above of the messenger making his way from one destination to another became a sign of normalcy in society. When societal norms broke down, communication often failed as well and the messengers ceased. The *Curse of Agade* recounts that when Enlil brought the Gutium to punish Sumer and Naram-Sin, "messengers no longer travel the highways, the courier's boat no longer takes to the rivers" (l.162-163).

In passing from the literature of Sumer to other areas in the ancient Near East, it should be stressed again that the extensive descriptions of messengers on their journeys are notably absent outside Sumer - with two exceptions at Ugarit. In the previous section where commissioning scenes at Ugarit were discussed, there were two occasions where an element appeared in which the journey itself was anticipated by the one who sent the messenger. We do not have the actual journey portrayed (the appropriate section is missing in each case). In the first text, we find Asherah ordering her attendant Qadish-wa-Amrar to go to the craftsman-god, Kothar-wa-Hasis, in order to ask him in Baal's name to build Baal's palace. The beginning is broken (*CTA* 3.6.3-19):

> A thousand [ ] in the sea, myriads [ ] in the rivers, traverse mountain (*'br gbl*), traverse hill (*'br q'l*), cross over the farthest peak of the heavens (*ibt np šmm*). Start away, oh fishermen of Athirat, come Qadish-wa-Amrar. Then thou shalt set thy face to the midst of Egypt . . . from a thousand fields, myriads of acres at the feet of Kothar bow down.

As in *Enmerkar and the Lord of Aratta*, the journey is here anticipated by the one sending the messenger. More explicit detail occurs when Gapnu-wa-Ugaru is sent to the Underworld (*CTA* 4.8.1-7):

> Then set your faces toward mount TRǴZZ, toward mount T̠RMG, toward the mountains which guard the underworld. Lift the mountain with your hands, the hill with your palms - and descend to the realm of the Underworld . . . .

Such epic voyages are manageable for divine couriers who can leap tall mountains in a single bound and with their bare hands lift the same. Nevertheless, there are still echoes of a delight in poetic description of the messenger's travels through exotic and distant lands, similar to that which was found in Sumer. As we saw in an earlier chapter, these passages are part of sections which also preserved the lengthiest addresses to a messenger in a commissioning scene.

The voyages of the messenger may have been an exotic treat about which to write, but others with a more realistic bent have left impressions which do not prompt jealousy of the messenger's task. In the myth *LUGAL-UD ME-LÁM-BI NIR-GÁL*, for example, Ninurta enters the conflict and targets certain individuals for destruction, among them the couriers: "He slew its (i.e. the rebel country's) couriers in the mountain" (*lú-ím-ma-bi kur-ra im-ra*).[4] The Egyptian wisdom text, *The Instruction of Cheti* (also known as *The Satire of the Trades*), in its pronounced bias against all professions apart from the scribe, may not describe the life of a courier with complete objectivity but is nevertheless illuminating:[5]

> The courier (*sḫꜣḫꜣty*) goes to the desert, leaving his goods to his children; fearful of lions and Asiatics, he knows himself only when he's in Egypt. When he reaches home at night, the march has worn him out; be his home of cloth or brick, his return is joyless.

Apparently Syria was not an especially popular locale for Egyptian messengers in the First Intermediate Period. The first danger cited would apply in any case to messengers of all nationalities. However, corresponding to the second danger, the presence of Arameans stifled messenger traffic between Babylon and Hatti in the 13th century and sheer force was the only remedy to safeguard one's messenger.[6]

---

[4] *[lāsim]ūšu ina šadî idūk* (*LUGAL-UD* 1.97); cf. T. Jacobsen, *The Harps That Once . . .*, 241.

[5] M. Lichtheim, *Ancient Egyptian Literature*, I 188. "Our text achieves its satirical effects by exaggerating the true hardships of the professions described, and by suppressing all their positive and rewarding aspects" (*Ibid.*, 184).

[6] *CTH* 172.36-43; "Had I provided a thousand chariots for your messenger, then I would have sent him safely to (the lower) Tuttul" *lū <ana> mār šiprīka līm narkabāti uqarribaššumma ina Tuttul [u]kaššidaššu* (1.42-43). The implication is that since the Babylonian king has so many horses (and hence chariots), he should provide armed escort for his messengers instead of stopping them. The syntax is certainly confused, as seen in the various translations offered, for

The slave in the *Dialogue of Pessimism* argues further for a less romantic view of a messenger's travels. He notes that it may not be wise to ride with chariot to the palace lest the king conscript chariot and driver to deliver messages, for the king(?) "will make you take a [route] that you do not know; he will make you suffer agony [day and] night" (*BWL* 145.8,9). Reluctant messengers may have been the source of the Babylonian king's remark when he explained why communication seemed to be faltering (*EA* 7.53-60):

> It is said that the way is difficult (*dannatu*[7]), the water in short supply (*batqū*), and the weather hot, therefore I have not sent many gifts . . . . When the weather improves, then I will have my future messenger who will go bring many fine gifts.

---

example: "Should I have had your messenger met by a thousand of my chariots?" (A. Oppenheim, *Letters From Mesopotamia* [Chicago: University of Chicago, 1967] 143); "A thousand chariots accompanied thy messenger" (D. Luckenbill, "Hittite Treaties and Letters," *AJSLL* 37 [1920-1921] 201); "Soll ich (da) für deinen Boten (noch) tausend Streitwagen herbeischaffen?" (J. Friedrich, "Briefwechsel zwischen Chatti und Babylon," *AO* 24 [1925] 26); "Your envoy brought one thousand chariots to him" (*CAD* N [1] 354). *Qurrubu* takes a dative of the person if the meaning is "to present something to someone" but an accusative if "to escort, let approach." If one takes the gemination of *uqarribaššumma* seriously (i.e. dative suffix) then *mār šiprīka* (not dative) is not its syntactic antecedent. But there is no other meaningful antecedent. The crux, then, is in which case is *mār šipri* to be understood: dative, accusative or *casus pendens*? Has *ana* been omitted before the noun, or is false gemination present on the suffix? The latter would mean no mistake in syntax, but there would be a double accusative, not appropriate to this verb. We consequently assume the latter syntactical slip or an omission of *ana*, understanding *lū* as indicating an unreal statement (*GAG* 152f).

[7] W. Moran pointed out to me that a subjunctive is required, restoring tu_4 instead of *tum*.

Great distances might seem the substance of which romantic descriptions are made, but the messengers themselves testify that the journey is longer than anyone can imagine. Burnaburiash in the same letter just cited is incredulous that during his illness no messengers came bearing condolences from the Egyptian Pharaoh (*EA* 7.16-32).

> Why did not he send his messenger to me when I was sick? My brother's messenger said, "This is not a place close by so that your brother can hear (you are sick) and send greetings. The country is far; who can tell your brother so that he can write quickly? Would your brother hear you are sick and not send his messenger?" I said to him, "Is there such a thing as a near or far land to my brother the great king?" He said, "Ask your own messenger if the way is far!" . . . . I asked my messenger and he said the way is far (*girru rūqatu*[8]), so I kept quiet.

A certain sense of comraderie seems to bind the messengers together in this text in the face of the naivete of the king - after all, they have measured off the 1,000 miles of caravan routes separating the capitals of Babylon and Egypt. Travelling forty to sixty kilometers per day,[9] even without hindrances or delays, meant that weeks at a time were simply spent travelling. The reluctant messengers visible between the lines of Burnaburiash's letter find a fellow sympathizer in the OB messengers of whom one writer laments, "You have sent (*tašpuram*) no one. The way is far (*girrum rūqma*) and no one wants to travel to me."[10]

---

[8] See preceding note; the following phrase is the translation of W. Moran.

[9] On the speed with which international messengers could travel, see C. Kühne's extensive excursus, "Das Zeitproblem in der Korrespondenz: Technische Erwägungen," (*Die Chronologie*, 105-124).

[10] *AbB* VII 144.4'-7'.

But the great distances were not the central discouraging element in being a messenger.[11] Messengers were not immune from the uncertainties which any traveller faced on the characteristically bad roads of the ancient Near East.[12] One must

---

[11] Note the occasional reluctance of later Greek messengers to serve (F. Adcock and D. J. Mosley, *Diplomacy in Ancient Greece*, 202).

[12] R. J. Forbes, "Land Transport and Road Building," *Studies in Ancient Technology* (2nd Ed.; Leiden: Brill, 1965) 131-192. Note the address to Shamash: "You stand by the traveller whose road is difficult," *temmid ana allāki ša šupšuqat ur[uḫšu]* (*BWL* 130-131 l.65). Although Sargon's description of the road between Babylon and Assyria is intended to indicate the poor conditions of a route in disuse, the fact remains that messengers often had to travel precisely such highways: "At that time, the road . . . to Babylon was not open, its road was not passable . . . going was cut short, the way was most difficult and there was no path prepared, in the inaccessible tracts, thorn thistles and jungle prevailed over all of them, dogs and jackals assembled in the recesses . . . . In that desert country Arameans, Suti, tent-dwellers, fugitives, treacherous, a plundering race had pitched their dwellings and brought passage across it to a stop" (C. J. Gadd, "Inscribed Prisms of Sargon II from Nimrud," *Iraq* 16 [1954] 191-193). The bliss envisaged in the *Lamentation over the Destruction of Nippur* belies the reality: "A day when (any) chosen(?) road can be travelled, the weeds having been ripped out, a day where man can travel where he wills, when even in the steppe(?) . . . will not be harmed, a day when all suffering will be gone from the land, light will pervade it" (S. N. Kramer, "Modern Social Problems in Ancient Sumer: Evidence from the Sumerian Literary Documents," *Gesellschaftsklassen im alten Zweistromland und in den angrenzenden Gebieten* [*ABAW* 75; 1972] 114-121). The motif of impassable roads is a feature in laments: in addition to the *Curse of Agade* cited above, note the lament of Ibbi-Sin: "no one sets foot on the roads, no one undertakes a journey" (A. Falkenstein, "Die Ibbi-Sîn Klage," *WO* 1/5 [1950] 376-384); cf. Judg 5:6. "There seem to have been very few periods in the history of the region when private letters could be sent from city to city (as in the Old Babylonian period) or a private person could move around freely" (A. L. Oppenheim, *Ancient Mesopotamia* [Chicago: University of Chicago, 1977] 120). See also L. Casson, *Travel in the Ancient World* (London: George Allen & Unwin,

not romanticize as did the Sumerian literary text. Indeed, the murmurings of dissatisfaction still echo from the Amarna letter mentioned above, for the messengers must have had the ear of the king on the day when that letter was written. We return once again to the Amarna letter from Babylon, a letter which suggests a candid perspective into the unadorned life of the messengers who did not always relish the commissions which they received from the king (*EA* 7.73-82):

> As for Ṣalmu, my messenger whom I sent to you, twice his caravan was plundered. Biriyamaza plundered one, and Pamahu[ ], the *šakin* of your land, the land *ki-is-ri*, plundered his second caravan. [Resolve(?)] that case! . . . Let them pay back what he lost.

It is important to recall in this context that messengers were more than simply bearers of words, for words were more often than not accompanied by goods. But a messenger's commission did not deter such a theft as was noted - and Ṣalmu was the messenger of the king of a significant power. Lesser messengers had more reason to tremble.

Ṣalmu was fortunate that he was merely robbed and remained alive to plead for justice. There is more than one reference to messengers losing their lives while on the road: Yasmah-Addu's messenger, Ili-iddinam, was slain by unnamed bandits along with fourteen others (of which one was a maid *amtu*) while travelling in a small caravan; ten managed to escape with their lives, leaving ten donkeys and one horse to their attackers (*ARM* II 123). A trio travelling from Carchemish to Mari became a solo when only the Carchemish messenger escaped with his life after four Ubrabians attacked them (*ARM* XIV 86). The king of Babylon feared lest his messengers and those of Egypt be

---

1974) 38-39. Note the (exaggerated) experiences of a *mhr/mariyannu* travelling in Syria-Palestine (Anastasi I) treated by A. H. Gardiner, *Egyptian Hieratic Texts* I/1 (Hildesheim: George Olms, 1911). Azitawadda's Phoenician inscription contrasts the peace of his reign with the former days when men feared to walk the highways (*KAI* 26 A II.1-8).

killed in Canaan (*EA* 8.31-32).[13] A Neo-Assyrian letter assures us that messengers have no special status when they are the enemy's messengers: "When you see his messengers, kill whomever you can kill, and capture whomever you can capture" (*SLA* 25.12-14). Diplomatic immunity was at best a messenger's dream. Immunity for the couriers between hostile powers was non-existent, a feature of society which repeated itself continually in the ancient Near East. This is noteworthy in so far as a general pattern in societies traditionally grants inviolability to such figures.[14]

Messengers were in danger of being seized *en route* before reaching their destination.[15] One OB woman begins her letter by grumbling that what she writes is a copy of a letter which she had sent earlier but which had never reached its destination: her two messengers were seized while on the road (*ina ḫarrānim*

---

[13] His merchants, often employed in the royal diplomatic corps, were killed in Canaan (*EA* 8.13-29).

[14] "[Primitive messengers], just like the diplomats of civilized nations, enjoy a number of special privileges. They are almost always personally inviolable . . . . A breach of the principal of inviolability of the messengers and envoys seems to be severely punished . . . even if the respective tribes are at enmity with each other" (R. Numelin, *The Beginnings of Diplomacy*, 147). See *Ibid.*, 147-152 for specific data (and rare exceptions to the generalization on p.150-151).

[15] In time of war, Kamose seized Apophis' messengers and their documents at the end of the Hyksos period (L. Habachi, "The Second Stela of Kamose and his Struggle against the Hyksos Ruler and His Capital," *Abhandlungen des deutschen archaeologischen Instituts Kairo - Ägyptologische Reihe* 8 [1972] 39-41). When returning from a campaign, Amenhotep II intercepted a Mitanni messenger in the Sharon plain (probably travelling to a south Palestinian ruler) and treated him as a prisoner (E. Edel, "Die Stelen Amenophis' II. aus Karnak und Memphis" *ZDPV* 69 [1953] 162). The aggressive posture of his father, Tuthmosis III, toward this region set an example for him early in his reign, but diplomatic relations were established by the end of his reign (*EA* 19.9-10). This precedent was followed by his successors, Tuthmosis IV and Amenhotep III, who each wed a Mitanni princess and submitted to diplomatic protocol.

iṣṣabtūšunūti).[16] Orders are given to seize the messengers of the Babylonian king Shamash-shum-ukin,[17] while the Hittite kings anticipate such seizures in time of war.[18] Indeed, the Hittites violated a messenger's rights and encouraged their allies to do likewise: "If any one sends a messenger from a hostile land, don't hide him but seize him and deliver him to the king."[19] A fragment of the Tukulti-Ninurta Epic records the imperative: "hold back the messenger [ ] keep the merchants from passing through."[20]

---

[16] *ARM* X 166.2-8. In *ARM* X 167.2-8, she composes the same introduction but addressed to a different party.

[17] *kī ḫantiš PN* [ ] *u mārē šipri ša Šamaš-*[*šum-ukīn lā t*]*aṣṣabtānimma lā taltaprā* [ ] "If you do not promptly seize PN and the messengers of Š. and send them" (*SLA* 41.6-8). See also *ABL* 1105.6,28-31, a documentary oath to be loyal to Ashurbanipal by seizing any of Shamash-shum-ukin's messengers and sending them to Ashurbanipal (cf. M. Dietrich, *Die Aramäer Südbabyloniens in der Sargonidenzeit* [*AOAT* 7; Neukirchen-Vluyn: Neukirchener, 1970], 82,174-175).

[18] "If the messenger is unable to come," then Murshili II stipulates that the vassal is to send troops immediately to the Hittite king when he hears of the subterfuge (*CTH* 68; *SV* I 126-127).

[19] A. Kempinski and S. Košac, "Der Išmeriga-Vertrag," *WO* 5/2 (1970) 193 (=*CTH* 133). The lacunae are reconstructed with the help of the Madduwattash treaty: "If Attarshiyash sends you a message, seize the messenger and send him to the Father of the Sun; and do not conceal anything which he writes to you, but write it out fully for the Father of the Sun. Do not send the messenger back to Attarshiyash without authorization" (A. Goetze, "Madduwattaš" [*MVAG* 32; 1927] 10-11 [=*CTH* 147]). See also the treaty with Mita: "Whatever enemy sends a messenger, hi[s messenger they seize] and dispatch him to my Majesty, and send him not back on their own initiative" (O. Gurney, "Mita of Pahhuwa," [*AAA* 28 (1948) 32-47] 36 [=*CTH* 146]).

[20] *kila mār šipri* [? ? *tamkā*]*rē etēqa šukli* (K. W. Chang, *Dichtungen der Zeit Tukulti-Ninurtas I. von Assyrien* [Frankfurt am Main: Peter D. Lang, 1979] 98 l.10-11). The preceding context speaks of a ratified treaty (*rikilta uktīn* l.9) and the benevolence of the one addressed (*damiqtaka* l.10). It is therefore likely that the detention of messenger and merchants is in response to the other party's

Ambushes and attempts to waylay messengers were an item to write home about if they were successfully avoided.[21] And although a messenger may not necessarily be seized, he might find that his passage was blocked by hostile forces, as in the case of a city under siege (*EA* 114.33-38):

> My messenger [ ] I repeatedly sent. How many times I sent him but he was unable to enter the city of Ṣumura! They have seized all the roads before him.[22]

The correspondence of Bahdi-Lim from Mari is replete with tales of messengers stopped *en route*, for that was part of Bahdi-

---

faithlessness. But it is unclear whose messenger is detained: the other party's messenger not allowed to return home, or the despatching of his own messenger, or even a third party's not allowed to pass through his territory? All three are attested elsewhere.

[21] "Since my lord sent me (*išpuranni*) to the land of Guti for information (*ana pîm u lišānim*), I departed safely/secretly (*naṣrum*) from Der for Susa and I ascended 6 double hours toward the city GN. 9,000 Elamites and 3,000 Gutians were in a ravine to seize me. Then out of their midst came 2 Elamites [ ] I approached [ ] they didn't approach. [ ] The mountain was near and they went there secretly. I approached the land of Guti and the 2 cities which belong to my lord, to Elam [ ] Send 5,000 men" (*AbB* VIII 92). This latter text was a model letter, now known from two exemplars (J. van Dijk, "Remarques sur l'histoire d'Elam et d'Eshnunna," *AfO* 23 [1970] 65-71). It is not certain the writer was a messenger, but he uses *šapāru* to describe his mission.

[22] *ṣabtū kali ḫarrānāti ana šâšu*. See also the Ugaritic letter from Puduhepa to the king of Ugarit which, though fragmentary, clearly pictures the breakdown of the caravan routes, so frequently used by messengers: "Concerning the fact that you sent word to the palace ["?]ed are the caravans of Egypt and they have stopped; moreover the caravans of Egypt through the land of Ugarit [are x-ed] and through the land of Nuhašše they must pass [ ](skip at least 8 lines) [ ]shall pass through the land of [X and through the land of] Qadesh and through the land of [X] and the land of [ ] shall not harm them (or 'shall not be harmed')" (D. Pardee, "Further Studies in Ugaritic Epistolography," *AfO* 31 [1984] 325 l.14-28').

Lim's service to the king. He occasionally gives a reason for not allowing messengers to pass, as in the following case where he fears that the messenger might see things which he should not (*ARM* VI 19.18-24):

> "Perhaps the auxiliary troops are not yet assembled before my lord, and should I send that man to my lord, he would discern the state of the troops" - for this reason I held him back. Now shall I send that man to my lord?

On another occasion he asks for a general policy decision from the king as to whether or not messengers travelling from Mesopotamian cities to Syrian destinations (or vice-versa) should be stopped.[23] In a similar vein, Hattushili III later anticipates the possibility of Assyria preventing Babylonian messengers from passing through Assyria in order to reach Hatti. But he reminds the Babylonian king that Assyrian military might was inferior to Babylon and messengers still should be sent (*CTH* 172.43-49). The implication of this text is that stronger powers could with impunity interrupt messenger traffic passing through their land (as at Mari; cf. *AbB* VI 24).

In both the second and first millennium, international law attempted to restrain the abuse of messengers.[24] The Akkadian text of a treaty between Hatti and Kizzuwatna stipulates that messengers sent between them, no matter their status (*lū mārašu lū ardašu . . . išappar*[25]), were not to be mistreated (*limuttam lā ippuš*) by the king who received the messenger.[26] A later Aramaic

---

[23] *ARM* VI 23.19f.; see N. Na'aman, "East-West Diplomatic Relations in the Days of Zimri-Lim," *RA* 75 (1981) 171-172.

[24] The notion of an international order established by imperialism motivated Amenhotep II's boast that "there is no hindrance to his envoy throughout all countries of the Fenkhu" (M. Lichtheim, *Ancient Egyptian Literature*, II 41).

[25] "Whether he sends his son or his servant . . . ."

[26] G. R. Meyer, "Zwei neue Kizzuwatna-Verträge," *MIO* 1 (1953) 114 1.11-13 (=*CTH* 26). This is reminiscent of later Greek behavior where envoys required the protection provided by a truce between

treaty (*KAI* 224.7-9) goes beyond reciprocal cordiality by guaranteeing any messenger from any land free access to the sovereign and vice versa. The vassal is ordered not to interfere or obstruct messenger traffic.[27]

The plea for diplomatic privilege in such documents belies the reality of frequent abuse documented in actual letters. Indeed, the possibility always existed that messengers might be slain upon arrival at their destination if the omen text reflects some reality: "Your messenger will be slain in the place to which you send him (*mār šiprīka ašar tašapparušu iddâk*).[28]

We will return later to the problems associated with avoiding the bureaucracy, but at present we wish to focus upon the alternatives open to messengers to avoid outright murder and plunder on the road as noted above. In response to the dangers just surveyed, messengers found an insurance policy in the custom of travelling with large groups. The caravan might be a safe way to travel for the messenger who might otherwise be travelling alone. Indeed, the caravan itself often took the place of messengers, for merchants and travellers were conveyors of information who might be given a message which they would pass on in the course of their travels: "May the caravan (*alaktu*) for Babylon bring me your message (*ṭēmu*) daily" (*AbB* III 65.24-25), or as in the following case (*SLA* 34.6-1r):

> A caravan went up from GN[1] - the sons of PN were bringing wool from GN[2] and they reported saying (*umma*): "The troops are . . . ."

---

formerly hostile states; the Greek herald, however, was always inviolate (F. Adcock and D. J. Mosley, *Diplomacy in Ancient Greece*, 202).

[27] "Now (as for) all the kings of my vicinity or anyone who is a friend of mine, when I send my ambassador (*ml'ky*) to him for peace or for any of my business or (when) he sends his ambassador to me, the road shall be open to me. You must not (try to) dominate me in this (respect) nor assert your authority over me concerning [it]" (J. A. Fitzmyer, *The Aramaic Inscriptions of Sefîre* [*BibOr* 19; Rome: Pontifical Bible Institute, 1967] 96-97 l.7-9).

[28] J. Nougayrol, "Textes hépatoscopiques d'époque ancienne," *RA* 44 (1950) 17-18 l.36.

The first example just cited is ambiguous as to whether or not messengers were the actual bearers of the message. However, compare the note which explains why other messengers would not be arriving immediately: "A caravan left the day before yesterday - the messengers will leave with the next caravan" (*ḫarrānim warkītim*; *ARM* II 133.19-24). The desire to travel with the caravan is so compelling in this case that the messengers are held back and their message delayed in order to wait for the next caravan.

Because caravans were constantly travelling the routes, a certain regularity or predictability was possible in despatching messages or messengers with the caravans (*AbB* II 162.13-23).

> Send me a letter with the caravan which comes to you (*ina gerrim ša illakam*) and send (*šuprānim*) a report about the tablets . . . . With the next caravan (*ina gerrim maḫrim*) write me (*šuprānim*).

This relative regularity removed any excuse from those individuals found in any age who simply are not faithful letter-writers: "Why do your caravans not bring news of you regularly?"[29] However, in defense of those who are often excoriated in Babylonian letters for failing to write, the caravans were fallible and subject to the same harassment and delays which were outlined above for messengers (*EA* 8.20-40; translation of W. Moran):

> (Your people in Canaan) killed my merchants and took their silver. . . . Pay back the money that they took, and the men who killed my servants you kill! . . . If you don't kill these men, they will kill again, whether it be your caravan or your messengers, and messengers between us will be cut off (*ipparras*). Shumadda . . . blocked the passage of one of my men and detained him, and Shutatna . . . forced another man into his service.

---

[29] *ammīni šulumki ḫarrānātuki kayyāna lā išpur* (*TR* 122.8-9).

This passage assumes that the treatment of messengers and caravans is a parallel phenomenon.[30] The degree of freedom for inter-urban mercantile ventures went hand-in-hand with the efficiency of information transfer: at Mari there was news that "the caravan was detained and he [couldn't] send" (*ARM* X 70.18-19).[31]

2.2 ASSISTANCE ON THE ROAD

2.2.1 MEANS OF TRAVEL

In spite of the frequent association of messengers with caravans, the caravan was not the sole option available for the transferring of information. A variety of choices was possible in determining the mode of transportation by which a messenger might travel. In fact, the caravan, although generally reliable, was

---

[30] By way of comparison, note the following observations with regard to Greece. "No theory of diplomatic immunity prevailed until the emergence of Roman power; until then, envoys relied on the traditional codes of religion and hospitality in their movements" (F. Adcock and D. J. Mosley, *Diplomacy in Ancient Greece*, 122). "Envoys passed readily between states which were not at war and relied on the traditional codes of conduct observed for strangers, but they did not possess freedom from arrest or immunity as such . . . . It was, of course, a serious matter and a risky enterprise to abuse envoys . . . . They could claim protection only if a herald first cleared the way. Furthermore, envoys conducting business between two states had no general right of immunity from arrest or interception by a third party. In cases of doubt, they would require permission to pass through the territory of third parties" (*Ibid.*, 154).

[31] Note Yarim-Lim's letter to Zimri-Lim with regard to a caravan detained at Hazor, apparently in reprisal for a theft at Hazor and in order to compel official compensation (A. Malamat, "Silver, Gold and Precious Stones from Hazor - Trade and Trouble in a New Mari Document," *Essays in Honor of Yigael Yadin* [ed. G. Vermes and J. Neusner; New Jersey: Allanheld, Osmun and Co., 1983] 71-79).

not the quickest way for an urgent despatch to travel.[32] In the earliest period, running fulfilled this objective. In the two Enmerkar tales, apart from the one time in which the herald accompanied a caravan of goods which his king sent to Aratta, we have already seen how the animal similes used to describe the messenger en route focus upon speed and determination as he runs. Running became the feature by which one type of messenger became known, namely the "runner" *lāsimu*.[33]

However, one must distinguish the runners of the third millennium B.C. from those of the later period. When Enmerkar's messenger used his feet to reach distant Aratta, there was no choice available for alternative, quick means of travel since the horse had not yet been domesticated. Clearly, he did not run the whole way non-stop, but it is quite likely that his feet were in fact his main source of propulsion. Later runners do in fact run, but the distances which they cover are shorter, although still requiring considerable stamina. In Israel it is the herald's feet which are worthy of praise (Isa 52:7; Nah 2:1), and when Gehazi deceptively passes himself off as Elisha's messenger, he runs after Naaman's chariot and successfully overtakes him (2 Kgs 5:20-22). The one who reports the capture of the ark and the defeat of Israel before the Philistines was such a runner (*wayyāroṣ*) who covered well over twenty miles in order to deliver his report on the same day in which the battle occurred.[34] Two runners also bring news to David of the defeat of Absalom (2 Sam 18:19-26):[35]

---

[32] For the Neo-Assyrian situation, see H. W. F. Saggs, "The Nimrud Letters," (*Iraq* 21 [1959] 158-179) 177.

[33] Long-distance running was early ennobled by Shulgi's remarkable prowess as a king who ran from city to city to perform his cultic duties (J. Klein, "Shulgi and Ishmedagan," [*Beer Sheva II*; ed. M. Cogan; Jerusalem: Magnes, 1985] 7*-38*).

[34] *wayyābo' šilôh bayyôm hahū'* (1 Sam 4:12). It is just over 20 miles from Ras el-'Ain to Khirbet Seilun as the crow flies, but the mountainous terrain prohibits a direct route.

[35] The distance which they ran could not have been more than several miles, if the allusions in Samuel are correctly interpreted to the effect that all of chapter 18 occurred on one day (v.6,7). If so, whatever ground the runners covered would have been covered already that

> Then said Ahimaaz the son of Zadok, "Let me run, and carry tidings to the king . . . ." (But) the Cushite bowed before Joab and ran. Then Ahimaaz the son of Zadok said again to Joab, ". . . . Let me also run after the Cushite." And Joab said, "Why will you run? . . ." He said, ". . . I will run." So he said to him, "Run!" Then Ahimaaz ran by way of the plain and outran the Cushite . . . . The watchman saw a man running by himself . . . and then saw another man running.

It is clear that running was always a means of transmitting communication in the Semitic world. But technology made the runner less than adequate in many cases. Mesopotamia was blessed with two great rivers which made boat travel an efficient transporter of messengers. We know of a messenger from Yamhad who took a boat downstream[36] and another order by the king of Mari to forward a messenger from Ekallatum on a boat.[37] It is noteworthy that in the latter case the order is not obeyed. The governor of Sagaratum explains his reticence in using a small boat for the messenger because "he bears in his hands a (valuable) gift" and it might be lost in the water.[38] Because the text is broken, it

---

morning by David's troops on their way to the battle. As to the two routes taken by the two runners, Aharoni notes: "The Cushite took the more direct, but up-hill-and-down-dale route of the 'forest of Ephraim,' whereas Ahimaaz ran by a longer, though much easier route passing through the Jordan Valley, and thus arrived first" (Y. Aharoni and M. Avi-Yonah, *The MacMillan Bible Atlas* [New York: MacMillan, 1968] 70).

[36] "The boats which were with Larim-Bahli arrived and Yammu-Qadum the messenger of Yamhad arrived with him" (*ARM* III 56).

[37] The king specifies a "small boat" (*maturru*, *ARM* XIV 127.5-11)

[38] *aššum šukuttam ina qāt[īšu n]ašû ādurma awīlam šâtu ina maturrim ul ušarkib umma anākūma assurrēma m[aturram u]šarkabšūma* [? ? *i*]*ṭbēma*, "Because he bears in his hands a (valuable) gift, I feared and so did not put that man in a small boat, thinking perhaps I might put him in the boat [ ] it sank [ ]" (*ARM* XIV 127.18-24). For *šukuttum* see *AHw* 1266-1267.

is unclear if the messenger is sent in a larger, more reliable boat or if he continues by land.

Not only is the trip effortless by boat, but under certain climactic conditions even necessary. Muddy roads resulting from intense rains could be impassable.[39] Messengers and boats are linked in Mesopotamia as early as Sumerian literature, where the *Curse of Agade* links the messenger (*kin-gi$_4$-a*) with the highways and the courier (*rá-gab*) with boats (l.162-163).[40] Wenamun's trip clarifies that messengers made use of merchant ships plying the Levantine coast.[41]

Refinements in technology soon put the chariot at the messenger's disposal.[42] We have already noted when discussing the messenger's preparation that the chariot could qualify a man to function as a messenger. Already at Mari we find the palace furnishing a foreign messenger with spare chariot parts.[43] The chariot was a preferred means of sending the messenger, since it

---

[39] Note how sheep travel under their own power if the ground is good, but with muddy roads they are to be transported by boat (*NBU* 309.18-25).

[40] For the significance of boats and communication at Mari, see S. Dalley, *Mari and Karana* (London: Longman, 1984) 169f. For southern Mesopotamia, see W. F. Leemans, *The Old Babylonian Merchant*, (Studia et Documenta 3; Leiden: E. J. Brill, 1950) 3.

[41] For other Egyptian messengers on boats, see M. Valloggia, *Recherche*, 170,186,187. See also C. Kühne (*Die Chronologie*, n.517) on the options in the Levant for travelling by land or by sea.

[42] See M. A. Littauer and J. H. Crouwel, *Wheeled Vehicles and Ridden Animals in the Ancient Near East* (*Handbuch der Orientalistik*, VII.1.B1; Leiden: Brill, 1979), and P. R. S. Moorey, "The Emergence of the Light Horse-Drawn Chariot in the Near East c. 2000-1500 B.C.," *WA* 18/2 (1986) 196-215. See C. Kühne (*Die Chronologie*, 106) with more precise data with special reference to the latter part of the second millennium.

[43] "A double yoke and a set of reins for PN the Qatna messenger," *1 tāpal ḫulli 1 appatum ana PN mār šipri Qatanāyi* (*ARM* XXIII 41.6-10). For the *tāpal ḫulli* as an accessory of chariots, see *ARM* VII 161.9.

maximized that most important of messenger qualities, speed.[44] "When Shindishugab my messenger reaches you, let him take chariots so that he can reach me quickly" (*EA* 10.37-39).[45] That the chariot was used for speed in such cases is clear at Nuzi where the king writes (*JEN* 494.3-14):

> Now PN I hereby send (*altaparšu*), so give him a swift (*qalla*) chariot. And (when he returns) from that place to which he is travelling, give him (another) swift chariot so that he can come to me.

As early as the OB period, the chariot seems to be employed by those who carry messages. However, the heavier chariots of this period were not designed for speed but for transport. In addition, the improving technology was inevitably accompanied by corresponding drawbacks when the chariot's sophistication became a liability. The *mariyannu* (who often served as messengers) experienced difficulties when travelling alone in a chariot through Syria-Palestine. They had to carry their chariots in poor terrain and suffer the consequences when the horse's groom deserted, the horse was stolen, or the chariot itself (or parts of it) broke down.[46]

The ass as a means of transportation is attested early, intimately tied with messenger activity. Two named *rākib imērī* are specifically called *mārī šipri* at Mari (*ARM* II 45.6-7), while the *rākibī imērī* from Larsa who escort Babylonians to Babylon with a message for Hammurabi are probably messengers as well (*ARM* II 72.6-7). Extispicy texts note that a messenger riding a donkey will

---

[44] J. Sasson notes two types of chariots at Mari, one of which is designated "fast" *ḫamuttim* (*The Military Establishments at Mari*, [Studia Pohl 3; Pontifical Bible Institute, 1969] 31,32).

[45] By the time of the Amarna age, chariots were employed as a major element in warfare. However, in the Old Babylonian period the evidence for chariots in battle is very limited (Littauer and Crouwel, *Wheeled Vehicles*, 61-65).

[46] A. Gardiner, *Egyptian Hieratic Texts* I/1 (Hildesheim: George Olms, 1911) 21*-22*,26*-27*.

arrive (*mār šipri rākib imēri errub*).[47] Already in Ur III provisions are made for the asses of a travelling *rá-gab* (*TEL* #55.25-26). Indeed, it may be that originally the riding of an ass lent its name to a specific type of messenger, namely the *rakbu*, who nevertheless was not confined to this mode of transportation, as seen above.

The association of messengers with horses is unquestioned in the first millennium. The Neo-Assyrian *kallāpāni* "couriers, carriers, despatch riders," and *raksūti* "escort riders" are both intimately connected with horses and messenger activity.[48] The biblical *rakkāb*-messenger who rides a horse (2 Kgs 9:17-20) and the Amarna messenger, Hani, who is given horses (and asses) for his journey (*EA* 161.23-24) confirm that at least some messengers used them. In the Neo-Assyrian period a *mār šipri* appears in conjunction with horse and mule lists (*TFS* 113.12)

Nevertheless, the crucial question concerns the precise time when the horse came into use as a mount.[49] "Horses were bred, trained, traded and used for a variety of purposes" already in the first half of the second millennium.[50] Considering the degree of sophistication of horse maintenance at this period, Lewy has suggested that the Haneans had already mastered the art of warfare on horseback,[51] and Sasson is ready to admit that horses may have been saddled at this time.[52] There is a general reluctance to acknowledge that horses were ridden this early, with a preference to see this innovation only in the first

---

[47] J. Aro and J. Nougayrol, "Trois nouveaux receuils d'haruspicine ancienne," *RA* 67 (1973) 41 l.2' and parallels cited in *CAD* I/J 113. See A. Salonen for his comments upon the lowly nature of this transportation (*Hippologica Accadica* [*AASF* B 100; 1956] 223).

[48] J. V. Kinnier Wilson, *The Nimrud Wine Lists* (London: British School of Archaeology in Iraq, 1972) 57-61. See also *TFS* p.229.

[49] In general, see Littauer and Crouwel, *Wheeled Vehicles*.

[50] S. Dalley, *Mari and Karana*, 159; see also p.161-165 for horses at Mari in general.

[51] H. Lewy, "On the Historical Background of the Correspondence of Bahdi-Lim," *Or* 25 (1956) 351 n.1, referring to *ARM* VI 76.20-22.

[52] J. Sasson, *The Military Establishments at Mari*, 63 n.100.

millennium.[53] But it is now clear that warriors mounted on horseback formed cavalry divisions in the Egyptian New Kingdom, and representations of mounted riders from the same period are numerous. Indeed, representations of deities mounted on horseback from this same period demonstrate that the mounted rider occupied a position of some status.[54] Unpublished Old Babylonian texts from Tell Leilan are reported to contain references to the extensive use of horses in battle.

In Mesopotamia, "horse bones have yet to be identified in a Near Eastern archaeological context before the later third millennium B.C."[55] At Nuzi a *sukkal* and a *šangû* priest ride horses when sent on a mission,[56] and when at Mari the king is counselled not to ride a horse (*ARM* VI 76.20-25), this certainly implies that the activity is possible. Indeed, the context of this letter implies that horse-riding was not uncommon for the nomadic elements of the population. Furthermore, pictorial evidence affirms that horses were ridden in a rudimentary fashion as early as the Ur III period,[57] a reality confirmed by an Old Babylonian fable.[58]

If the horse is introduced and ridden by the end of the third millennium, can we assume that they became a regular means of transportation for messengers? As Moorey points out, the typical rations for Ur III individuals in the so-called "messenger texts" do

---

[53] L. Casson, *Travel in the Ancient World*, 51-52.

[54] J. LeClant, "Astarté à cheval d'aprés les représentations égyptiennes," (*Syria* 37 [1960] 1-67) 18. The horse is known in Egypt only from the Hyksos period onward (*Ibid.*, 17-18).

[55] P. R. S. Moorey, "Pictorial Evidence for the History of Horse-Riding in Iraq before the Kassite Period," *Iraq* 32 (1970) 36.

[56] "Have them mounted on a pair of fine horses and . . . send" (*ina ištēnūti ANŠE.KUR.RA damqāti šurkibšunūti u . . . šupur*; *HSS* XIV 14.3-5).

[57] P. R. S.Moorey, *Ibid.*, 47-49.

[58] "The horse, after he had thrown off his rider, (said): 'If my burden is always to be this, I shall become weak!'" (E. Gordon, "Sumerian Animal Proverbs and Fables: Collection Five," (*JCS* 12 [1958] 1-21) 18-19.

not make allowance for feeding a quadruped,[59] although as we noted above some rations are made occasionally for asses. It is reasonable to assume that some messengers were using the horse in the Old Babylonian period;[60] can we be sure that the horse accompanying one messenger was a gift between monarchs (*ARM* II 123)?[61]

There is no evidence to connect early messengers with the camel, for it was not in use even as a beast of burden until the end of the Middle Assyrian period at the earliest.[62] Even then, it never gained popularity until the Persian period.[63]

2.2.2 PASSPORTS

We noted above that messengers could be easily detained due to bureaucracy. Since the network of city states and independent kingdoms or empires in the ancient Near East could only be sustained by an adequate exchange of information and goods, formal protocol developed which, although compounding bureaucratic complexities, served to facilitate the movement of messengers. In order to ensure safe passage through territories far removed from the point of departure, the wise messenger would carry documents (in addition to any written communiqués) which specifically identified him as a messenger in the service of an influential person. Such documents would naturally have had little influence on brigands who constantly harassed travellers. Rather, their main function would be to allow the messenger to bypass any bureaucratic delays and unnecessary monetary

---

[59] P. R. S. Moorey, *Ibid.*, 48.

[60] "But generally speaking messengers travelled by foot or boat making best use of the network of rivers and canals to speed their journeys in Iraq until at least the Old Babylonian Period" (P. R. S. Moorey, *Ibid.*, 48).

[61] As S. Dalley does in *Mari and Karana*, 161.

[62] A. Salonen, *Hippologica Accadica*, (*AASF* B 100; Helsinki: 1956) 84.

[63] L. Casson, *Travel in the Ancient World*, 55-56.

charges which he might encounter along his route. One OB example will suggest the nature of the problem, even though in this particular case no messengers are involved (*AbB* IX 112.28-34).

> I await you two in GN accompanied by soldiers of the king and letters of the king saying that nothing should be an obstacle to you up to Larsa.

This note underscores that the document which grants safe passage is valid only for a certain defined area and for specific individuals. Such a document for a messenger would specify his point of departure, his name, who sent him, those who accompany him along with their point of origin and their destination (M.8990 in *ARM* XXIII p.20):

> Yaspuq-Il, messenger of Ṣura-Hammu, from Ahuna. One hundred *beḫrum*, one *šagatum* his guide (*ālik pānīšu*) from Ashlaka. To Mari.

Iṣi-Haru of Ekallatum traveled to Carchemish without such a permit and suffered the consequences when the governor of Sagaratum stopped him (along with the four female slaves he escorted and an accompanying Marian[64]) and asked (*ARM* XIV 52.11-15):

> Without (the permission of) my lord, a transport (*šubultum*) can not pass through to another land; why do you (sing.) not bear a tablet [of my lord]?

---

[64] Sakummi-El is simply *ša bēlīya* and is probably not an escort supplied by Zimri-Lim (mentioned only here although the name recurs in *ARM* IX 289.7). Only the Ekallatum messenger is addressed in the singular in contrast to the plural for messengers with escorts (*ARM* XIV 122.5-7). The Marian is not only of no assistance to the messenger in this scuffle with Mari red-tape, but the messenger is said to travel "with Sakummi-El" in contrast to the usage described below.

The messenger's reply to this query is lost, but since the governor wrote a letter to Zimri-Lim about this circumstance, it is likely that the messenger was not permitted to pass until Zimri-Lim gave the governor appropriate instructions.[65]

Several such "passports" for messengers are preserved from the second part of the second millennium. The following is such a document which a (probably[66]) Mitanni messenger bore on his way south to the Egyptian court (*EA* 30):

> To the kings of Canaan, servants of my brother: Thus (says) the king: "Now, I have sent Akiya, my messenger, to the king of Egypt, my brother, to speed post-haste. Let no one hinder him. Provide him with safe entry into Egypt and hand him over to the fortress commander of Egypt. Let him go on immediately and as far as his presents[67] are concerned, he is to owe nothing.

This passport, like all others which we possess for messengers, is messenger-specific and valid for only the immediate task; it is not reusable, and for that reason it was left behind in the Egyptian

---

[65] The antiquity of the concept is clear. From the Ur III period, note the comment, "Why is it (that although) he did carry my tablet someone detained him?" (*TCS* 1 166.7-9). From the OAss material, a passport is specifically made out for the messengers from *kārum* Kanish to "every single *kārum*" (*ana kār kārma qibīma*). The passport indicates that each *kārum* along their journey is to provide the designated messengers with two escorts (*muqarribu*) to accompany them safely from *kārum* to *kārum* (*BIN* 6 120). See the discussion in K. R. Veenhof, *Aspects of Old Assyrian Trade and Its Terminology* (Leiden: E. J. Brill, 1972) 252-253, where he calls the document a "circular letter".

[66] The Mitanni background of this document is argued by P. Artzi, "El Amarna Document #30," *Actes du XXIXe Congrès Internationale des Orientalistes - Assyriologie* (Paris: L'Asiathèque, 1975) 1-7. However, the OB and OAss evidence clarifies that such documents were not an innovation of the Amarna period as he claims.

[67] W. Moran suggests *kad-<ru>-su*, and the translation is his.

archives where it was found. Styled like a letter, it is similar to another letter of introduction which identifies a certain Ili-milku as a bona fide messenger of the king and queen of Ugarit as he travels on ultimately to the Hittite king (*PRU* IV 294). Found at Ugarit, one may presume that the trip was never made. The archives of Ugarit contain a passport left behind by the messenger of the kingdom of Beirut when he was sent on a mission to Ugarit (*PRU* III 12-13):

> Thus says the King of Beirut to the *šakin* of the land of Ugarit, my son: Greetings to you, may the gods protect you well. My son, I have sent this my messenger to your country in order to accomplish my desires. You, my son, watch over him (*īnēka damqūta ana muḫḫīšu šukun*).

The messenger is not specified by name, as was the case in the former document from Mitanni. Furthermore, the address is not to the king but to one of the highest officials at Ugarit, the *šakin* of the land.[68] The purpose of the messenger's trip is not stated, for it is essentially carte blanche according to this document. By addressing the document to the *šakin* of the land, potential bureaucratic delays for the messenger in the fulfillment of his mission would be minimized.

One such delay not specifically mentioned in the above text but which is found in the following passport (also found at Ugarit) is the avoidance of any tax. After the typical address and greeting to the *šakin* it reads (*PRU* IV 196-7):

> Is all well with you? Send me news. Now I sent (*aṭrussu*) my man to my son. Everything that he needs on his trip he is to receive - let no one stop him. Let no tax-collector collect any tax from him. As long he remains there, watch over him.

---

[68] For this office at Ugarit, see M. Heltzer, *The Internal Organization of the Kingdom of Ugarit* (Wiesbaden: Dr. Ludwig Reichert, 1982) 141-152.

The concern that the *awīlu* be neither hindered nor taxed and be watched over while under the jurisdiction of the *šakin* is repeated in the closing lines of another letter which is also such a passport carried by the man to whom it refers.[69] It was the responsibility of the post stations to regulate messenger traffic. Officials were recognized as having the authority to inquire as to the business of all who passed. When Bahdi-Lim, for example, asks foreign messengers for their commission when they pass through Mari territory, they provide him with the desired information (*ARM* VI 27 *et passim*). If one wished to relay secret information, alternate steps had to be taken as will be discussed in section 4.3.

2.2.3 LODGING

Taverns[70] no doubt served as lodgings for envoys *en route*. This is apparently the case in 12th century Syria, for Wenamun,

[69] *PRU* III 15-16 l.22-31. A further document contains similar features (*Ugar.* V 92,93), although it is addressed directly to the king of Ugarit from a Hittite prince. He is sending a group of men (*ṣa-ri-b/pu-tu*) from a certain city to perform sacrifices, after which the king of Ugarit is to send them safely on to the *ḫazānu* of Salmiya. There is a request that no one rob them while in the mountains (*uḫabbatšunūti*; the editor translates this as "tax", but the locale and the different vocabulary do not make this similar to *PRU* III 16 as he argues) and that all their requests be granted. See also other passports in *EA* 39, 40; *PRU* IV 193.

[70] For bibliography on the Sumerian *(é)-èš-dam*, Akkadian *aštammu* and *bīt sābīti*, and Hittite *arzana* see H. A. Hoffner, "The Arzana House," *Anatolian Studies Presented to Hans Gustav Güterbock on the Occasion of His 65th Birthday* (K. Bittel, Ph. H. J. Houwink ten Cate, E. Reiner, eds.; Istanbul: Nederlands Historisch-Archaeologisch Instituut in het Nabije Oosten, 1974) 113-121. For the OAss *bīt wabri/ubri* see P. Garelli, *Les Assyriens en Cappadoce* (Paris: Adrien Maisonneuve, 1963) 303f. with additional texts cited in K. R. Veenhof, *Aspects of Old Assyrian Trade and Its Terminology* (Leiden: E. J. Brill, 1972) 250.

spurned by the Byblian king, finds lodging in a sea-side tavern[71] in a fashion similar to the two spies (called *mal'ākîm* in Josh 6:17,25) sent out by Joshua to reconnoiter Jericho (Josh 2:1f.). It is not true that there was necessarily any opprobrium attached to such establishments (in spite of their use as brothels), for individuals of substantial stature dined and spent the night there,[72] and they have been described as the "social center of the estate or village," and "a place in which the inhabitants would typically gather for talk and recreation after the end of work."[73]

But from the third millennium, it is already apparent that a strong government did not leave the maintenance of inns to chance. The Persians were not the first - although they are the most famous[74] - to realize the importance to the state of reliable communication. Shulgi already boasts of building secure government hostels for travellers along the road,[75] and the "courier

---

[71] Goedicke, *Wenamun*, 49. Goedicke translates it "tavern" (*Ibid.* 45) and considers *ỉmw* in this context a "lowly accommodation", being tempted to see it as "a kind of boarding house, possibly in the nature of a khan." In addition to the Hittite evidence locating the *arzana* outside the town proper cited by Hoffner (*Ibid.*, 120), it is possible that the same holds true for Mesopotamia on the basis of the Middle Assyrian Law A 14 (reading *tal-be-te* with *CAD* A (2) 473 instead of *ri-be-te*).

[72] See H. Hoffner, *Ibid.*, 119-120; G. R. Driver, *The Babylonian Laws* (Oxford: Clarendon, 1952) 202; L. Casson, *Travel in the Ancient World*, 37. Driver may overstate the opposing case from a modern perspective, as the example he cites suggests.

[73] T. Jacobsen and S. N. Kramer, "The Myth of Inanna and Bilulu," (*JNES* 12 [1953] 165-181) n.68.

[74] R. J. Forbes, Land Transport and Road-Building," *Studies in Ancient Technology* (Leiden: Brill, 1965) II, 131-192.

[75] "I . . . proceeded along the roads of the lands, . . . built there (lodging-)houses, planted gardens by their sides, established resting places, installed in those places experienced (men); (he) who comes from 'above', (he) who comes from 'below', may refresh themselves in their cool shade; the wayfarer, who passes the night on the road, may seek haven there" (Shulgi A 29-35). Shulgi texts "may reflect the celebrations of the opening of a newly constructed road between Ur

stations" (*é-kaš*$_4$) were centers where rations and lodging were provided for state envoys.[76] The regulation of messenger traffic implied in the passport *EA* 30[77] is made explicit in Papyrus Anastasi III vs.6.1-5.9 where a border-post official recorded messenger traffic passing between Canaan and Egypt.[78] The Neo-Assyrian *bīt mardīti* is some type of road station (*CAD* M (1) 278) or post station (*LAS* 294.r4) whose maintenance, functioning and staffing is the subject of *SLA* 90. Its use as a relay station for official letters (and in this case its breakdown) is evident when an official writes to the king (*LAS* 294.r4-11):

> Alongside the road the (personnel) of the post stations entrust my letters [to] each other (and) bring

---

and Nippur provided with a system of parks and caravanserai along the way" (J. Klein, "Shulgi and Ishmedagan," 9*).

[76] L. Casson (*Ibid.*, 36) notes (citing T. Jones and J. Snyder, *Sumerian Economic Texts from the Third Ur Dynasty*, [Minneapolis, 1961] 293-302) that Lagash provided for "efficient movement of her administrators, couriers, and army personnel between the capital and the subject cities, most of which were 100 to 250 miles away and one even more than 400. Each man's travel orders included an issue of food rations, which were enough to carry the recipient just one day's march; at the end of this he presumably found himself at a government hostel where he put up for the night and received food for the next day on the road. The amount and quality of the rations went according to rank: administrators, for example ate distinctly better and more than ordinary dispatch riders. The men travelled on foot except for the very highest officials, whose allowance included fodder for animals; it is very likely that they got fresh mounts as well at each stage."

[77] For the Amarna period in particular, although incorporating much other data, see C. Kühne, *Die Chronologie*, 108-110, especially n.532.

[78] One Semitic messenger carries two despatches north, one of which is going to the ruler of Tyre. Seven days later, three messengers go south with a despatch for pharaoh, another in the same direction carrying two letters for Egyptian officials, while another travels north with two letters. For translation, see R. Caminos, *Late Egyptian Miscellanies* (London: Oxford University, 1954) 108-109.

> them to [the king], my lo[rd]. (Yet) for two or three times (already) my letter has been returned [from] the towns of GN^1,GN^2, (and) GN^3! [Let a sealed order be s]ent to them (that) they should entrust my letter [to each oth]er (and) bring it to [the king my lord].

Such post stations no doubt granted provisions and mounts only for royal and official business;[79] one may assume that private correspondence was not a concern of such posts. The Assyrian kings placed a premium upon good roads primarily for the maintenance of the empire and the efficient operation of their war machine,[80] providing a foundation for the future Persian communication network.

Finally, one must not discount the generous hospitality available from non-institutionalized lodgings apart from private enterprise or state-operated inns. In early second millennium Syria, more than one official envoy travelling between Egypt and Syria found lodging in Sinuhe's bedouin tent.[81] Such private hospitality toward travellers reappears in later Israelite texts (Gen 19:2 24:22-34; Judg 19:15-21) as well as in classical sources[82] and likely served the needs of many messengers.

2.3 SAFETY IN NUMBERS?

2.3.1 AKKADIAN

In the light of the material discussed in the preceding sections regarding the often adverse conditions on the road, the

---

[79] See also E. Weidner (*AfO* Bei 6, 11-13) for the Neo-Assyrian posts. Messengers rest at Mari in *ARM* V 26.9-10, presumably provisioned from the palace inventories.

[80] L. Casson, *Travel in the Ancient World*, 50-51.

[81] "The envoy who came north or went south to the residence stayed with me. I let everyone stay with me" (M. Lichtheim, *Ancient Egyptian Literature*, I 227).

[82] L. Casson, *Ibid.*, 87.

phenomenon of messengers travelling in groups is hardly mere coincidence. Several times at Mari, Shamshi-Adad makes a specific request for exactly two messengers to be sent on a mission, and in each case the mission is clearly fraught with danger: intercepted correspondence, despatches regarding troop movements, and covert travel by night.[83] A letter from southern Mesopotamia records the threat that "if you do not help me, two messengers (*našparu*) will come and will cause trouble for you."[84] One may deduce from such examples that two men were sent together if there was reason to expect opposition or resistance.[85]

---

[83] "Send two swift men (to PN)," *2 awīlī qallūtim ana ṣēr PN šupram* (*ARM* I 39.17'; II 10.4',5'); *2 qallūtum ṭuppam ana PN liblūnim* (*ARM* I 93.14-17); *2 ṣuḫārūka qallūtim* (sic!) *ṭuppātīka lilqû* (*ARM* I 97.16-17); although broken, [ ] *qallūtum liblūšunūti* (i.e. carry tablets; *ARM* I 93.11-12), it is possible that "two" should be supplied since such a request recurs later in the same tablet. It is clear from *ARM* I 97 that the two messengers travel together and are not going to two different sections of the country; see W. von Soden, "Zu den politischen Korrespondenz des Archivs von Mari," *Or* 21 (1952) 75-86 82.

[84] *Ša elīkunu marṣu ippušū* (*AbB* I 97.3'-6'); see *CAD* N (1) 71.

[85] It has been suggested that there was "die sicherheitspolitische Praxis, mehrere Boten gleichzeitig zu entsenden, um die Nachricht sicher zum Empfänger zu bringen, selbst wenn das Kontingent der Botschafter dezimiert werden sollte" (*TWAT* IV 890-891). But there is no evidence to suggest that messengers were sent separately in order to insure the safe-arrival of at least one, as is certainly attested in other cultures. Geniza material does show that in the Middle Ages one would send several copies of a letter to insure its safe arrival when sent by boat, but this was not done with overland mail which was quite secure (M. Larsen, *The Old Assyrian City-State and its Colonies* [Copenhagen: Akademisk, 1976] 93). There is also no evidence to affirm that more messengers meant greater accuracy in the delivery of message or response (as argued in *TWAT*). Those with experience in oral communication can testify quite the opposite: the more messengers, the greater confusion ("a man with two watches can never be sure what time it is"). This may be why in ancient Near Eastern embassies sent as groups, one figure tends to dominate as spokesman.

Presumably, if one messenger is waylaid, the other can continue[86] or even extricate his fellow from danger.[87] As in the letter cited above, two men can be more threatening than one. A wisdom text from Ugarit reflects such an attitude:[88]

> Make your journey with a companion (*ibri*); the one who goes with a companion, he is concerned for him, he who goes with a troop (*UGNIM*) goes in security (*šulumšu illak*).

It is important to observe that the individuals in the above citations seem to compose a pair sent out together, originating in the same locale. Such a commissioning of two messengers is to be differentiated sharply from the custom of a single messenger making a round trip who is escorted home by a messenger from the city to which he was sent. At Mari we are well-informed of this traditional diplomacy from the *ṭēḫītum*[89] texts in *ARM* VI which

---

[86] The Greek herald always functioned alone since he was inviolable, while Greek messengers in general tended to work in groups, not possessing the herald's immunity (F. Adcock and D. J. Mosley, *Diplomacy in Ancient Greece*, 154). The size of embassies varied, with Sparta consistently sending three men as messengers while Athens sent embassies of two, three, five, or ten men (three and ten dominating); the size of a group also could be dictated by its relative importance (*Ibid.*, 155).

[87] In the Aegean world, Diomedes volunteers to spy at night with the following proviso reflecting such a perspective (*Iliad* X.221-227: "Gladly will I visit the host of the Trojans over against us, but if another will go with me I shall do so in greater confidence and comfort. When two men are together, one of them may see some opportunity which the other has not caught sight of; if a man is alone he is less full of resources, and his wit is weaker."

[88] *Ugar.* V 278-280 l.14-16.

[89] *ṭe$_4$-ḫi-tum*. The following three types of phrases introduce each letter after the traditional greetings:

A) *ṭēḫītum ištu GN^1* (*ARM* VI 79.5) (*u GN^2*) *ikšudam* (*ARM* VI 16.5-end; 21.5-22; 62.7-15; 78.5-6).

Bahdi-Lim writes to the king, informing him of the arrival and departures of messengers at Mari.

TABLE A

Origin	Goal	Messengers	Escort	Letter
Qatna	Mari	1 Qatna	none	14
Yamhad	Babylon	3 Bab.	1 Yamhad	14
Yamhad	Ekallatum	1 Ekallatum	1 Yamhad	14
Qatna	Mari	1 Mari	1 Qatna	15
Qatna	Babylon	1 Qatna	none	15
Qatna	Arrapha	1 Arrapha	1 Qatna	15
Babylon	Mari	3 Mari	[broken]	16
Babylon	Mari	2 Mari	2 Babylon	21
Qatna	Elam	2 Elam	1 Qatna	22
Qatna	Qabara	1 Qatna	1 Qabara	22
Karana	Mari?	1 [Mari]	1 [Karana]	62
Babylon	Mari	3 Mari	1 Babylon	63
[Babylon]	[Mari]	2 [Mari]	1 [Bab.]	70
Hazor	Mari	2(+)Mari	1 Hazor	78
Hazor	Babylon	2 Babylon	1 Hazor	78
Qatna	Mari	1 Mari	1 Qatna	78
Qatna	Babylon	2(+?)Bab.	1 Qatna	78
Ekallatum	Mari	3 Mari	3 Ekal.	79
Ekallatum	Mari	1 Mari	1 Kakmum	79

B) *mārū šipri ṭēḫītum ištu GN ikšudūnim* (*ARM* VI 15.6; 63.3; 25.5; 70.3 - latter two broken after *ṭēḫītum*).

C) *ṭēḫītum mārū šipri ištu GN^1 (u GN^2) ikšudūnim* (*ARM* VI 14.7-28; 22.6-21).

A similar list of individuals occurs in *ARM* VI 19 but the expected *ṭēḫītum* is missing. Note that in these three phrases, only two of them specify that the groups are messengers, but even where not indicated, messengers are explicitly involved according to the context.

The first striking feature of the list is that the escorts[90] are usually comprised of only one man who is mentioned after the messenger he escorts, and he is nearly always escorting some other country's messengers back to their place of origin.[91] It is irrelevant how many messengers he must escort (one, two or three messengers). There are only two exceptions where more than one escort is found. However, it is significant that in both cases the number of escorts corresponds precisely with the number of messengers, suggesting that at some point the group with 3 escorts[92] was originally 3 groups which joined together along the route (and similarly the group with 2 escorts once was 2 groups).[93] The two occasions when a messenger is travelling alone without escort conform to the pattern since in both cases the messenger is setting out from his own country (Qatna in these cases), not returning. Indeed, one messenger above from Qatna who was sent alone to Mari is given an escort as he travels further in Mari territory.[94]

There is evidence that single messengers (or even groups of messengers) often would join with other messengers along the

---

[90] All of the individuals in the column marked "Escort" are explicitly so labelled in the texts with the exception of those in letters 22 (where it does not occur), 62 and 63 (where both texts are broken). However, the format of the letters suggests the presentation in the table; for the problem this poses in the case of letter 22, see the text below. For the reconstruction of letters 62 and 70, see below.

[91] The bearer of the Hurrian name mentioned after the Amorite in a *ṭēḫītum* from K[arana] permit the reconstruction of text 62.

[92] The messengers (and presumably escorts since the text is broken) are described as a *sikkum*, a sufficiently vague term when applied to messengers, given its few known occurrences, which does not allow precision; see *AHw* 1042.

[93] One can predict that the two groups of messengers in letter 78 from Qatna and Hazor travelling to Babylon will continue together to their mutual destination, escorts included.

[94] "PN, the Qatnean messenger, is on a mission to my lord (*ana ṣēr bēlīya šapir*) and he arrived without an escort; now one escort I have joined to him (*uštaṣbitamma*) and so send him to my lord" (*ARM* VI 14.22-28).

route and so compose a larger entourage. For example, a certain messenger (Nipram) brings news from Shamshi-Adad to Shamshi-Adad's Hurrian vassal Kuwari. Kuwari is then given advice by a fellow chieftain as follows (*SH* 827.33-41):

> Let Nipram, Kubiya, and Ullamtashni come up together with the messengers of Shamshi-Adad, Ja'ilanum, and Shimurrum. Inasmuch as the messengers of these kings came up to me voluntarily, then (also) there should be no reason why we should worry.

Later, in the Amarna period, Ahu-ṭabu travels in company with Burnaburiash's merchants (on diplomatic missions?) only as far as Canaan, since that is their destination; if they had lived to travel on to Egypt, they might have done so with other messengers passing through.[95] There are many texts which simply speak of messengers (plural) without further clarifying how many or supplying sufficient context to determine their significance.[96]

It is clear that the escorts accompanied their "wards" all the way back to the home country of the messenger. From the above list, one may note that the Yamhad escort, for example, does not hand over the Babylonian envoys to someone else at Mari and then return to Yamhad. On the contrary, the texts explicitly note that the entire group continues on its way.

Even though columns one and four correspond to each other and likewise columns two and three, one glaring exception is found in letter 22 where the two roles are reversed. It is noteworthy that this is one of the exceptional cases where the *ālik idi* is not specifically identified as such: *Iašlim-Ia*[ ] *mār šipri Qatanāyyu u Iasmaḫ-El mār šipri Qabarāyyu ana Qabarā illakū* (l.14-18). There is no mistake in the direction, for the rubric which heads the letter is describing messengers arriving

---

[95] Thus, when a large entourage arrives at a royal court (e.g. *EA* 20.64-69), it is not always clear that they all left at the same time as an inflexible group.

[96] *ARM* II 36.5-17; 105.6-17; VI 17.3-5; 18.10-4r; 42:5-19; 59.4-8; 61:4-7; XIII 131.r.

from Qatna. Because the pattern of the other texts would lead one to expect the messenger from Qatna to appear second, has the order of the two names accidentally been reversed? More likely, it is significant that this is an occasion when Bahdi-Lim writes the king for instructions as to whether or not these envoys should be allowed to pass, as we will see below.

The second variation in the columns is that in which the messenger coming from Ekallatum is said to be escorted by a man from Kakmum.[97] One may presume that Kakmum is geographically or politically in sufficient proximity to Ekallatum to allow it to be subsumed under the rubric, "*ṭēḫītum* from Ekallatum."

In international politics,[98] then, one may conclude that the escort was a diplomatic gesture provided for the safe conduct of foreign messengers in one's own country in order to accompany them safely back to their place of origin. A king never provides escorts for one of his own messengers in his own country. For messengers who are arriving from a foreign land, an escort is similarly provided at some point in the host country in order to guide him to his destination.[99]

We began this discussion by noting that 2 messengers were often sent on missions which anticipated some opposition. But

[97] The reference is further peculiar in that the name of the Kakmum escort is not given.

[98] The *ālik idi* in common parlance usually means simply "companion"; see *CAD* A (1) 343.2.

[99] The fact that Bahdi-Lim states that the Qatna messenger had no escort in *ARM* VI 14:22-28 seems to imply that he should have had one by the time he reached Bahdi-Lim at Mari; someone up the river should have supplied the escort. Yaqqim-Addu of Sagaratum does just this: "One messenger from Haya-Sumu arrived at Sagaratum . . . . Now, because no escort (*ālik id*[*īšu*]) goes with Haya-Sumu's servant (*ṣuḫār*), I supplied a man to safely conduct him (*mušallimšu*) and am having him brought to my lord" (*ARM* XIV 120.7-24). *EA* 30, the "passport" discussed earlier, requests that the messenger be given safe conduct to the border of Egypt where he is to be entrusted to the *ḫalzuḫli ša Miṣri* (l.10), which Moran translated as "the fortress commander of Egypt." Such an official would supply the escort.

from the list above, half (9) of the messengers are travelling alone (with their escort, of course, who represents a different political entity). The concept of the escort may thus echo the notion of protection, for the escort helps the messenger through unfamiliar territory. Three times, two messengers from the same court are travelling together, while four times there are three such messengers travelling as a group; in three cases, the text is broken but clear that at least two (if not more) compose such an entourage. Can anything more be learned apart from the *ṭēḫītum* texts?

Bahdi-Lim is also the expediter of *ētiqtum* texts which resemble the *ṭēḫītum* type[100] (*etēqu* "to pass on/through/by, advance, go beyond" and *ṭeḫû* "to arrive"). But it is not accurate to label the latter as a "group of messengers travelling together with Mari as destination" and the former as "same, passing through Mari to their destination."[101] It is more likely that the *ṭēḫītum* should be described in these contexts as an "embassy returning from its mission" and the *ētiqtum* as an "embassy setting out on its mission."

This perspective clarifies why the *ṭēḫītum* texts are in large part homogeneous. Exceptions which are observed in the chart

---

[100] For the *ṭēḫītu* pattern refer to the note accompanying Table A. Note the form which does not occur there and which we label here D) *mārū šipri GN¹ u GN² ētiqtum ištu maḫar sukkalim ikšudūnim* (*ARM* VI 19.4-5). Close to form B is *mārū šipri ētiqtum ištu GN¹ (u GN²) ša ana GN³ (u GN⁴) wu''urū ikaššadūnim* (*ARM* VI 23.19-24; cf. *ARM* VI 27.4-5). The word occurs elsewhere in a *ṭēḫītum* text (*ARM* VI 15.11).

[101] So A. L. Oppenheim, "The Archives of the Palace of Mari II," *JNES* 13 (1954) 147. But the *ētiqtum* is not necessarily a group, as VI 15.10-11 demonstrates: it can be one man without even an escort. The same text underscores the problem with these two terms since the solitary *ētiqtum* just mentioned is classed as a sub-group of a *ṭēḫītum*, the rubric which heads the letter. Oppenheim incorrectly observes that the verb *etēqu* is characteristic of the *ētiqtum* (e.g. of the *ṭēḫītum* in VI 14.7-29), and he overstates the case that *kašādum* is characteristic of *ṭēḫītum*, for it also applies to the *ētiqtum* (see preceding note). Furthermore, the *ṭēḫītum* is demonstrably a group which does not have Mari as destination; see Table A.

above actually fit in to this scheme. For example, the lone traveller from Qatna which we placed first in the chart above actually occurs last in enumeration in *ARM* VI 14, a distinction reinforced by the syntax where he alone is described with the stative of *šapir*. In the same way in which the *ētiqtum* of *ARM* VI 15 is subsumed under the rubric of the *ṭēḫītum* with which he travels (without it being explicitly so indicated in the rubric), it is also likely that the Qatna traveller of letter 14 should be understood as an *ētiqtum* travelling with a *ṭēḫītum* (even though he is the only party from Qatna). Both men are without escort and are setting out on their mission.

A further confirmation of this perspective is the way in which the *ētiqtum* is treated in contrast to the *ṭēḫītum*. Below we list the details associated with messengers in the *ētiqtu* texts of *ARM* VI.[102]

TABLE B

Origin	Goal	Messengers	Escort	Letter
Qatna	Babylon	1 Qatna	None	15
Elam	Qatna	Elam	Qatna	19
Babylon	Yamhad	Babylon		23
Eshnunna	Qatna	Eshnunna		23
Ekallatum	Hazor	Hazor		23
Karana	Carchemish	Karana		23
Qabra		Qabra		23
Arrapha		Arrapha		23
Yamhad	Babylon?	Yamhad		23
Qatna	Eshnunna?	Qatna		23
Hazor	Ekallatum	Hazor		23
Carchemish	Qabra?	Carchemish		23
	Karana?			23
Eshnunna?	Ekallatum	3 Eshnunna?	?	27
	Kurda?			

[102] For reconstruction of letter 23, see N. Na'aman, "East-West Diplomatic Relations in the Days of Zimri-Lim," *RA* 75 (1981) 171-172.

Letters 15 and 27 stand quite alone in their format. However, it is in letters 19 and 23 that one finds that the *ētiqtu* are in a position of real or potential detainment[103] - Bahdi-Lim either detains the messengers in question or holds them until someone gives him the authority to let them pass. On the other hand, in the many texts in which a *ṭēḫītu* is mentioned, there is never any question of detaining them. Letter 22 is the only apparent time, but under investigation it also conforms to the pattern.[104] Therefore, a messenger who is sent out on his mission could be subject to detention *en route* by intervening kingdoms. No doubt the reason would be to determine what type of correspondence is passing between one's neighbors. Messages would be intercepted on their way to their destination and envoys would have to give some account of their activities.[105] Embassies

---

[103] The *ētiqtum* of letter 15 is undistinguished, while the *ētiqtum* of letter 27 is distinct in so far as its destination includes more than one city, perhaps resembling a circular mission whose trip also includes a visit to Mari according to l.13-14.

[104] The problem is the initial rubric identifying a *ṭēḫītum* from Qatna. But two groups of messengers are described. The first conforms to the *ṭēḫītum* pattern, but the second is very awkward: a Qatnean messenger is said to be going to Qabra along with a Qabran messenger, who is named second but not described as an escort. Following this pair, Bahdi-Lim asks for guidance as to whether "these men" should be detained. We suggest that the deictic pronoun refers only to the last-named pair and not all the messengers in the letter. The last pair is technically an *ētiqtum*, while only the first is the *ṭēḫītum*. This perspective allows a clear understanding of another anomalous text (*ARM* VI 19) where the first pair of letter 22 (possibly restoring Ebi-Il in 22.11) is travelling this time from Elam to Qatna, but the Qatna messenger is the escort! This delegation is detained by Bahdi-Lim, and it is explicitly called an *ētiqtum*. We would suggest that the Qatna escort is not a returning messenger from Elam, but has met the Elamite messenger en route in order to conduct him to Qatna.

[105] Note in the Mari archives such an intercepted letter which was not permitted to pass, as interpreted by its editor G. Dossin ("Une lettre de Iarîm-Lim, roi d'Alep, à Iašûb-Iaḫad, roi de Dir," *Syria* 33 [1956] 63-69).

returning from delivering their message would be of presumably lesser import and hence not detained, for the subject of their mission would be known. Presumably a returning delegation would be stopped if their outbound detention revealed matters of vital importance,[106] but such messengers may not have been allowed even to reach their destination at all.

In addition to Bahdi-Lim, the governor of Sagaratum (Yaqqim-Addu) has left behind reports of messenger traffic cast in a different format. The data may be summarized as follows:

TABLE C

Origin	Goal	Messenger	Escort	Letter
A[ ]	Mari?	1 Mari?	1 A[ ]	XIV 19
Ilanṣura?	Mari?	1 Mari?	1 Ilan.	" 118
Suda?	Mari?	1 Mari?	1 Suda	" 119
Ilanṣura	Mari	1 Mari	1 Ilan.	" 125
?	Mari?	1 Mari?	1 ?	" 129
Carchem.	Mari	2 Mari	1 Carch.	" 86
Ilanṣura	Mari?	1 Ilanṣura	none	" 120
?	Mari?	4 ?	2 Mari	" 123
?	Mari?	2+ Babylon	1 Mari	" 126
?	?	1 ?	1 ?	" 129
Kurda	Babylon	2 Kurda	1 Babylon	" 97
Qatana	Mari?	3 Qatana	1 Mari	V 26

As with Bahdi-Lim, the escorts[107] above again tend to be single, even when escorting groups of two or three messengers. In the

[106] A Babylonian messenger returning from Kurda is stopped by the governor of Suhum who writes Zimri-Lim for further instructions. He does not tell the messenger why he is being detained, providing an all too realistic glimpse into the bureaucratic trauma to which international messengers were exposed (A.2983 in G. Dossin, "*Adaššum* et *kirḫum* dans des textes de Mari," *RA* 66 [1972] 111-130).

[107] All escorts so labelled in the chart are explicitly called *ālik idi* with the exception of *ARM* XIV 86, 123 (where it is likely to be restored) and *ARM* V 26.

chart above, almost two-thirds of the messengers are themselves solitary.

On the other hand, only rarely does Yaqqim-Addu specify the ultimate destination (*ARM* XIV 86,97), and in the other cases one can not be sure that Mari is the ultimate destination. Where it is a Mari messenger accompanied by a foreign escort, one may assume that the destination is Mari (*ARM* XIV 125). Consequently, the first five texts in the chart above fit the pattern seen elsewhere, namely, columns one and four correspond and columns two and three correspond. The escorts from abroad are returning Mari messengers to Mari.

The order of presentation in letter 86 might be understood as presenting one Carchemish messenger escorted by two Marians.[108] But this letter, instead of reporting the arrival of messengers at Sagaratum, describes the murder of messengers en route. It is thus not to be classed as the other documents. The letter does not identify any party as ***ālik idi***, although it does mention the Carchemish messenger before the two Marians on their way to Mari from Carchemish. If the Marians were the escorts, we would have an exceptional case of two escorts for one messenger. We suspect that had these men safely continued onward, the report of their arrival would likely have read, "PN^2 and his one companion, (servants) of my lord, and PN^1 the messenger of Carchemish, his escort, arrived from Carchemish." The reason for listing the apparent escort first in this case may be because he alone escaped with his life to be sent on to Mari (l.15-16).

Less than half of the texts above (the bottom half of Table C) show correspondence between columns one and three and/or two and four in contrast to the upper section of Table C. In particular, Mari escorts appear surprisingly in the last column. Nevertheless, *ARM* XIV 120 also fits the pattern in so far as the Ilanṣura messenger represents an "initiating"[109] embassy to Mari -

---

[108] *PN^1 mār šiprim awīl Karkamiš PN^2 u 1 tappûšu ša bēlīya ištu Karkamiš ana ṣēr bēlīya illakūnim* (l.5-9).

[109] We do not mean to imply that this marks the beginning of contact between Ilanṣura and Mari. Rather, there were no doubt many

he has no escort, but is supplied with one at Sagaratum. The group in *ARM* XIV 123 is clearly travelling toward Mari (though it may not be their final destination), and it appears that the Mari escorts must have been provided to them further upstream, perhaps at Qattuna. *ARM* XIV 126 has some perplexing unique features: the group of Babylonian messengers (with Mari escort north of Mari!) is said to have been earlier conducted to the Turukku by Ishme-Dagan, and upon arrival at Sagaratum the governor writes: "upon their arrival I hereby write to my lord" (l.17-19). If these Babylonians represent an embassy sent throughout the entire northern Euphrates and Tigris area on a circular mission (cf. *ARM* VI 27), the escorts may be filling a different role than normal.

The single inexplicable exception is letter 97 where a Babylonian escorts two Kurdans to Babylon. But remarkably, as in the Bahdi-Lim correspondence, this is the only time in which Yaqqim-Addu prevents an embassy's passage and asks Zimri-Lim for instructions as to whether or not they should be allowed to continue.

ARM V 26 comes from the Assyrian period at Mari (addressed to Yasmah-Addu). Although no one is identified as ***ālik idi***, the Marian clearly fulfills this role. Again, one may assume that this is an "initiating" embassy from Qatna, supplied with an escort upon entering Mari territory.

The correspondence of Yaqqim-Addu also makes explicit some of the functions of the ***ālik idi***. It was noted above that one messenger, having no ***ālik idi***, was given a ***mušallimum***, "one who provides safe conduct" (*ARM* XIV 120.19-22). Another messenger in *ARM* XIV 117, bearing tablets to the palace (***ṭuppātim ana ṣēr bēlīya naši*** l.8-9), is supplied by Yaqqim-Addu with ***maṣṣarī***, "guards" (l.12) since he was travelling alone (***kīma ēdiššišūma illak*** l.11-12). Both of these references indicate that at least part of the responsibility of the ***ālik idi*** was to provide protection. Furthermore, some messengers required special escort if their mission was of great import, as when Zimri-Lim (*ARM* XIV 127) orders an exceptionally strong guard to bring an

---

times when a message had to be sent and there were no guest messengers present to escort home.

Ekallatum messenger to Mari. This messenger was bearing valuables and consequently Yaqqim-Addu obeyed the royal order by assigning "three trustworthy men" to accompany him.[110]

We turn to the remaining letters at Mari which supplement the evidence given above. With this information in hand, it is clear that in *ARM* II 123 the bandits kill and rob the messengers as they are returning to Mari from Elahhutum. The messenger from Mari is accompanied by an escort from Elahhutum. This text, however, provides further valuable information. As the text begins, we read simply "PN[1], my lord's messenger, whom my lord sent to Elahhutum, and PN[2], the man from Elahhutum, his escort, were conducting ten asses etc." Were the messengers left unharassed, we would never have been provided with the following information which details who was killed and who managed to escape. The total entourage consisted of 24 individuals, of which ten survived. The Mari messenger had taken along two men in the Mari king's service, four aids (*ṣuḫāru*), and two Haneans - only the first pair escaped. The escort from Elahhutum brought along a total of fourteen (including one maid) of whom only eight managed to escape with their lives. Clearly, the bandits had to be of considerable strength to plunder successfully a caravan with 23 males. In any case, this text warns us that a simple reference to a messenger travelling with an escort may imply that a much larger group is actually travelling.

On the other hand, a later text from Mari after the Assyrian period (*ARM* XIV 86) details not only the size of the messenger's entourage but also the number of bandits. A messenger from Carchemish travelling to Mari with two Marians only is overwhelmed by four Ubrabeans who kill the two Marians. Clearly in this case a larger entourage would have deterred the Ubrabeans and granted safe passage. It is evident from this text

---

[110] *3 awīlī taklūti[m a]pqidam* l.14-15. If these men could be described as *ālik idi*, this is an unusual case of the escorts outnumbering the messenger, but they are simply called his guards (*awīlī maṣṣarīšu*, l.9).

that an official messenger did not always travel with a large entourage.[111]

Hammurabi is reputed to have insulted some Elamite messengers by threatening to send them back to Elam without an escort. It is noteworthy again that though the messengers are a group, the issue is the withholding of a single escort.[112] The essential role of the escort appears in another OB letter written by envoys who have been ignored and detained far too long by their host. In frustration they ask for permission to leave:[113]

> The king answered me as follows: "Since you have been quite unable to come to an agreement with one another, go and do as you have been ordered. No one is going to listen (to you any more)." In the morning we approached Semme-atar and requested an escort (*ālik idi nīriš*). But he answered us as follows: "From now on for three days no court will be functioning in Eshnunna . . . ."

Apparently no escorts were forthcoming. The fact that this letter was written suggests that the envoys decided to sit out the three-day period, and no doubt they encountered further abuse. This letter must have been sent by one of their servants. The specific request which they made for an escort underlines its import for the returning ambassadors. Presumably without such a figure, their trip out of the host country might be beset with a multitude of bureaucratic hurdles which otherwise would be avoided easily by an official representative of the king.

---

[111] S. Dalley (*Mari and Karana*, 171-175) suggests that one may distinguish tablet-carriers (between local officials and the king) from an envoy or royal emissary by the fact that the former (often called *ṣuḫāru*) may have travelled quickly and alone while the latter travelled with the caravans. But this text proves otherwise.

[112] Unless *ālik idim* is here collective, or simply singular by nature of the negative: "I shall send the Elamite messengers to their lord without an escort (*balum ālik idim*; *ARM* II 73.7-9).

[113] M. Rowton, "Watercourses and Water Rights in the Official Correspondence from Larsa and Isin," *JCS* 21 (1967) 269-270 l.12'-17'.

This diplomatic custom of providing an escort for the messenger's homeward trip may be reflected in other sectors of society. Although the person in the following letter is not called an "escort" as such, the activity is what one would expect of an *ālik idim* (*AbB* VI 57.7-20):

> Now I send PN to you. The man I sent (*ašpurakkum*) to you is someone I need - don't detain him! When you send him back to me, a trustworthy man of yours send with him and so join them together[114] and send them to me. And so, your man who will come with PN, I'll let him bring to you whatever you write that you need from me. And I have a request of you . . . .

This text makes explicit that the one who accompanies a messenger on the return trip has a larger task than merely providing safe-conduct. In this letter, he is himself to carry out a task for the one who sends him. He is a messenger who bears a message from his lord and whose task will not be complete until he also has made a round trip in his turn. The same perspective is also suggested by the above *ṭēḫītum* texts, for those who are designated as escorts are often explicitly labelled as messengers[115] in their own right.

It thus appears that once communication begins, it may be very awkward to stop the momentum, for presumably the escort must be escorted back in his turn. This feature seems to form a major part of the correspondence of the Amarna age a few centuries later where the custom of the escort appears in full vigor. Messengers returning to their homeland often travel with messengers from a host country. An Assyrian messenger goes to

[114] In spite of Frankena's note a in the edition of *AbB* VI 57, it is preferable to see *šutaṣbitaššunūti* as referring to the messengers joining each other, not to the messengers joining a caravan which is not mentioned; see *CAD* Ṣ 39 where the form is used of gathering groups of messengers.

[115] This is explicit in letters 14 (the group going to Babylon), 21, 22, 63, 79. In the other letters, we are not told the status of the escorts.

Hatti and, after being detained for three years, returns to Assyria accompanied by a Hittite messenger.[116] The Queen of Egypt sends a messenger to Shuppiluliuma which results in the Hittite king sending his messenger to Egypt who again returns accompanied by an Egyptian messenger (*DS* 28). The kings of this period on occasion request that their fellow kings send a messenger to accompany their own messenger on the return trip,[117] or they may make explicit that they are doing so.[118] Indeed, when this courtesy is denied, it is ground for complaint (*EA* 47.14-20):

> [To] all royal messengers you give your tablet (and) you send (*tašappar*), and you send as well your messenger to them. But to mine - [to] my messenger you give [no] tablet, nor do you send your messenger [to m]e![119]

In all of these passages, only one messenger from each country is described as travelling, consequently comprising a pair (with their entourage not mentioned).[120] But as at Mari, larger groups of messengers do occur[121] accompanied by their escorts.

[116] O. R. Gurney, "Texts from Dūr-Kurigalzu" (*Iraq* 11 [1949] 131-142) 139.

[117] *mār šiprīka itti mār šiprīya arḫiš uššer* (*EA* 35.16-17); the same phrase recurs in l.40-41 with the addition of *naṣriš* before *arḫiš*; *mār šiprīšu lišpuram itti mār šiprīya* (*EA* 160.34-35 and cf. l.41f.); "send your messenger and the messenger from me quickly and let them come" (*CTH* 151.19-24). A different nuance in one letter emphasizes that the two messengers should physically travel and bring the gifts together: *kī mār šiprīya u mār šiprīka illaka itti aḫamiš lilqûni* (*EA* 10.41-42).

[118] *mār šiprīya itti mār šiprīka ana muḫḫika altapar* (*EA* 35.8-9).

[119] See note on this translation in section 1.3.7.

[120] An accompanying entourage is assumed, rarely made explicit as in *EA* 20.64-65.

[121] "May my brother let my envoys go as soon as possible and they should be on their way! And may my brother send Mane along, and may he be on his way together with my envoys. Any other envoy may my

Never, however, do we find the actual term *ālik idi* used of messenger escorts in the Amarna period. The messengers are simply listed in tandem, neither marked specifically as in the care of the other. Nevertheless, a certain hierarchy is observable in the way in which the messengers are joined. A king returning another's messenger says "I send mine with yours"[122] but never "I send yours with mine." When a king requests that his messenger be returned, he asks that *with* his messenger the other king send his own along.[123] When such a distinction is made,[124] the evidence points to the returnee as the one *with* whom the other king joins his messengers.

However, although the evidence is unified in the Amarna texts with echoes in later material, in the thirteenth century (with a new idiom *qadu* instead of *itti* "with"), the old hierarchy has broken down. For example, when they deliver a message, the

---

brother not send, may he send only Mane" (*EA* 24.IV.51-54). *Pirizzi u* [*Tulubri itti mārī šiprīšu ša aḫīya*] *ana aḫīya ana kalli*[*mma altaparšunu*] (*EA* 27.89-90). *Mane itti mārī šiprīya aḫu'a lišpuršūma* (*EA* 29.167). *Anākūma itti mārī šiprīka attū'a mārī šiprīya ana muḫḫi abīya ašpuršunūti* (*EA* 44.20-22). See also *CTH* 159.2.7. It is instructive to note that in one letter, at first only two individuals are mentioned as travelling: "Keliya my envoy and Mane your envoy I have let go and they are coming to my brother . . . . I heard from Keliya and Mane, when they left . . . ." (*EA* 24.I.114-II.7). But later in the same letter, Tushratta notes with greater precision: "I have now dispatched most magnificently Mane, my brother's envoy, now, too, Keliya and Ar-Teshub and Asali my envoys" (*EA* 24.IV.35-39).

[122] "I send with yours mine" (*EA* 44.21) or "mine with yours" (*EA* 27.89; 35.8f.; *CTH* 164.1.10r [cf. E. Edel, "Ägyptischer Namen," 19]; *CTH* 159.1.1-6 [cf. E. Edel, "Weitere Briefe aus der Hieratskorrespondenz Ramses' II.," *Geschichte und Altes Testament* (Tübingen: J. C. B. Mohr, 1953) 32-35]).

[123] *EA* 24.IV.52-53; 29.167; 35.16; 35.40; 160.34-35; *CTH* 152.10-12.

[124] There are cases where the simple conjunction "and" is employed. In such cases, the sender names his own second (*EA* 24.IV.35-39) or first (*EA* 10.38 20.18-19 24.I.114f.), or in requests mentions his own first (*CTH* 151.23).

returning messenger speaks *with* the guest messenger.[125] Narrative descriptions of such embassies also reverse this form, and the returning messenger comes home *with* the other messenger.[126]

In the light of this evidence, some continuity with the OB material from Mari may be observed. In the Amarna material, the escort is joined *with* the returning messenger. The very notion of one "going at his side" (*ālik idišu*) underscores that the escort is defined in terms of the returning messenger and not vice versa. Even though a special term such as *ālik idi* does not occur in the later period for such envoys, the syntax still persists in affirming that the returning messenger is the one with whom the other messengers are joined. In diplomatic terms, this implies that up through the fourteenth century B.C., the higher status of the returning messenger is reflected in the idioms describing how he is accompanied home. However, this distinction breaks down so that by the following century (with a new idiom "with" *qadu*), no hierarchy is observable.

We have found, furthermore, that it is quite normal for one messenger from one country to travel with one messenger from another country. On occasion, two messengers from the same country may make the journey together and sometimes even more do so.[127] The situation remains similar to that in the OB period.

In the later period in Mesopotamia, groups of messengers are mentioned but few details assist in their analysis.[128] Periodically

---

[125] *KBo* XXVIII 4.19. Compare also lines 10-11 with *KBo* XXVIII 8.11'-12'; 11.8'-10'; 14.14-17; 24:8-9; *CTH* 157.10-13; 158.11-15; 159.2.7-8; 164.1.r9-11; 164.2.14-16.

[126] O. R. Gurney, "Texts from Dūr-Kurigalzu," 139; *DS* 28. Note the pharaoh's description of the arrival in Egypt of the messengers of Hatti and Egypt (*CTH* 159.7): "My messengers arrived before me with the messengers of my sister."

[127] Note the two Hittite messengers travelling with three Egyptian messengers in *CTH* 158. Compare the Hittite text *CTH* 15.1-3: "Two men from Zalpa sit before [him and he says:] 'Go and speak to the ruler of Haššu saying, [message follows]'."

[128] "PN[1] and PN[2] with the messengers - all of them I am detaining" *NBU* 154.16-21.

some light shines through, such as the lone messenger who should not travel alone because he needs a guide (*NBU* 211.5-11):

> I send PN to the Persian Gulf. He doesn't know the land. May my brother send a man with him (*lišpur*) who knows the road.

And noteworthy as well are references to the institution of the escort even in the first millennium B.C. Ezazu is sent to the Assyrian king as the messenger of Ayanur, an official (possibly the king) of the land of Ṭab'el. He reaches one of the Assyrian administrators in the Levant with a message of hostile incursions along the Moabite border. Ezazu is said to bear a sealed document (***kanīku***), whose contents he reveals[129] to the Assyrian administrator. This synopsis is then recorded in a separate letter to the king from the administrator, entrusted to his own messenger who then escorts Ezazu on to the king ("I have just now entrusted him to the care of my messenger").[130] In addition to Ezazu, note the following:

> Now PN the messenger of the king and my messenger I send to my lord (*NBU* 186.18-22).

> Bag-Teshub sent my messenger with his messenger into the land of Urartu (*ABL* 139.r8-10).

> Let a messenger of the king my lord be sent with the messenger of Elam concerning the matter unto Ummanaldash the king and unto Elam for our report, as follows . . . (*ABL* 1286.11-14).

[129] Presumably the document itself could be read, voluntarily surrendered by the messenger as part of the exigencies of participating in the Assyrian administration and using their messenger service. The Assyrian official notes "the words in the tablet" and not "the messenger said" or the like.

[130] H. Saggs, "The Nimrud Letters," *Iraq* 17 (1955) 131-132.

2.3.2 BIBLE

Biblical sources provide abundant material on messengers travelling in groups, but unfortunately the data are often too vague and stereotyped to assist in detailed analysis. No human *mal'āk* so designated in the Bible is ever given a personal name (Haggai is a prophet in Hag 1:13), and one often reads simply that a king "sent messengers."[131] Such groups, if they relate a message or speak, are schematically depicted as if they were a Greek chorus in unison ("The messengers said"[132]) which certainly can

---

[131] *wayyišlaḫ (PN) mal'ākîm* - Sennacherib to Hezekiah (2 Kgs 19:9 = Isa 37:9), Balak to Balaam (Num 22:5), Saul to Jesse (1 Sam 16:19) or in pursuit of David (1 Sam 19:11,14-15,20,21 *bis*), David to Hanun (1 Chr 19:2; cf. 2 Sam 10:2), Hiram to David (2 Sam 5:11 = 1 Chr 14:1), Ahaziah to inquire of Beelzebub (2 Kgs 1:2), Ben-Hadad to Ahab (1 Kgs 20:2), Ahaz to Tiglath-Pileser (2 Kgs 16:7), Necho to Josiah (2 Chr 35:21; *'ēlāyw* inserted after verb), David to Jebusites (2 Sam 2:5) or Ishbosheth (2 Sam 3:14), David fetching Bathsheba (2 Sam 11:4). The same stereotyped phrase recurs with non-royal figures: Jacob to Esau (Gen 32:3), Moses to the king of Edom (Num 20:14), Jephthah to the king of Ammon (Judg 11:12,14), Joshua (Josh 7:22), Zebul to Abimelech (Judg 9:31), Abner to David (2 Sam 3:12), Joab to Abner (2 Sam 3:26), Joab to David (2 Sam 12:27). Note "Israel" (Num 21:21 Judg 11:17,19) in parallel passages in place of "Moses". The plural form of the verb is used when a group sends messengers (1 Sam 6:21 1 Chr 19:16). Without the *waw*-consecutive (as a result of an introductory particle), the phrase occurs as *šālaḫ (PN) mal'ākîm*: David to Nabal (1 Sam 25:14; *hinnēh*), Amaziah to Joash (2 Kgs 14:8; *'āz*), Hoshea to So (2 Kgs 17:4; *'ăšer*). Striking in its consistent irregularity is the phrase *ūmal'ākîm šālaḫ* of Gideon (Judg 6:35 *bis* 7:24). The first person singular (Deut 2:26 Neh 6:3) form of the dominant cliché appears, as does a use of the first person plural referring to the future (1 Sam 11:3).

[132] Speaking to Jacob (Gen 32:6; cf. v.4), to Balaam (Num 22:7,16), to Balak (Num 22:14), to Ahaziah (2 Kgs 1:6-8), to Ahab (1 Kgs 20:5), to the inhabitants of Gibeah (1 Sam 11:4), to the men of Jabesh-

not be taken literally. On occasion a novel feature appears, such as Balak's decision to send a second embassy to Balaam "more numerous and distinguished than the former" (*śārîm rabbîm wĕnikbādîm mē'ēlleh* Num 22:15), suggesting that the greater the size of the delegation, the more honor applies (or pressure is applied) to the recipient (as in *EA* 11.13-14).

On the other hand, when one moves from stereotyped narrative to the actual depiction of messengers in action in the Bible,[133] it is the solitary messenger who dominates. In spite of the fact that such individuals identified by their personal name are not called *mal'āk*, their behavior clearly identifies them so. Joab reports the victory over Absalom by sending only the Cushite; another runner is sent (and then reluctantly and separately) only when the second messenger insists on going (2 Sam 18:19-32). Uriah is depicted as a solitary messenger on a round trip (2 Sam 11:6-15) just as the lone messenger who reports his death (2 Sam 11:18-25). A single messenger reports the defeat of Israel before the Philistines (1 Sam 4:12-18), and a different messenger is sent out alone on two separate occasions by Joram to determine Jehu's intentions (2 Kgs 9:17-20).[134] A single messenger is sent by Ahab to summon Micaiah (1 Kgs 22:9,13), and a single messenger is sent by Ahab to Elishah (2 Kgs 6:32).[135]

Gilead (1 Sam 11:9). The messengers of Sennacherib in the second embassy do not speak (though given an oral message!) but in unison hand over the letter to Hezekiah (2 Kgs 19:14).

[133] Freedman and Willoughby overlook this literary distinction when affirming that the cliché is normative while the singular messenger is abnormal in the Bible, occurring "wenn der Absender Mitwissen um eine Sache verhindern vollte" (*TWAT* IV 890-891). But this feature is not defensible in the nine cases discussed below and would make any solitary messenger suspicious.

[134] The first *rakkāb* sent is explicitly described as a *mal'āk* (and a *rôkēb sûs*) who delivers a message (v.18): "Thus says the king, 'Is it peace?'"

[135] Although the consonants *ml'k* appear in v.33 also, one should perhaps read *mlk* as implied by Josephus' account (*Antiquities* IX.70); see D. Barthélemy, *Critique Textuelle de l'Ancien Testament*

Furthermore, the cliché "he sent messengers" as noted above does admit exceptions. Twice in the MT, the object of the verb appears as a singular messenger. In one case (2 Kgs 5:10), the sheer weight of the context makes the standard cliché awkward, for not only is Naaman merely standing outside Elijah's door when he receives the message, but in the rest of the narrative Elijah has only one servant, Gehazi. The second text is probably defective, for although the Masoretic text reads, "Jezebel sent a messenger to Elijah" (1 Kgs 19:2), the Old Greek omits the noun "messenger" while Josephus reads the familiar cliché "messengers."[136]

A clear case of a pair of messengers appears in the two figures, Ahimaaz and Jonathan. David insists that Zadok return "and your two sons with you" for "by them you shall send me everything that you hear" (2 Sam 15:27,36). When they are sent with a message, both travel together in great haste (2 Sam 17:16), avoiding search parties by any ruse. This case parallels the situation in the OB Babylonian period where an explicit preference for two occurred in situations of danger or where opposition was anticipated, for Ahimaaz and Jonathan must report information from behind enemy lines. As with descriptions in the Bible of groups of messengers, the pair of Jonathan and Ahimaaz are schematically depicted as if they delivered their message in unison ("they said" 2 Sam 17:21). The despatching of two spies by Joshua to investigate Jericho seems to fit the picture as well: although in the narrative proper they are described as *meraggĕlîm* (Josh 2:1), they are later described as *mal'ākîm* (Josh 6:17,25). No narrative context is supplied for the two envoys sent by king Zedekiah to Nebuchadnezzar (Jer 29:3).

A unique narrative is the first embassy sent by Sennacherib to Hezekiah. The three individuals who are sent[137] call in unison to the king for an audience from outside the city walls (2 Kg

(*Orbis Biblicus et Orientalis* 50/1; Göttingen: Vandenhoeck & Ruprecht, 1982) 388-389.

[136] The only other occurrence of the third feminine singular form of the cliché is used of Israel personified (Ezek 23:16).

[137] Only the Hebrew representations of their Akkadian titles are known (*tartān*, *rab-sārîs*, and *rab-šāqēh*).

18:17,18). However, when the king's representatives make their appearance, it is the *rab-šāqēh* who more realistically does the talking, and for the rest of the narrative the other two men are completely forgotten[138] except for one side comment (19:6).

Consequently, biblical literature, when uninterested in messenger activity *per se*, employs a limpid cliché assuming more than one messenger. However, when biblical literature treats specific messengers, they tend to function alone. Nevertheless, one or two narratives may ratify an observation made above that two messengers tend to go where there is expected opposition. This may inform the exceptional narrative of the two messengers sent to Sodom as well (Gen 19). However, in the latter case we are moving toward the realm of the divine which calls for special treatment.

2.3.3 DIVINE MESSENGERS IN MESOPOTAMIA

In examining the issue of travelling singly, in pairs or in larger groups, it may be instructive to turn to the divine realm and depictions of divine messengers.[139] In the literature which stems from Mesopotamia, the gods who are sent on missions as

---

[138] Glaringly so. Note v.19,22,23,26-28,36,37 and 19:4 and especially 19:8. The Chronicler had a text before him which included a group embassy (2 Chr 32:9f.), but the third parallel passage in Isa 36 indicates only the *rab-shāqēh* is sent as the messenger. See J. A. Montgomery, *The Books of Kings* (ICC; Edinburgh: T & T Clark, 1951) 486, for the expansion in the text of Kings.

[139] In the Egyptian tale of Ashtarte, Ptah sends a single messenger, unique in Egyptian literature (so M. Valloggia, *Recherche*, 118-119) and likely of Semitic influence. The only divine messengers in Egypt noted by Helck in *Wörterbuch der Mythologie II* are Buchis (*Bḫ*), the herald of Re, along with the bovines Apis (*Ḥpy*), herald of Ptah, and Mneris (*Mr-wr*), herald of Re (p.336-337,345,377,388). Note also O. Keel's *Vogel als Boten* (*Orbis Biblicus et Orientalis* 14; Göttingen: Vandenhoeck & Ruprecht, 1977) which presents the data for birds as symbols of deities, bearing news.

messengers tend to be the *sukkal*'s and are always pictured as travelling alone. Enki sends Isimu (*IE*), Anshar sends Kakka (*EE* III), Enlil sends Nuska (*Atra.* I.118f.), Ereshkigal sends Namtar (*STT* 28), Anu sends Kakka (*STT* 28), Marduk sends Nuska (*UL* 96f.), Inanna sends Ninshubur[140]: each of them travels as a single messenger. In addition, the scholastic enterprise enshrined in the god lists tends to identify one ***mār šipri*** with a god: Enlil's Ninmara (*CT* XXIV 11.35; 24.52), Mashtabba's Har (*CT* XXV 6.22) and Shamash's Shagadulla (*CT* XXIV 31:92; XXV 26:29).[141] In descriptions of illness, the affliction may be described in terms of a single messenger sent by one's personal god.[142]

Exceptions to this pattern seem to occur. The demons from below (the *ekur*) who are unleashed upon an unsuspecting world are described as the messengers of Enlil (*UL* 4f.). All seven of these are pictured as simultaneously coming upon their unfortunate victim ("they approach . . . , they cast . . .") and they are simultaneously removed ("these evil ones will be put to flight") by the solitary but more powerful messenger of Ea (*UL* 4-7).[143] A further coalition of seven sent by Anu also wreak havoc: "these seven are the messengers of Anu" (*UL* 88-91). Like most bullies, they too attack as an ensemble (*UL* 90-97),

---

[140] S. N. Kramer, "'Inanna's Descent to the Nether World' Continued and Revised," *JCS* 5 (1951) 1-17. For Kakka, described as "a messenger god," one "among the thousands of deities that formed the lower echelon of the Mesopotamian pantheon", see P. Steinkeller, "The Mesopotamian God Kakka," *JNES* 41 (1982) 289-294. *An=Anum* equates Kakka with Ninshubur and Papsukkal, respectively. Kakka is neither a Sumerian nor an Akkadian deity, and Steinkeller argues for a West-Semitic origin, "most probably Amorite" (*Ibid.*, 292).

[141] Note the fragmentary "[ ] *LÚ KIN.GI*$_4$*.A* [ ]" (*CT* XXV 5.48).

[142] *Mār šipri ša ilīšu* referring to the afflicted (*TDP* 168.2; 244.12). Note also in the same context the "messenger of Sin" (*TDP* 224.57).

[143] J. V. Kinnier Wilson seeks unnecessarily to find a literal reality behind these figures in the exposed natural gas fields (*The Rebel Lands*, [Cambridge: Cambridge University, 1979] 93-97). In general, however, see H. W. F. Saggs, *The Encounter with the Divine in Mesopotamia and Israel* (London: Athlone, 1978) 97-105.

> Bearing gloom from city to city, . . . they take their stand for evil, and none oppose . . . . When the seven evil gods forced their way into the vault of heaven, they clustered angrily round before the crescent of the Moon God, and won over to their side Shamash the mighty and Adad the warrior . . . . The evil gods, the messengers of Anu the king, raising their evil heads went to and fro through the night, searching out wickedness.

These characters show by their behavior that they are not actual messengers. Though they may be called messengers, they speak no words, communicate no messages, and behave like no other messengers already discussed. Rather, in so far as they do the will of the one who despatches them (namely plunder, kill, ravage, and inflict pain) they are his "messengers" in a metaphorical sense.[144] They are thus of no help in analyzing travelling groups of messengers. Indeed, the real messenger who emerges in these texts is the solitary messenger of Marduk or Ea who banishes the Gang of Seven by the spoken message of his lord.[145]

We noted above that in the god lists, only one messenger is found for some gods. However, a clustering of seven messenger

---

[144] Later Syriac and Mandaic incantation bowls continue the tradition: "I say against all the messengers (*'ašgandā*) of the idol-spirits" (T. Harviainen, "A Syriac incantation bowl in the Finnish National Museum, Helsinki," *StOr* 51 [1981] 12,17). The Semitic *ml'k* is also used to describe these infernal denizens who may bear names (e.g. Qarqiel and Harbiel in E. Yamauchi, *Mandaic Incantation Texts*, [*AOS* 49; New Haven, CN: American Oriental Society, 1967] 22.141,155f.) or occur in groups of seven (*Ibid.*, 5.7; 6.7) or twelve (*Ibid.*, 22.255). Note the Angel of Fury (*ml'k rwgz'*) who is commissioned along with Misfortune (*qry'*) and Destruction (*ḫrb'*) to "strike", "seize" and "continually oppress" (*Ibid.*, 22.84) but who is stopped by the solitary envoy of God. When confronting them, one queries, "Why have you been sent (*'štlḫtwn*) against the sons of Adam?" (*Ibid.*, 10.13 11.24). It goes without saying that *ml'k* also refers to good angels in these contexts.

[145] *UL* p.8-11,98-103,110-113,132-135.

figures around a deity recurs in the god lists also: the chthonic goddess Manungal has at her disposal Shushaduga, Gishu, Gishgir, Gishgu, Gishe, Gishardibdib, and Unuk/lu.[146] Seven deities are marked off as messengers in *CT* XXIV 33.24-31 (Ubdalah, Ashanugia, Amatur, Malak, Shedu, Lamassu, and Dudu), of whom the fourth may be a West Semitic loan. Larger groups of divine messengers appear, as in the last noted case where although only seven deities are marked off by the scribe, eighteen deities is the final sum indicated (l.31).[147]

The phenomenon of death and associated ills may be personified as the messengers who come from the Netherworld to claim a victim: "the messenger, the sons of death (*lú kin-gi₄-a dumu namtar me*[*š*?]) leave by the great gate of the Land of No Return, they overcome the man."[148] In another context, the two messengers (*našparū*) of Ishtar, lions who accompany her (*ālikūt idīša*), Dan-bitum and Rashub-bitum by name, are also to be understood in this same metaphorical sense.[149]

---

[146] One tradition gives a total of seven where the five central figures have initial *giš*- ("Handcuffs, foot-shackle, neck-iron, etc. *CT* XXIV 35.23-26). An expansion is represented in *CT* XXV 4.15-22 where a total of eight is given, with six central figures with initial *giš*- (see also the fragmentary *CT* XXIV 47.37-42).

[147] Cf. *TCL* XV 10.243-254 and an unpublished text noted by W. G. Lambert in "A List of Gods' Names Found at Mari" (*Miscellanea Babylonica - Mélanges offerts a Maurice Birot* [J.-M. Durand & J.-R. Kupper, eds.; Paris: Éditions Recherche sur les Civilisations, 1985] 181-190) 187.

[148] J. Nougayrol, "Une amulette de Syrie et un nouvel 'oeil'," *RA* 64 (1970) 67. In addition to "messengers of death" in Prov 16:14, note the Egyptian "Instruction of Ani" where Death comes as a messenger: "When your messenger comes looking for you, may he find you ready to depart for your place of rest, (as you) say, 'Behold the one who prepared himself for your arrival.' Don't say, 'I'm too young for you to take me.'" (M. Valloggia, *Recherche*, 118).

[149] R. Kutscher & C. Wilcke, "Eine Ziegel-Inschrift des Königs Takil-iliśšu von Malgium, gefunden in Isin und Yale," *ZA* 68 (1978) l.42-44.

2.3.4 DIVINE MESSENGERS IN THE BIBLE

Do divine messengers in the Bible prefer to work alone or in groups? The biblical literature is problematic due to the complex issues associated with the *mal'āk* of Yahweh. At first glance, it is noteworthy that this figure is consistently singular in the formulaic presentation of his office. However, it seems likely that much of the material with respect to this figure is unreliable for our purposes. The originality of the word *mal'āk* in many places has been legitimately questioned.[150] In any case, this figure's solitary nature is echoed in the more revealing account of the deceitful spirit who misleads Ahab through the lying prophets (1 Kgs 22:19-23). The divine messenger normally travels alone.[151]

There is no doubt that God is pictured as having a multitude of messengers at his disposal: "Praise the Lord all His messengers!" (Psa 148:2).[152] The question is rather are there occasions in which such plural messengers are sent in teams and not as single ambassadors?

Exceptional is the case of Abraham's three visitors in Genesis 18 who become two messengers in chapter 19 (both J). But as noted earlier, the unusual presence of two messengers may reflect the notion of crisis inherent in the narrative of Sodom and Gomorrah. The winds are God's messengers in Psalm 104:4, but the metaphor here is reminiscent of that seen in the Mesopotamian examples. Although a number of messengers appear in Jacob's dream in Genesis 28:12 (E), it is unlikely that

---

150 See D. Irvin, *Mytharion* (*AOAT* 32; Neukirchen-Vluyn: Neukirchener, 1978) 91-104 for a study with regard to Genesis in particular.

151 Later rabbinic interpretation continues this perspective (e.g. *Aboth de Rabbi Nathan* 12.3).

152 So Job 4:18 Psa 91:11. The translation of *mal'āk* as "messenger" is not likely in these later texts, given the development of angelology. We retain the word "messenger" for the sake of continuity simply because the same Hebrew word is employed, as well as the fact that if these references are dismissed then half of the citations for plural divine messengers disappear.

they are pictured as all travelling to the same destination; each angel employs the heavenly stairway in order to accomplish his own individual task, whatever it may be. Indeed, the picture is precisely parallel to the stairway of heaven which the individual messengers travel in the Akkadian myth of *Nergal and Ereshkigal* (STT 28). In Genesis 32:2 (the E counterpart to the much more detailed J narrative where Jacob wrestles with a solitary figure in v.25-31), there is unfortunately no context remaining in which to evaluate the significance of the group of messengers from God who meet Jacob.

Finally, although Hebrew and Akkadian early lost a functioning dual,[153] remnants of the dual are preserved in both languages in predictable pairs. The dual is not used with messengers, reaffirming the above data that messengers were not customarily sent out by two's.

2.3.5 DIVINE MESSENGERS AT UGARIT

The description of Anat's reception of Baal's embassy in *CTA* 3.4.76-81 is perhaps the best starting place for describing the phenomenon of the divine messenger at Ugarit. It is a wise place to start since it provides indisputable evidence for messengers who do not travel alone and since it also occurs in a parallel passage where Kothar-wa-Hasis receives El's embassy in *CTA* 1.3.17-21:

wy'n PN
lk lk 'nn ilm
atm bštm wan šnt
GN lrḥq ilm GN lrḥq ilnym
ṯn mṯpdm tḥt 'nt arṣ

[153] A case of the old dual personal pronoun applied to messengers does occur in an early text from Tell Asmar (Asmar 30.13). However, the pair is composed of "Ahi-ṭab, the messenger of my lord, and Balalati, my messenger." This must represent a pair of which one functions as an escort for the other, a phenomenon discussed above.

ṯlṯ mtḥ ǵyrm
idk lytn pnm ʻm . . . .

The first line occurs only in *CTA* 1, clarifying what is otherwise implicit: this is the acknowledgement to the messengers that their message has been heard and their task fulfilled. The personal pronoun *'atm* coupled with the plural participle *bšťm* in the third line proves that at least two messengers delivered the message. Certainty is enhanced by moving back to the arrival of these messengers in *CTA* 3.3.33, for there (unlike the fragmentary *CTA* 1) the messengers are named as Gapnu-wa-Ugaru. A double name is not necessarily indicative of plurality,[154] but in this case it provides us with the total number of messengers, namely two. When *ǵlmm* (*CTA* 3.3.5 3.4.49) or *ilm*[155] appear in the rest of the

[154] Kothar-wa-Hasis is clearly only one god with a double name. The compound form of his name interchanges freely with simple Kothar and simple Hasis and simple Hayyan (*CTA* 6.6.48-49 17.5), he speaks of himself in the first person singular (*CTA* 4.6-7: *ašt* 4.6.5, *bwty* 4.6.15 4.7.25, *lrgmt* 4.7.23), and when spoken of he is described with third singular pronouns (*CTA* 4.5-7: *qdmh* 4.5.107, *pnh* 4.5.108, *gh* 4.7.22, *hwt* 3.6.20; cf. *ahlh* and *mšknth* *CTA* 17.5.32-33). See in this regard H. L. Ginsberg, "Baal's Two Messengers," *BASOR* 95 (1944) 25. His explanation of the use of *hmt* in *CTA* 17.5.20,30 to describe this god is strained; more likely is the fact that we have here typical unevenness of mythology as represented in different works. It is conceivable that the double name encouraged splitting up the deity, and it is quite possible that in the Aqhat material he is presented as dual (actually a trinity!). But in the Baal cycle he is consistently singular. For evidence of this phenomenon outside Ugarit, note Shullat and Hanish treated as a unit on occasion (I. J. Gelb, "Shullat and Hanish" *ArOr* 18 [1950] 189-198).

[155] *CTA* 3.3.29. This is not a decisive piece of data since the final *m* could be an enclitic particle; even the singular god Kothar/Hasis/Hayyan is so designated (*CTA* 17.5.20,29), even though some translate it as plural (G. R. Driver, *Canaanite Myths and Legends* [Edinburgh: T & T Clark, 1956] 53). But see the preceding note. The only other occurrence not yet mentioned of the 5 occurrences of the name Gapnu-wa-Ugaru is in *CTA* 8.6-7, a passage parallel to 4.7.54.

narrative as a consistent identification for these deities, this must be construed as dual in accord with the preceding data.

CTA 4.8, in which Gapnu-wa-Ugaru reappear, also confirms that more than one god is present. Baal sends them (cf. 1.47 and 4.7.54) off, warning them to approach Mot with caution, "lest he pop you (plural - *y'dbkm*) in his mouth like a lamb" (l.17-18). In accord with the preceding evidence, the suffix pronoun should be construed as second person dual.

Elsewhere, the evidence corroborates the fact that this god with the double name is in fact two gods: the third person plural (better: dual) suffix pronoun is used when describing them (*CTA* 5.2.17 *ghm*), and they are always referred to as *ilm* (*CTA* 5.1.9 5.2.13). Gapnu-wa-Ugaru, as the messengers of Baal, may find their counterpart in the god lists found at Ugarit even though they do not appear under this designation. Ranking 25th in a list of 33 gods occurs the Ugaritic *il* [*t*]*'dr b'l* which corresponds to the Akkadian *ilānu tillat Adad*.[156] This sounds very much like the retinue which is associated with the storm and warrior god who enters battle.[157] It is likely that this is the source of the imagery for Baal's two messengers. That is, the mythology has dictated the number of messengers which the storm god requires and not sociology or any social paradigm by which two messengers are somehow requisite. The solitary divine messenger as well as the solitary human messenger we have seen to be normative; it is the groups of messengers which require explanation.[158] The explanation in the human realm seemed to focus upon the aspect

[156] Following *'ṯtrt*/Ishtar and preceding *ršp*/Nergal (*Ugar.* VII p.3).

[157] Hab 3:5, *EE* IV, Shullat and Hanish assisting Adad in Gilgamesh XI.98-99. Note Ninurta's assistants: "Udanne, the all-seeing god, and Lugalanbadra, the bearded lord(?), go before him, and the awesome one of the 'mountains', Lugalkurdub, the [ ] of lord Ninurta, follows behind him" (J. S. Cooper, *The Return of Ninurta to Nippur* [*AnOr* 52; Rome: Pontifical Bible Institute, 1978] l.63-68).

[158] In spite of a general consensus to the contrary: "Messengers used to travel in pairs" (J. C. de Moor, *An Anthology of Religious Texts from Ugarit* [*Nisaba* 16; Leiden: Brill, 1987] 10).

of danger or opposition being a motive to increase the number of messengers. This fits in well with a god of battle such as Baal.[159]

We noted above that the double-name Kothar-wa-Hasis was not a guarantee of duality of persons. What about the name Qadish-wa-Amrar? Like Kothar-wa-Hasis, the name interchanges with simple Qadish and simple Amrar (*CTA* 4.4.16-17) unlike Gapnu-wa-Ugaru which never splits up its elements (probably fortuitous). Beyond this feature, no clues surface which are unambiguous as to the number of gods behind this name. One might cite *CTA* 4.4.17 where the simile is introduced of Amrar being like a single star (*kkbkb* - singular). But this occurs in a line where the double name is split up into two poetic parallels. As in the case of Kothar-wa-Hasis, one must be prepared to find that the duality or singularity of such a god may even vary from work to work.[160]

---

[159] Gaster notes that major gods are attended by two servitors when they stir abroad, *because* of a so-called ancient practice of dispatching messengers in pairs "lest one alone meet with mishap en route" (T. H. Gaster, *Myth, Legend, and Custom in the Old Testament* [New York: Harper and Row, 1969] 670). His last remark conforms to the data, but we have seen that there is no such "ancient practice," for single messengers are more common than dual or plural. His few citations are instructive: in addition to citing Shullat and Hanish accompanying Adad (see note above), he cites Ares (a god of war!) accompanied by Deimos and Phobos as well as Mars (same!) accompanied by Pallor and Pavor. How does one account for the solitary Hermes/Mercury figure (or the female version in Iris)? It is the latter who is the messenger par excellente. Similarly, C. H. Gordon in *The World of the Old Testament* (Garden City, NY: Doubleday, 1958) 110, overstates the case when he says that "another common bond between the Homeric world and the ancient Near East is the regular custom of sending messengers in pairs; thus Il.1.320ff.(etc.), 2 Kgs 5:23 (etc.) and at every turn in Ugaritic." 2 Kgs 5:23 is not clearly a messenger pair, and we have yet to see how common pairs are at Ugarit. The pair which accompany the storm god may not be paradigmatic.

[160] Is this an accidental slip on Driver's part when he treats Qadish-wa-Amrar as singular in *CTA* 4.4 but dual in 3.6 (G. R. Driver, *Canaanite Myths and Legends*, 91,95)?

Unfortunately, the Ugaritic texts are not helpful outside the divine realm. One may certainly point to *CTA* 14 where messengers are mentioned in the plural/dual *mlakm* (14.3.124,137; 14.6.300) and clear plural/dual pronouns are used (*tšan ghm w tṣḥn* - 14.6.303-304). However, this must not be pressed too far, for this sounds exactly like the schematization found in biblical literature. On the other hand, all see a single messenger in "your messenger" *mlakk* in *KTU* 1.124,[161] and rightly so since its verb is singular *ymǵ*. The arrival of the single *ml'k* named *nmy* (or *amy*) before Ugarit's last king, 'Ammurapi,[162] further confirms that each case must be taken on its own merit.

2.4 SUMMARY

Extensive narrative descriptions of messengers on the road were found only in Sumerian literature, with echoes at Ugarit. Perhaps literary descriptions diminished because the life of the messenger in transit was not an easy one to idealize. It was a harsh life, and one which many sought to avoid. The dangers from thieves and murderers compounded the trauma of travelling through unfamiliar country with accompanying bureaucratic imposts and delays. Escorts mitigated the tension, and proper documentation for those with influential patrons facilitated transit. But diplomatic immunity from political manipulation was not a reality for the messenger on the road (nor upon arrival as will be seen).

The evidence confirms that the Persians were not the initiators of a sophisticated postal and relay system but were the heirs of a long tradition. Ur III, Old Babylonian and Neo-Assyrian

---

[161] *Ugar.* V 563-564; see also P. Xella, "L'influence babylonienne à Ugarit, d'après les textes alphabétiques rituels et divinatoires," *Mesopotamien und seine Nachbarn* (XXVe Rencontre Assyriologique Internationale; ed. H-J. Nissen and J. Renger; Berlin: Dietrich Reimer, 1982) 329-331.

[162] P. Bordreuil, "Quatre documents en cunéiformes alphabétiques mal connus ou inédits," *Semitica* 32 (1982) 10-12.

monarchs are known to have maintained a communication network which permitted the rapid flow of information essential to the welfare of the palace. The transfer of information of any other nature could perhaps benefit to some degree from the stability which such government posts provided, but often as not, the bureaucratic complications inherent in such a system no doubt tried the patience of many a messenger. Messengers readily found hospitality and rest in local taverns and in private dwellings.

The messenger was accommodated with transportation in accord with the available technology and status of his employer. In addition to the messenger's own feet, boats plying the Mesopotamian river valley also carried him as a passenger. The donkey was utilized by messengers already in the OB period, when the horse or chariot was apparently only just beginning to make their appearances in this capacity.

It appears that travelling in groups was a feasible way to diminish potential opposition and make harassment less enticing. When we hear of a royal messenger travelling (or even a messenger travelling with an escort), we should often (although not always) picture him as travelling with an entourage of considerable size - if not large enough to make a caravan, perhaps travelling in conjunction with caravans. However, there is no justification for the notion that normally two messengers were sent on missions. This might hold true for dangerous missions where one repeatedly does find two messengers in action. But for normal communication, one is the norm. An exceptional case in the divine realm occurs in the Baal cycle where the storm god characteristically has two messengers. However, this feature seems to characterize this figure in general in the ancient world and is certainly not paradigmatic in the light of what we know of divine messengers.

3

THE MESSENGER'S ARRIVAL

3.1 ANTICIPATING THE MESSENGER

Did one always look forward to receiving a messenger? The answer is conditioned upon variable factors. If one is a monarch, the constant flow of messengers bearing greetings and accompanying gifts was an occasion for joy. The monarch looked forward to a constant flow of messengers from his allies as a sign of normalcy.

But for those who were not in an environment where messengers were regular, the arrival of a messenger may have been a sign of foreboding. It represented a break in normalcy, and change in the ancient world was not an enviable state in which to find oneself. If the following report is not unusual, it may suggest that in such contexts, "no news is good news" (*AASOR* XVI 7.2-6):

> The messenger of the palace (*mār šipru ša ekallim*) came to me and said, "On account of the bridge which broke down, produce two sheep, the mayor's fine."[1]

At Ugarit, the phenomenon of dismay before approaching messengers surfaces more than once. In *CTA* 3.3-4, Baal sends messengers to Anat with a conciliatory message, ultimately to have

---

[1] For messengers who collect on debts owed to their senders, see for example *Nbk* 257; *Dar* 380,458; *AnOr* 8 40,62; *YOS* VII 84.

a house built for himself. However, Anat's response upon seeing the messengers is out of all proportion to the message to be delivered. She undergoes an extended physiological breakdown and delivers an eloquent soliloquy anticipating conflict and tragedy. But the messengers soothe her traumatized imagination when they begin, "No enemy has risen against Baal, nor any foe against the Cloud-Rider" (*CTA* 3.4.49-50). They repeat Baal's invitation, which she accepts, heading for Zaphon where a banquet awaits her.

Although Baal and Anat are not messengers in another context (*CTA* 4.2), Asherah reacts similarly upon their arrival, only rejoicing when she sees the gifts they brought for her - it is not a message of conflict or tragedy which they bring. In another literary work, however, messengers elicit a mournful response when they arrive, and this time the sorrow is justified. In *CTA* 19.2, messengers bring news of Aqhat's death, and the response to their news is described with the same dramatic imagery as employed above. The arrival of unexpected messengers did not necessarily mean good news.

Elsewhere, the gods react strangely when Yam's messengers arrive at the divine banquet. When they are spotted from a distance, the gods immediately go into mourning, lowering their heads at what should be a festive occasion. A rebuke by Baal raises heads again, at which point the messengers arrive. Because we do not have the larger context, it may be that the gods had good reason to expect the worst, knowing what message was on its way. But as it stands, it conforms to the pattern we have seen in the other Ugaritic texts: the arrival of messengers may be a sign of foreboding. The fear of the gods is justified in this case, for the message of Yam is hostile.

Although such descriptions may be a characteristic West Semitic phenomenon, there is little interest in describing reactions of individuals who see approaching messengers in Mesopotamian literature. Instead, the arrivals of messengers figure prominently in omens. It is not so much the reactions of people which are described in the omens as it is the fact that these omens reflect or even condition attitudes toward envoys. For example, it is the first messenger who will bring the good news when many envoys arrive ([? *mā*]*rī šipri maḫrûm bussurāt ḫadêm našikum*; *YOS* X

25.28), but otherwise good and bad news alike come with different portents.[2]

Israelite literature follows the lead of Ugarit with several narrative descriptions of people anticipating the arrival of messengers. As in the two cases in the Baal cycle where those waiting for the news guess wrongly what type of news is coming, so also in Israel, both the narratives of David waiting for news of Absalom (2 Sam 18:19-33) and the account of Adonijah as he is crowned king (1 Kgs 1:41-49) depict men who fail to discern correctly. These two narratives are bound together in several other features: the one to whom the message is addressed is involved in a struggle for the throne; both messengers, each the son of a priest, had once worked together for David as messengers (2 Sam 15:27,35,36; 17:15-22); both are active on a day of ill-tidings for the ones they serve; and the message which each brings confirms the security of the Israelite throne. It is likely that these narratives come from the same pen as part of the succession narrative.

Both narratives are constructed such that the reader knows the reality of which the central character is ignorant. Consequently, the wishful thinking of each man is made to appear foolish in its naivete. Adonijah optimistically misjudges the messenger: "Come in! For you are a worthy man (*'îš ḫayil*) and you'll have good news!" (1 Kgs 1:42). But the tidings break up the celebration and send everyone running for their lives. David's misperception is also based on the character of the one who comes: "He is a good man (*'îš ṭôb*) and comes with good tidings" (2 Sam 18:27). It is true that Ahimaaz tells the king what he wishes to hear, but he has not told all, and sorrow rules the day.[3]

---

[2] For example, bad news in *YOS* X 25.35; good news in *YOS* X 26.ii.15-16; 26.iii.6. Presumably the messengers who will arrive before the king from a far land (*YOS* X 25.59) or the entrance of messengers (*YOS* X 25.6) are good omens. The frequent reference in omens to the messenger arriving on a donkey is unclear; see the discussion in section 2.2.1 on means of transportation. We will note below the omen regarding the treacherous messenger.

[3] David's identification of solitary runners as bearers of news is not a part of his optimism. The root *bśr* in each case is unqualified

Elsewhere, Shiloh waits for news from the battle-front (2 Sam 4:12-18), with none more eager than Eli (v.13). As in the episodes above, Eli is unable to discern accurately the news which has come. His blindness may prevent him from seeing the mourning garb of the messenger, but his ears also fail to interpret accurately the outcry of mourning from the city: "What is this uproar?" (v.14).

In summary, the arrival of a messenger was not an emotionless event. It appears that a significant literary topos in evidence in the West Semitic world dealt with the apprehension of individuals to whom messengers come. In particular, there is a marked tendency to depict such scenes when the individual fails to perceive accurately the news which is about to be delivered. In its extreme form, individuals over-react either positively or negatively when in fact neither response is ultimately justified.[4]

3.2 RECEIVING AN AUDIENCE

3.2.1 FINDING THE ADDRESSEE

It was noted earlier (section 1.1) that messengers might be chosen based upon their prior experience as travellers and their acquaintance with the terrain they might traverse. For such envoys, and in particular those sent between monarchs, finding the intended addressee would pose no problem. But an envoy bearing messages to private individuals might have difficulty locating them if they were unknown to him. In fact, such a

---

(v.25,26); they are bearers of news and whether good or bad is not evident. Only in v.27 does the adjective "good" (*ṭôb*) appear. In addition to *bussurāt lā ḫadê* (W. Mayer, "Ein altbabylonischer Opferschaubericht aus Babylon," [*Or* 56 (1987) 245-262] 247 l.11) and *bussurāt lumnim* in contrast to the well attested *bussurāt ḫadê* or *bussurāt dumqim* (*CAD* B 346-347), see A. L. Oppenheim, "Mari II," 145.

[4] 2 Kings 9:17-23 does not deal with the arrival of a messenger, but it may represent a variation on the theme. King Joram is unable to discern that the vigorously-driven chariot which approaches brings his death; he naively goes out to meet it.

situation provides the framework for a literary composition addressed to a messenger (*kaš*$_4$) where the sender observes: "If you do not know my mother, I shall give you some signs: the name is Shat-Ishtar . . . ." Five stanzas follow this statement, elaborating in detail descriptive praises glorifying the sender's mother, each introduced by the phase, "I shall give you a second/third/fourth/fifth sign about my mother."[5]

This text is peculiar in that the sender, though not a king, is found commissioning a royal courier (*lú-kaš*$_4$*-e-lugal-la* 1.1). The literary fiction of a courier needing a description of the intended recipient provides the excuse for the paeans of praise. But it also suggests that royal couriers could carry private despatches, without doubt for a fee. This may explain also why this courier bears a letter without knowing its contents.[6]

Without addresses, a description of the individuals themselves (as in the text above) or their estate within a city would be the messenger's key guide to locating the addressee. Addresses on Aramaic letters from the Persian period may specify the city in which the addressee lived.[7] Finding a private individual would not necessarily be an awkward experience for a messenger who did not know the recipient, for the experience of Saul with his servant, when sent to look for his father's donkeys, probably indicates the customary and universal technique which messengers no doubt used in such circumstances (1 Sam 9:11-12):

---

[5] M. Civil, "The Message of Lú-Dingir-Ra to his Mother," *JNES* 23 (1964) 1-11. For further treatment, note S. N. Kramer, "Poets and Psalmists: Goddesses and Theologians," *The Legacy of Sumer* (ed. Denise Schmandt-Besserat; Malibu: Undena, 1976) 19-21.

[6] Utilizing messengers not in one's direct employ was probably more common than the explicit evidence suggests. When a man sends one shekel of silver and two sila of sesame oil to a woman, he does so by the mediation of Ishum-malik, *mār šipri ša Ekallatum* (*AbB* VII 15). Ishum-malik is neither "my messenger" nor "your messenger" but is instead identified with a city-state. Jeremiah's letter to the leaders of the Babylonian Jewish community is carried by king Zedekiah's messengers sent to Nebuchadnezzar (Jer 29:1-3).

[7] Cf. the Hermopolis Letters (Hermopolis 1.14 2.18 3.14 4.15 5.10 6.11 7.5).

> They met young maidens coming out to draw water, and said to them, "Is the seer here?" They answered, "He is; behold he is just ahead of you."

In the case of correspondence associated with the palace, finding the recipient would be less problematic. Furthermore, the arrival of the messenger himself would not always come as a surprise, for we have already seen how the arrivals and departures of messengers were part of a well-supervised enterprise by palace bureaucracies, well-attested at OB Mari and in the Neo-Assyrian empire. As noted in section 2.3.1, word was often sent ahead that an arriving messenger soon would make his appearance in the palace. Biblical narratives (2 Sam 18:24-27; cf. 2 Kgs 9:17-20) portray an advance warning announced by strategically located watchmen.[8]

The time of day when messengers arrived was only rarely of significance to correspondents. However, Mari correspondents (particularly Yaqqim-Addu), more frequently than elsewhere in our sources, do note that messages arrive in the evening,[9] at meal-time,[10] at mid-day,[11] or at dusk.[12] Other notices outside Mari usually are prompted by extenuating circumstances, such as the presence of hostile elements which forces the messengers to make their arrival surreptitiously under cover of darkness.[13]

---

[8] As the text stands in 2 Kgs 6:32-33, Elisha's awareness of the arrival of the king's messenger beforehand is curious (cf. 1 Sam 9:15 or 1 Kgs 14:1-6); but see discussion of this passage in section 2.3.2.

[9] *Šamaš erbēt* (*ARM* XIV 9.8). "It was night and the palace bolts were in place when my lord's tablet arrived" *inūma ṭupp*[*i bēl*]*īya i*[*k*]*šudam mušītumma sikkāti ekallim nadê* (*ARM* XIII 9.26-28).

[10] *ina simān naptanim* (*ARM* XIV 16.19).

[11] *muṣlālam* (*ARM* XIV 37.8).

[12] *pān mūšim* (*ARM* XIV 45.9; 70.11).

[13] "I brought them in by night," *mūša šūribtîšunūti* (*EA* 116.24). "By night the messengers of the king, because of the dog, bring (news) and by night they return (news)" (*EA* 108.52-56). Note the two *ṣuḫārū* who carry tablets and are to "slip in to GN by night," *mušītamma libbi GN lirḫiṣūnim* (*ARM* I 97.18-19).

The actual arrival of the messenger at his destination is most pleasingly displayed in one of our earliest sources: "Joyfully he set his foot in Aratta's courtyard" (*ELA* 172). Of the seven known trips by this particular messenger, three times[14] in Aratta and twice in Uruk[15] it is recorded in similar words that he is glad to have reached journey's end. The joy of road's end, however, would not likely lull a messenger into the false comfort that his job was over. In many ways, it was just beginning.

3.2.2 PROTOCOL IN GENERAL

The messenger's initial reception by the ones to whom he was sent could very well determine the success of his mission. Messengers no doubt longed for the grand reception at road's end. Such a fortunate messenger is known from the protocol which the king of Mitanni recorded when Mane, the Egyptian messenger, arrived (*EA* 24.II.15-27):

> When earlier Mane brought what my brother had sent as my gift, I assembled my entire land, and my nobles, as many as there were present . . . . And I addressed Mane . . . and I addressed my land . . . .

Mane was no doubt the object of considerable jealousy by messengers with less appealing tales to tell. For example, the entourage of "five thousand standing at his right and left" witness Shulgi's messenger as he is shamed by his host.[16] A protocol for the reception of the messenger[17] is most often evident on such

---

[14] *ELA* 172-176 438-440 511-515.

[15] *ELA* 299-303 417-419.

[16] F. A. Ali, *Sumerian Letters: Two Collections from the Old Babylonian Schools* (Ph.D. dissertation, University of Pennsylvania, 1964), 33.

[17] In Greece, "little courtly etiquette surrounded the despatch and reception of envoys or representatives. Such developments were reserved for the Romans and Byzantines" (F. Adcock and D. J. Mosley,

occasions when it is violated and hence made explicit. Thus one emissary sent by Shulgi writes back to his lord: "when I came to thc gatc of thc palace, no one took notice of the greetings of my king; those who were sitting did not rise (and) did not bow down."[18] If the one destined to receive the message wished to avoid the messenger, he could refuse to grant an audience.

> I continually write him (*aštanapparaššum*) but he does not come to me nor does he meet with my messengers (*itti mārī šiprīya ul inna*[*mmar*]) . . . I sent him my letter, but he said, "I threw your tablet in the water" (*ṭuppam ana mê addi*).[19]

The decisive destruction of the message clarifies that it was no accident that this messenger never received an audience. The recipient wanted no communication and the messenger was consequently helpless. The kings of Canaan find this to be a problem with pharaoh, for he simply ignores the messengers that are sent and fails to meet with them, even an ambassador of such stature as the sender's own son: "I sent (*ušširtî*) my son to the majestic palace; after four months he has not seen the face of the king!" (*EA* 138.77-78). The problem recurs again in the first millennium as well when one writer threatens, "I shall not salute your messenger, nor shall I send greetings to the king my lord" (*SLA* 12.16-11r).

In international diplomacy, it became an explicit policy among allies to repulse messengers from non-allied third parties.

Diplomacy in Ancient Greece, 163). They first presented themselves to the council's committee who decided if and when they should appear before the assembly (*Ibid.*). "It was a serious affront to turn away an envoy abruptly . . . . It was unusual for an envoy to receive such a cold reception [as when Athens failed to offer any hospitality to a Theban messenger], for even when there was a complete failure to establish any diplomatic rapport, it was usual to observe the customary niceties . . . . When a firm rebuke was intended, envoys could be formally requested to leave within a specified period [e.g. before sundown]" (*Ibid.*, 164).

[18] F. A. Ali, *Sumerian Letters*, 32.

[19] *AbB* III 21.10-32.

Hattushili recounts how both he and Kadashman-Turgu once formed an admirably united front against Egypt, such that Kadashman-Turgu "prevented the royal Egyptian messenger" ([*mār šipri ša šarri*] *miṣri iptaras*)[20] from even entering his kingdom. Hattushili is consequently dismayed when the next Babylonian king upsets the coalition, complaining:[21]

> But when you, my brother, [became king], you sent [your messenger to the king of Eg]ypt, and the words of the [Egyptian king's] messenger [? ? and the king] of Egypt [accepted] your [gifts and you] accepted [his gifts]. Now [? ? if you] send [your messenger to the king of Egypt], shall I indeed hinder you?

Creative insults when declining an audience to a messenger underscore that the life of a messenger was not always an attractive one. The commandant of Babylon threw several citizens into prison because "you threw lumps of clay at my messengers."[22] Provocation to war was the result of the outrage which Hanun committed toward David's envoys: he cut off half of their beards as well as their garments before sending them on their way (2 Sam

---

[20] *CTH* 172.71; for the reconstruction of this and the following note, see E. Edel, "Die Abfassungszeit des Briefes *KBo* I 10 (Hattušil - Kadašman-Ellil) und seine Bedeutung für die Chronologie Ramses' II," (*JCS* 12 [1958] 131-133) 131.

[21] *CTH* 172.71-75. For the chronological issues associated with this text, in addition to E. Edel, *Ibid.*, see also M. Rowton, "The Material from Western Asia and the Chronology of the Nineteenth Dynasty," *JNES* 25 (1966) 247.

[22] *LAS* 276.23-15r. We don't know that this actually happened since this information comes from a source which insists that the commandant is lying. In any case, the accusation was perceived as a legitimate ground for imprisonment. For the historical context of this incident reflecting the social and political tensions during Babylon's restoration after Sennacherib destroyed it, see J. A. Brinkman, *Prelude to Empire*, (Philadelphia: Occasional Publications of the Babylonian Fund, 1984) 76-77.

10:2-5). The text makes explicit their extreme humiliation (*kî hāyû hā'ănāšîm niklāmîm mĕ'ôd* v.5).[23]

The most memorable account of the messenger who can not arrange a reception is found in Wenamun's autobiography. His rapid reception at the northern Egyptian court contrasts markedly with the reception which he received at Byblos where the first words to greet him from Zakar-Baal (via messenger!) are "Get out of my harbor!" (*Wenamun* 1.34,35). A curious narrative describes how the Egyptian messenger first finds lodging for himself, even before checking in with Zakar-Baal: "I got myself shelter in a tavern at the shore of the harbor [of the Sea] of Byblos" (*Wenamun* 1.33).[24] Consequently, with accommodations outside the palace and unable to have an audience with the ruler, Wenamun must endure twenty-nine days of daily reminders sent to him from Zakar-Baal: "Get out of my harbor!" (1.37,38). Wenamun replies by messenger (1.35-37): "Where [shall I go?] . . . If [you find a ship] to transport me, let me be taken to Egypt again!"

But Zakar-Baal grants no response to this request. That is, until Wenamun actually does find a ship and is preparing to load it under cover of darkness. The comedy of coincidences continues with the Byblite ecstatic raving that the messenger must not depart. Wenamun is baffled (1.43-47).

> The harbor master came to me and said: "Stay until morning, says he, the ruler!" And I said to him, "Aren't you the one who always spent his time coming

---

[23] "The 'half' is not half in length, but half in breadth, one entire side, to make them look ridiculous" (S. R. Driver, *The Books of Samuel*, 287). Their undergarments are in view according to Meir Malul, "Some Comments on B. Margalit's 'Ugaritic Lexicography II'," (*RB* 93 [1986] 415-418) 416.

[24] Goedicke (*Wenamun*, 48-49) notes that this is a problematic sentence - many translate as, "I celebrated in a tent." It is clear from the context that wherever this place is, it is for the deposit of the sacred things of Amun and the statue itself. Goedicke prefers to see this as a lowly accommodation, perhaps a boarding house in the nature of a khan.

> to me daily saying, 'Get out of my harbor!' Aren't you saying, 'Stay the night!' in order to let the ship, which I found, depart? And then you shall come out and say again, 'Move on!'" And he went and told it to the ruler. And the ruler sent to the captain of the vessel, saying: "Stay until morning, says he, the ruler!"

Finally an audience is granted. The next morning, Zakar-Baal sends for Wenamun who enters the ruler's presence to find him seated[25] with his back to the Mediterranean. The first words are spoken by the messenger ("Amun will be merciful!"[26]) while the response from the ruler is to inquire how long Wenamun has been on the road.[27] At this point, Zakar-Baal asks for Wenamun's credentials, specifically the edict of Amun and the letter of the High Priest of Amun, both of which he repeats "should be in your hand" (1.52).[28] Dealing with the bureaucracy in one's own land is

---

[25] "It seems that the chief of Byblos was sitting near the floor, possibly even squatting, because Wenamun could not have seen the breakers, if he had to look up" (Goedicke, *Wenamun*, 59).

[26] 1.50. As for Wenamun's greeting: "Although the term is undoubtedly a greeting, it is not attested in this form in any other place . . . . [It] is not an established form of greeting but is apparently an individual formulation chosen by Wenamun to convey something" (Goedicke, *Wenamun*, 59-60). Goedicke proposes that Wenamun wishes to stress that quality of Amun upon which he depends for success in this venture.

[27] "[The ruler of Byblos] opens his speech suddenly and without amenities like a greeting, posing the question of how much time Wenamun has spent since leaving Thebes. This is hardly an inquiry motivated by concern or politeness. It is rather aimed to convey the following: first, it makes Wenamun realize how far he is removed from the place where Amun might have significance, and second, it tests Wenamun's veracity" (Goedicke, *Wenamun*, 60).

[28] "The request for the letters of introduction shows the existence of established diplomatic procedures. Their absence . . . is taken by Zeker-Baal as an insult, because Amun's request was not directed to him as it should have been. It is noteworthy that Zeker-Baal did not expect a letter from the Pharaoh, i.e., Ramesses XI; his concern

often a nightmare in itself, but this unfortunate incident illuminates the compounded complexities which confronted international messengers in dealing with two (and more) bureaucracies. The system in Egypt had kept the document which the system in Byblos now required. And it was not simply Zakar-Baal's whim,[29] for "he was really irate" (1.53) and launched into a barrage of insulting rhetorical questions, the last of which may be paraphrased: "Who asked you to come?" (1.57).

In the light of these problems which delays foster or exacerbate, it is therefore not unexpected to find messengers (or those who send them) making the request that they be brought into the presence of the person to whom they are sent. At Ugarit, a letter is addressed to a friend to make sure that he can personally bring his messenger (known elsewhere as a merchant) into the king's presence and have his request granted (*Ugar.* V 98-99r):

> Now I send Amutaru to the king my lord. May my lord introduce (*lušēribšūma*) Amutaru to the king; may my lord speak his words as persuasively as possible before the king and introduce him as pleasingly as possible (*amatēšu kī ša ṭābiš . . . lidbub u kī damqiš lišēribšu*). Let my lord speak before the king so that he sends 2 fine horses and a fine bow in the hands of Amutaru and you too send . . .

When an audience is granted, it is the first item of import which a messenger reports back to his lord: "Upon my arrival in Carchemish, I met with Aplahanda (*itti PN annamer*; Apla. 5-7).

In the cumbersome bureaucracies of the great empires, it is understandable that some messengers might accidentally be

---

is restricted to the cult and its representative, the First High Priest of Amun . . . . There seems to be a vague hint that Zeker-Baal would have acted differently if Wenamun had brought the documents with him and had not handed them to Smendes" (Goedicke, *Wenamun*, 63).

[29] Goedicke (*Wenamun*, 63-64) notes the issue here is that since Smendes received the divine order, that makes him responsible, hence Wenamun must now write to Smendes.

overlooked and end up cooling their heels simply on account of bureaucratic oversight. Therefore, we have records of the messengers themselves applying through the proper bureaucratic channels to assure themselves of a hearing. The following tablet is devoted entirely to informing the king that a messenger is being forwarded by the provincial officials, having requested an audience with the king:

> To the king: That Babylonian (*mār Bābili šū*) has come to me saying, "I am the bearer of a message (*dibbī ina pîya*); let them bring me into the palace (*ina ekalli lūbilūni*)." Consequently I have sent him into the presence of the king my lord. The king my lord may ask him what his message is. On the 28th from the city of Zaddi I sent him into the presence of the king.[30]

In the Neo-Assyrian empire, a personal meeting with the king was a significant privilege.[31] Commoners were not permitted to see the king face to face, and entrance into his presence with head covered may not have been unusual if we may judge from the readiness with which one fellow bringing a message accepts such treatment.[32]

Even if a personal interview was granted to a messenger, the host could still exhibit considerable disdain and use the occasion to shame the messenger. Shulgi's messenger, to whom none showed respect upon arrival as noted above, meets with further

---

[30] *SLA* 157. See also *CT* 53.68.9-3r: "Bel-udu'a the messenger of Eteri the *šatammu* who came before the king my lord once, twice, now has come again, saying: I am being sent to the palace (*šaprāku*) [ ] I have dispatched him to the king my lord. May the king listen to his words." (Edited by F. Fales, "New Assyrian Letters from the Kuyunjik Collection," [*AfO* 27 (1980) 136-153] 139).

[31] See *TCAE* 125-126 for a survey of the king's reception of foreign embassies.

[32] *ABL* 1091 treated in S. Parpola, "The Murder of Sennacherib," *Mesopotamia 8* (XXVIe Rencontre Assyriologique Internationale, ed. B. Alster; Copenhagen: Akademisk, 1980) 171-182.

abuse when ushered into the presence of the Subarian A-WI-illa. The latter "seated himself on a throne (placed upon) a dais covered(?) with noble cloth . . . , put his feet on a golden footstool, (and) did not move his feet from it."[33] A-WI-illa's proud and staid immobility here is not the deferential treatment which Irmu expected.[34] Further details suggest the proper expressions of hospitality, such as the messenger being offered a seat in a "golden chair (with) a foot rest" and provided with a meal in the king's presence.

However, Irmu's response is to refuse rest and refreshment until he delivers his message: "In accordance with the instructions of my king, I will remain standing, (and) will not sit down." He declines to eat food which is placed before him. The messenger's posture at this point need not be considered provocative,[35] for a legitimate response to offers of hospitality could be that one conclude business before pleasure. Such a ritual is found, for example, in biblical literature when Abraham's messenger receives hospitality from Laban (Gen 24:31-34):

> And he said, "Come in blessed of the Lord! Why do you remain outside since I have prepared the house and a place for the camels?" So the man entered the house and he (Laban) unloaded the camels and gave straw and fodder to the camels and water to wash his feet and the feet of the men who were with him, and food was set before him to eat. But he said, "I cannot eat until I have spoken my affairs (*'ad 'im dibbartî*

---

[33] F. Ali, *Sumerian Letters*, 32-33.

[34] This is clear not only from subsequent events but also from Shulgi's comments in another letter, that if A-WI-illa were behaving properly, "he would not have seated himself on a throne (placed upon) a dais covered(?) with noble cloth, would not have put his feet on a golden footstool" (*Ibid.*, 40).

[35] Ali feels that the messenger's response represents a direct reaction to the insults he had received (*Ibid.*, 10). One must be cautious in noting similarities between the reception which a Subarian grants to a Sumerian in the third millennium and how a Semitic patriarch of northern Mesopotamia behaves in the second millennium.

> *dĕbārāy*)." So he (Laban) said, "Speak (*dabbēr*)." Then he said, "I am Abraham's servant . . . ."

Offers of hospitality consequently precede the delivery of the message, but the offers may not be accepted for several reasons. First, there can be no question that the host was eager to hear whatever news came from afar, but the offer of food and rest proceeded from the host's sense of traditional propriety.[36] On the messenger's part, the postponement of needed refreshment lent a greater urgency and significance to his mission and the message he bore. A response to the messenger's report was certainly not necessary before dining (although this did in fact occur in Gen 24:50-54) and the interval provided by dining may often have given a host the necessary time for reflection or council on how to respond. We will return later to the issue of wining and dining the messenger, but here we only wish to point out that on the occasion noted above with regard to Irmu, such a custom was employed to insult the messenger: soldiers overturned the messenger's table such that he became "afraid and terrified."[37]

A glimpse into the palace bureaucracy is afforded by the late second millennium harem edicts of the Assyrian court. In so far as they affect messengers, at least one particular type, we read:[38]

> If the king sends (*išappar*) a eunuch to the harem, he shall not enter the palace without the knowledge of the *rab ekallim*. He shall speak with the *rab ekallim*. Until he enters and comes out, the *rab ekallim* shall stand at the entrance of the *bīt-musate*. If they are on the way (*ḫūlu*), he cannot enter without the permission of the *rab ekallim* and the *rab zariqi*. If the eunuch enters without permission, he is guilty and liable for punishment.

---

[36] Evidence from the Aegean is instructive: "Taste food and be glad, and after you have eaten we will ask what men you are" (*Odyssey* IV.60-62; cf. I.123-124 V.87-96).

[37] Ali, *Sumerian Letters*, 33.

[38] E. F. Weidner, "Hof- und Harems-Erlasse," 277-278.

It is therefore clear that the personal reception of the messenger was a matter of significance, regulated by the bureaucracy of the palace and normally necessary for the completion of the messenger's task. To avoid an envoy deliberately was a substantial insult.

An envoy may not necessarily be avoided deliberately by a king, for lesser bureaucrats could intentionally keep messengers from him. We noted above the protests of the Canaanite kings that their messengers are not granted an audience. The palace bureaucracy in this case may have filtered through only those messengers who were desirable, without pharaoh's knowledge. Aziru recognizes this in writing to pharaoh's official in charge of messengers, asking him not to allow his enemies into the king's presence (*EA* 158.20-31). Tutu acknowledges in his tomb autobiography that when messengers came to pharaoh,

> I would report their words to the palace, since I was daily in [ ] and I would exit again to them as a royal messenger with all of his Majesty's instructions."[39]

There was thus clearly a screening of messengers, both by a monarch as well as court functionaries. One's office as messenger did not guarantee that one would be heard.

An Assyrian text connected with the ritual for the New Year contains instructions on the special reception of messages during this event:[40]

> [When] a message (*našpirtu*) comes to Ashur from a campaign,[41] he brings (*ušerrab*) the message (i.e. the messenger[42]) into the *qersu* and has him sit down (*ušeššab*). He performs a sacrifice, brings cooked

---

[39] M. Valloggia, *Recherche*, 108.

[40] E. Ebeling, "Kultische Texte aus Assur," *Or* 22 (1953) 32-35, l.1-9.

[41] Reading *ištu (TA) ḫūl*[*i*] (*CAD* N (2) 71) for Ebeling's *ta-ḫu-ú-m*[*u*] "von der Grenze".

[42] Ebeling notes that "message" here = "messenger" (*Ibid*., 35).

> flesh, roasts a kid, opens the *ḫariu*-container, puts the message in the box[43] of the chief of the chancellery (*rab šipirte*), (and then) he goes within the city (Ashur).

The specifically cultic context of this description cautions against generalizations. On special days when all activity is to cease, the arrival of a message (thus breaking the solemnity) can be a sign of disaster,[44] and the ritual outlined above may be designed to neutralize the danger.

Perhaps the most detailed literary text recounting the reception of messengers is the Neo-Assyrian version of *Nergal and Ereshkigal*. When Kakka,[45] the messenger of Anu, reaches the gates of the Underworld, a dialogue between messenger and gate-keeper occurs (*STT* 28 I.18'-19').

> "[Porter!] O[pen] the gate [for m]e!"
> "[Enter, Kakka,] and may the gate [bless you."]

Upon being ushered through the seven gates of the underworld (*STT* 28 I.27'-29'):

> He entered her spacious courtyard. He knelt, k[issed] the ground before her, straightened up, took his stand and said to her" (*īrumma ana p*[*al*]*kî kisallīša ikmisi i*[*ššiq*] *qaqqaru maḫrīša īšir izzazz*[*īma*] *izakkarša*).

---

[43] Ebeling translates *g/qub-ba-ni* as "in den (die) Kasten(?)", citing as a parallel *ABL* 1042, "you are like a sealed document which one conceals in a box (*gub-ba-ni-ka*)". *CAD* N (2) 71 and L 12 read *li-ba-ni* for normal *labānu*, as if the document is placed around the neck.

[44] F. Thureau-Dangin, "Les fêtes d'Akītu d'après un texte divinatoire," *RA* 19 (1922) 145-146.

[45] The appearance of Kakka in the NA version in place of the nameless messenger sent in the earlier Amarna text (*EA* 357) can be explained as an Assyrianism. Kakka's cult never gained ground in Babylonia although it did so in Assyria (P. Steinkeller, "The Mesopotamian God Kakka," [*JNES* 14 (1982) 289-294] 292).

Namtar in his turn is sent from the Underworld to heaven in a missing section of the tablet, but we can still gather from two later sections that all of the gods (except Nergal) bowed to him since he was carrying the divine decrees:

> [The gods], all together, [knelt before] him, [even the great gods], the lord(s) of destinies; for he carried the authority, the authority of [the gods, the god]s who dwell in Irkalla. Why do you not [kneel] before him? [ ] I kept winking at you but you acted as if you didn't notice. (*STT* 28 II.4'-10')

> My lady, after you sent me [to] your father, on my entering the courtyard [of Anu, all the gods] were kneeling humbly [. . . the gods of the land] were kneeling [ ] the gods before me [ ].[46]

Nergal is then sent as a messenger from Anu,[47] but he is detained at the gate for a considerable length of time - four messages must be relayed within the gates before he can be allowed to enter! While the messenger waits outside, the porter reports his arrival to the queen of the underworld who then sends Namtar to identify the messenger. Namtar returns to say it is Nergal, at which point the queen sends him to bid Nergal enter. Like Kakka before him, he is ushered through the seven gates[48] and makes his appearance (bowing and standing) in identical words.[49]

---

[46] *STT* 28 III.24'-27'; H. Hunger, *Spätbabylonische Texte aus Uruk* (*ADFU* 9; Berlin: Gebr. Mann, 1976) 1.3.1'-2'.

[47] *STT* 28 III.50' modified according to H. Hunger, *Ibid.*, 1.4.5.

[48] The gates are described differently in each case: for Kakka, the gates are simply numbered, while for Nergal the demonic porter identified with each gate is also noted.

[49] *STT* 28 III.48'-49, H. Hunger, *Ibid.*, 1.4.4. The last three words, omitted in the Sultantepe text by scribal error, are found in the Uruk text. Other variations are insignificant: the vocalic glide on *ikmisi* is omitted in Nergal's description, *qaqqara* appears in Sultantepe and

We can begin to see that as the poem progresses, the descriptions of the messengers' arrivals become increasingly more complicated, reflecting the increasing tensions between heaven and hell. The cordial initial invitation from heaven is reflected in an ease of access through the seven gates of hell for that first messenger, even though his message is unknown. This *entente cordiale* is marred when the ambassador from below is not accorded due respect in heaven by Nergal who refuses to bow. From this point on, messengers do not travel so freely as tensions rise. Instead, the porter in the underworld does not allow Nergal to enter freely but makes him wait for permission from the throne. Tension develops to its highest pitch as far as messengers are concerned with the next embassy from Ereshkigal (*STT* 28 V.14'-16'):

> On his arrival at the gate of Anu, Enlil and Ea, Anu, Enlil and Ea saw him and (said): "What have you come for, Namtar?"

It is arresting that the message which Namtar is commissioned to deliver is presented while he is standing outside the walls of heaven. He is not even allowed the courtesy to enter. Furthermore, this is no mere gate-keeper who is preventing him access, but it is the great trinity of authority peering down rather comically[50] from the gate upon this lone envoy. After his threatening message is complete, Ea (reluctantly?) recognizes that the gods have no choice and only then invites the messenger in: "Namtar, [enter] the courtyard [of Anu]". His reception then follows the normal protocol (*STT* 28 V.31'-33'):

> On his entering the [courtyard of Anu], all [the god]s knelt [humbly . . .] [The god]s of the land k[nelt . . . .]

---

qaqqar at Uruk, the Uruk text reads *maḫar-*, the suffix pronoun *-šu* for the three occurrences of *-ša*, and *izzazzu*. Instead of Hunger's *i-šar* read *i-šìr* with W. Moran.

[50] This contrasts with the regal aloofness of Ereshkigal where a gate-keeper does her bidding.

> (*ana* [*kisalli An*]*im ina erēbīšu kam*[*su ašru . . . ilāni*] *kališunu k*[*amsu . . . ilāni*] *ša māti*).

Namtar must make another journey to heaven, and he finds the gate barred again with the same triumvirate asking him the same question ("What have you come for?"), the message again delivered outside the gate and the same (reluctant?) command to enter.[51]

Against this interpretation of the varying receptions, it may be argued that we have no coherent text preserved of a messenger from the underworld arriving before the gate of heaven who is then ushered in to the courtyard before he delivers his message. However, the fragments which remain do suggest that this is the situation.[52] Furthermore, narratives elsewhere reinforce the impression of the less than cordial protocol emanating from this text. In *Enmerkar and the Lord of Aratta*, a peculiar stress is repeatedly placed upon the messenger physically setting foot in the courtyard where he delivers his message.[53] In *Enmerkar and Ensuhkeshdanna*, the messenger enters the *gipar* into the presence of the lord (l.49-53) or the holy place (l.114-117). In the *Marriage of Sud*, Nuska "arrived at Eresh, entered the Ezagin, Nanibgal's residence" (l.45-46). In later Hittite treaties, a cordial relationship between sovereign and vassal can be maintained only if they "admit not the enemy's messenger within their gate."[54]

---

[51] *STT* 28 V.43'-45'. The note as to the prostration of the gods before the messenger is one of two elements missing. It likely was originally in the text, but like the other element (the identity of the god who speaks the command to enter), it was probably omitted for the sake of brevity; see notes above for other omissions. The final entrance of Nergal into the underworld (*STT* 28 VI) is not a mission on which he is sent as a messenger but rather as one summoned.

[52] Note the traces *i*]*k*!-*šu-du i*[*na* (*STT* 28 II.2') just two lines before the gods are reported to have bowed. It is to be observed, however, that this is a report in the mouth of Ea of what occurred and not the actual description.

[53] Lines 299-303 (emphatic here), 172-176, 438-440; cf.352-356.

[54] *CTH* 146.22r; O. R. Gurney, "Mita of Pahhuwa," *AAA* 28 (1948) 36. Note also, "that man's messenger into my gate [I will] not [ ]" (*CTH*

A close parallel to the drama at the heavenly gate is Sennacherib's embassy to Hezekiah: high officials[55] line the wall while the envoy must deliver his message outside the gate. In this latter case, the tension between envoy and hearers is obvious, for they are at war. Also instructive in this regard is the letter to the king from two Assyrian messengers who were sent to the rebel Babylonians:

> "We came to Babylon. We took our stand before the Marduk gate and argued with the Man of Babylon. So-and-so the servant of Ukin-zer was present at his side. When they came out they were standing before the gate with the Babylonians. We spoke to the Babylonians in this way:". . . ." We said to them: "Open the great gate! We would enter Babylon". He was not willing."[56]

The Babylonian behavior is here no different than the way in which Assyrians themselves are counselled in another letter (*CT* LIII 76) to respond when an unwelcome man or his messenger arrives at a military encampment - he is not to be allowed in but is to be addressed outside (r.5'-9').

One cannot ignore the many parallels of *Nergal and Ereshkigal* with the Akkadian *Descent of Ishtar*. Even though Ishtar is not functioning as a messenger but goes of her own will, her reception at the gate adds perspective to our discussion. Her opening words - "Open the gate!" - are supplemented by the provocative, "Or else I'll smash it!" Had her approach been more civil, one wonders if she might have entered with less fuss. As it

---

146.13; Gurney, *Ibid.*, 34), in addition to, "[and the enemy's messenger] you shall not admit within your gate" (*CTH* 146.41r; Gurney, *Ibid.*, 38).

[55] Hezekiah preserves his dignity by not appearing on the wall, unlike his counterparts in the myth of *Nergal and Ereshkigal*. Note that Hezekiah is in fact summoned (2 Kgs 18:18), but sends his representatives in his place.

[56] H. W. F. Saggs, "The Nimrud Letters," *Iraq* 17 (1955) 23-24.

is, she is left to wait while the porter gets orders from his queen, Ereshkigal.[57]

It is difficult, therefore, not to see in the reception of Namtar by Anu, Enlil and Ea a reference to the chilling relations between heaven and hell.[58] It should also be observed that not only does Ereshkigal play the role of the more regal of the monarchs in regard to never showing up at the gate, but her messenger receives the homage of those to whom he is sent while the heavenly messengers on the contrary themselves must bow down. This brings us, however, to a distinct feature of the reception of messengers which requires a separate discussion.

3.3 WHO BOWS TO WHOM?

There is only one known messenger who bows when he leaves the presence of the one who sends him, namely, the Cushite sent by Joab to inform David of the defeat of Absalom (2 Sam 18:21). This is quite peculiar and the reason for this unique description is no doubt to be found within the narrative itself. The polarization between David and Joab in the concluding chapters of 2 Samuel seems to echo in the phenomenon of the two runners sent to David by Joab. One runner shows his allegiance to David by desiring to run and cushion David against the bad news; the other runner in contrast shows his insensitivity

---

[57] Inanna's hostile behavior (similarly rewarded) is also explicit in the Sumerian *Descent*: "She acted evilly at the door of the nether world, spoke evilly in the palace of the nether world" (S. N. Kramer, "'Inanna's Descent to the Nether World' Continued and Revised," *JCS* 5 [1951] 4-5).

[58] One might also cite 2 Kgs 7:10f. in this regard, for four men come bearing good news that the enemy had fled. They call to the gate-keepers who will not open the gates; is this because it is night or because they are at war? In any case, the king is aroused in much the same way as Ereshkigal is summoned in *Descent of Ishtar* and *Nergal and Ereshkigal*. A thorough study of door-keepers' behavior would be needed to decide the precise nuances of what is normal and aberrant.

toward David in cheerfully informing the bereaved father that his son is now dead. It is a part of the high literary art of the narrator, reflected in much of the succession narrative, that this polarization is reflected in the individuals to whom each messenger bows: the Cushite bows to Joab before departing but not to David on arrival, while Ahimaaz bows not to Joab but only to David. It is the literary artistry which prompts this unique reference to a messenger bowing before departing. It is likely that messengers did bow before leaving, as a sign of subordination, but it was never of interest to narrative apart from this one example.[59]

Passing from the unique, we are confronted with actual descriptions of messengers bowing only in narrative and poetic literature, not in the letters themselves. We turn first to mythic narratives which form a category by themselves. In these, it is normal for messengers to bow rather than to receive homage: Baal's messengers bow to Anat (*CTA* 3.3),[60] Asherah's to Kothar (*CTA* 3.6), Enlil's to Nanibgal (*Sud* 47), Anu's to Ereshkigal (*STT* 28 I.28'; III.49), Anshar's to Lahmu and Lahamu (*EE* III.68-70), Enlil's to the Igigi (*Atra*. I.122-4,134-136; p.54-55).

---

[59] Mayer Gruber misinterprets the prostration as reflecting a real hierarchy, i.e. "Ahimaaz the priest, being of the same status as Joab, does not bend over to Joab" and although "we might expect that . . . the Cushite must bend over to the king also," Gruber suggests that prostration is used only to "affirm . . . relationships of direct subservience [sic], not to affirm relationships which logically derive from these" (*Aspects of Nonverbal Communication in the Near East* [Rome: Biblical Institute, 1980] I 195). But Ahimaaz depends on Joab for his orders and is hardly an equal, while the suggestion that the Cushite does not bow to the king because he is a subordinate only of Joab is ludicrous. It is exceptional to depict messengers bowing in the Bible. When they do so, that narrative fact requires explanation.

[60] Their prostration is commanded by Baal but omitted in the actual narration.

3.3.1 UGARIT

A certain formulaic regularity emerges in these scenes where bowing occurs. At Ugarit, seven times[61] prostration is commanded or performed with messengers in view:

<u>*CTA#*</u>

2.1 *[lp'n il] al tpl al tšt*ḥ*wy p*ḫ*r [m'd qmm a ? am]r* ṯ*ny d'tkm*

2.1 *lp'n il l tpl l tšt*ḥ*wy p*ḫ*r m'd qmm a[] amr w*ṯ*ny d'tbm*

1.2 *balp ḥṣr [rbt kmn lp']n 'nt*	*[yhbr*	*wyql*	*yšt]ḥwyn*	*wy[kbdnh]*
1.3 *balp šd r[bt kmn lp'n kṯr]*	*hbr*	*wql*	*t[štḥwy*	*wkbd hwt]*
3.3 *lp'n 'nt*	*hbr*	*wql*	*tštḥwy*	*kbd hyt*
3.6 *balp šd rbt kmn lp'n kṯ<r>*	*hbr*	*wql*	*tštḥwy*	*wkbd hwt*
4.8 *balp šd rbt kmn lp'n mt*	*hbr*	*wql*	*tštḥwy*	*wkbd hwt*

The unity of the phrasing between tablets 1, 3 and 4 stands in contrast to the phrasing in tablet 2, one of several features which confirm that CTA 2 is not a literary unity with the Baal cycle found in CTA 1,3-6.[62] One marked distinction between the texts is the presence of the participle *qmm* when the messengers obey Yam's command. This is not a finite verb and does not readily translate as a parallel event following the preceding verbs of falling and bowing. Since it is not finite, it is not precisely parallel to the Akkadian formula to be discussed below, where in fact messengers arise after they have bowed. In CTA 2 the messengers do not stand up because they are already standing (stative participle).

Although there is room for doubt as to the meaning of *'l* or *l* in any given context, whether it be emphatic or negative, the deviation of our text from the formula elsewhere is significant even if it be in a distinct cycle. Why would a master emphatically

[61] The following twelve references exhaust the occurrences of the root *ḥwy* at Ugarit; *hbr* occurs elsewhere only in *CTA* 2.1.47 (broken context) and *CTA* 23.49,55 in an unrelated context.

[62] S. Meier, "Baal's Fight with Yam (*KTU* 1.2.I,IV) - A Part of the Baal Myth as Known in *KTU* 1.1,3-6?" (*UF* 18 [1986] 241-254).

wish to charge his messengers to bow, when that is what messengers normally do in other epic cycles without requiring such emphasis? Certainly the negative would be the most likely candidate for preference in this context as we will argue below. But if so, why is Yam commanding them not to bow? Precisely for the reason just noted, that this is normally what messengers do. These messengers are not to show their submission or exhibit any type of servile behavior to the divine council.

This behavior is not unique, for it appears that *CTA* 2 is one form of the mythic tradition which is known elsewhere: the infernal deity requires one of the divine beings to spend time in the underworld, a request which is resisted but eventually acceded to with some form of compromise. Parallels from the classical world are familiar, but in the Near East they are equally common. The *Descent of Ishtar* and the myth of *Nergal and Ereshkigal* are immediately obvious; it is not accidental that so much in the former finds echoes in the latter. What makes this discussion necessary is that the narrative of Baal and Yam has many features which are precisely parallel to the story which we have preserved of *Nergal and Ereshkigal*.

In both myths, the following elements appear: a divine council sits at meal, the chthonic deity is not present, an embassy is sent from the absent deity to claim one of the gods, the gods are threatened by the embassy, and the desired god is delivered over to the embassy. Finally, the peculiar feature of the myth of *Nergal and Ereshkigal*, namely that the messengers of heaven bow in hell while the messengers of hell stand in heaven, is echoed in *CTA* 2 where the gods at meal do homage to the messengers from below. We will discuss this further below in regard to the Akkadian story.

The description of bowing can not be labelled a specific feature characteristic only of messengers at Ugarit. Other individuals besides messengers bow five times in the Ugaritic texts: Anat to El (*CTA* 4.4.25-26; 6.1.36-38; 17.6.49-50), Athtar to El (*CTA* 2.3.5-6) and Kothar-wa-Hasis to El (*CTA* 1.3.24-25):

<u>*CTA #*</u>

1.3 *l*[*p'n il yhbr wyql*] *yštḥwy* [*wykbdnh*]
2.3 [*lp'n il yhbr*] *wyql* [*y*]*štḥwy wykbd*[*h*]
4.4 *lp'n il thbr wtql tštḥwy wtkbdh*
6.1 *lp'n il thbr wtql tštḥwy wtkbdnh*
17.6 [*lp'n il t*]*hbr wtql tštḥ*[*wy wtkbd*]*nh*

It is clear that the regularity of phrasing is of a formulaic mold, agreeing with the majority of cases seen above describing messengers, a formula which underscores the aberration in *CTA* 2 noted above. It should also be noted that not all descriptions of messengers at Ugarit require that they be described as bowing; Gapnu and Ugaru do not bow to Baal when sent by Mot (*CTA* 5.1) nor to Mot when sent by Baal (*CTA* 5.2), Anat does not bow when sent by Shapshu to El (*CTA* 6.3), and King Pabil's messengers bow to neither Kirta nor Pabil (*CTA* 14.6). It is thus an optional feature of narrative, exploited for verisimilitude and color or to reflect social relationships.

3.3.2 AKKADIAN

The Akkadian myths, though formulaic, feature less of a regularity in their six known descriptions of messengers bowing or being commanded to do so:[63]

ikmisi iššiq qaqqaru maḫrīša īšir izzazzīma izzakkarša *STT* 28.1.28'-29'
ikmis iššiq qaqqara maḫrīša *STT* 28.3.49'
iššiq qaqqara maḫaršunu īšir izzaz izzakkaršun *EE* 3.69-70

[63] The reading for *Atra.* 1.135 is a proposal by W. Moran. The Sumerian account of Enlil's betrothal to Sud (supplied with a partially preserved Akkadian translation) pictures Enlil's messenger, Nuska, bowing before Sud's mother: "[ ] he prostrated himself before her on her throne (*ki mu-na-ni-ib-za/uštekeni*), Enlil's emissary stood before her" ([ ] *gub/izzizma*; *Sud* 47-48). Similarly when Nuska returns to Enlil he again bows, although expressed in different words: "He kissed the ground before Enlil" ([*ki*] *mu-un-su-ub*; 1.87).

kimis	*iziz*	*qibâ šunūti*	*Atra*.1.123
ikmis	*izziz*	*tertam ipšur*	*Atra*.1.135
kimis [ ]		*qibâššunūti*	*Atra*. p.54-55

The correspondence between *Nergal and Ereshkigal* on the one hand and the *Enuma Elish* on the other is striking. The contrasts between the Ugaritic and Akkadian phrases are greater than their similarities. Where every phrase in Ugarit revels in synonyms for "bow" (*npl*, *ql*, *ḥwy*, *hbr*), the Akkadian phrasing is satisfied with one root (*kamāsu*) on occasion supplemented by "kiss the ground" (a common Akkadian idiom). From the Ugaritic formula, one would suppose that the message is delivered in the prostrate position (we will return to the exceptional *CTA* 2), but all the Akkadian myths indicate that the messenger resumes the upright position (*izuzzu* occurs in all; *ešēru* in two myths).

In contrast to the above, at least one messenger stands while others bow to him: Ereshkigal's messenger to Anu (*STT* 28 II.4'-11'; III.25'-27'; V.31'-33'; H. Hunger, *Spätbabylonische Texte*, 1.3.1). This peculiar reversal is known as well outside literature. For example,[64]

> Tammaritu, the king of Elam, said, "How could Ummanigash kiss the ground before the messengers of Ashurbanipal?"

A different idiom which moves in the same semantic sphere is preserved in a Neo-Assyrian text of daily blessings to the king; for the eleventh day we read: "To your messenger may they [all lands] do homage" (*ana pān mār šiprīka appa lilbinū*).[65] The tradition is old, for Shulgi's envoy expects it when sent abroad, and he notes the insult when such homage is not granted:[66]

---

[64] Streck II.34-35, 1.19-20.

[65] *STT* 340.11; see E. Reiner, "Another Volume of Sultantepe Tablets," (*JNES* 26 [1967] 177-200) 195.

[66] F. Ali, *Sumerian Letters*, 32 1.9-11.

> When I came to the gate of the palace, no one took notice of the greetings of my king; those who were sitting did not rise (and) did not bow down.

Clearly, bowing toward the messenger is a sign of submission to the one who sent the envoy. Murshili II acknowledges the submission of Manapa-Dattash who not only bows to Murshili himself but sends messengers who do the same.[67] This attitude of homage is reflected as well in the greetings which prefaced Akkadian and Ugaritic letters in the second millennium:[68] "I fall at PN's feet" (*ana šēpē PN amqut - lpʻn PN qlt*[69]), "I fall at PN's feet from afar X number of times" (*ana šēpē PN ištu rūqiš 2-šu 7-šu amqut - lpʻn PN mrḥqtm šbʻd wšbʻd qlt*[70]). The notation "from afar" describes the respectful distance which a supplicant maintains when in the presence of a superior.[71] No doubt, the messenger who delivered the letter actually performed the genuflection on behalf of the sender. Such expressions, however, occurred only in letters addressed from a relative inferior to his superior. It is unlikely that the messengers of the Hittite sovereign bowed to the king of Ugarit. Based upon the first millennium example cited above of Ashurbanipal, it is likely that the king of Ugarit would be the one on his knees.

---

[67] *CTH* 69.I.38-40.

[68] For details see O. Kaiser, "Zum Formular der in Ugarit gefundenen Briefe," *ZDPV* 86 (1970) 10-23, to which add "we fall at PN's feet from afar" (*lpʻn PN mrḥqtm qlny*, *CTA* 51). For the many Akkadian variations, see E. Salonen, *Die Grüss- und Hoflichkeitsformeln in babylonisch-assyrischen Briefe* (*StOr* 38 [1967] 66-70). Note also the Middle Assyrian *ultaka''in* (E. Salonen, *Ibid.*, 77).

[69] Add *KTU* 2.72 to Kaiser's data above.

[70] *UT* 2115 is abnormal with *ṯnid sbʻd* (as Akkadian) in place of *šbʻd wšbʻd*. Add to Kaiser's corpus *KTU* 2.68.

[71] S. E. Loewenstamm, "Prostration from Afar in Ugaritic, Akkadian and Hebrew," *BASOR* 188 (1967) 41-43. See also A. Herman, "Jübel bei der Audienz," *ZAS* 90 (1963) 49-66 for discussion and figures of Egyptian reliefs depicting such prostration; note in particular the un-Egyptian manner of prostration which Syrians assume before pharaoh.

The unanimous testimony of the evidence affirms, therefore, that it was appropriate for a messenger to bow when he was despatched by his lord to one who was of greater rank than his lord. The messenger sent by a sovereign to his vassal would have the honor of receiving the bows of the vassal.[72]

There still remains the problem as to why the messenger from heaven bows while the messenger from below receives homage. In the light of the suggestion earlier that Ereshkigal is depicted in a much more favorable light than the heavenly trinity of ruling gods, the issue of bowing messengers reaffirms this impression. But how could one attribute relative superiority to Ereshkigal? It is likely that the etiological concerns of the story (i.e. how Ereshkigal acquired a husband or how Nergal ended up below) point to a locale such as Cutha where the deities of the Underworld were of paramount importance. It is possible that in such a context, the gods of the Underworld could be depicted more favorably than their celestial counterparts. Ereshkigal is clearly pictured as wielding ultimate veto power over heaven's decrees: the threat to make the dead more numerous than the living is not taken as an idle boast by the gods.[73] In the Ugaritic myth, we seem to have a variation of this theme.

The secondary[74] nature of *CTA* 2 as opposed to the *Nergal and Ereshkigal* myth may be seen in the command (in *CTA* 2) not to bow. In the Akkadian accounts, it is assumed that the messengers from below will receive the homage of heaven. When

---

[72] The offending god in the Amarna version of *Nergal and Ereshkigal* "did not rise" (*lā itbû EA* 357.26). Some have been perplexed at this apparent reversal of custom, as if respect were shown by standing (M. Hutter, *Altorientalische Vorstellungen von der Unterwelt* [Göttingen: Vandenhoeck & Ruprecht, 1985] 80; O. R. Gurney, "The Sultantepe Tablets," *AnSt* 10 [1960] 128). However, the nuance is best understood as, "he didn't get up (in order to do homage)", clear in another messenger's experience: "those who were sitting did not rise (and) did not bow down" (F. A. Ali, *Sumerian Letters*, 32).

[73] *STT* 28 V.11'-12',26'-27'. Cf. the Akkadian *Descent of Ishtar* l.19-20 where this is used as a trump card *against* the Underworld!

[74] We can derive neither one from the other; we are speaking of secondary only with regard to this feature of the messenger.

it is denied, all hell literally breaks loose. Yet this is such a striking cosmology (for hell to receive the homage of heaven) that to be in a text where it is unexplained argues for primacy. *CTA* 2 is more apologetic, supplying a reason for the lack of respect, namely, the command of Yam. The text leaves open the possibility that the chthonic messengers on other occasions do homage to the divine council; the *Nergal and Ereshkigal* myth does not permit such a possibility.

3.4 SUMMARY

Having reached his destination and located the individuals to whom he was sent, a messenger could never be sure what type of reception he would receive upon arrival at his destination. If he was an international envoy, the changing winds of politics could blow insult or honor in his path. If insult was his fate, an appreciation for creativity would hopefully help him bear his shame; if honor, the whole world could be at his feet. Offers of hospitality would await the well-received ambassador, who could politely decline them until he had stated his business. Usually, the rules of politics, regulated through the bureaucracy, permitted the messenger the access he needed to the palace. An awareness of bureaucratic rules was essential, not only to achieve an audience, but also (as in the case of the harem edicts) to avoid harsh punishment. Embassies of hostile or threatening powers were traditionally kept waiting outside the city gate; it was a sign of tension when the messenger was compelled to deliver his message from without.

The messenger was received with due signs of respect exchanged between messenger and the one receiving him. Prostration was the mark of submission rendered to the relative superior (the messenger representing his sender in this capacity), although the message itself was delivered while standing.[75] When

[75] Cf. the instructions from the tomb inscription of the Egyptian vizier Rekhmire, specifying that the vizier's messengers are to stand while giving the message (M. Valloggia, *Recherche*, 95).

prostration is omitted in narrative, it normally has no significance. However, a failure to show proper respect by prostration forms an essential element in plot development in an Akkadian and a Ugaritic myth.

4

PRESENTING THE MESSAGE

4.1 TRANSLATORS

In the light of frequent messenger activity between mutually unintelligible language speakers, the problem arises as to how precisely the messenger verbalized his message in such diverse linguistic environments. Was the messenger expected to be conversant in more than one language? If not, did he travel with an interpreter or was an interpreter assumed to be waiting on the receiving end? The frustration of the language barrier surfaces when Ashurbanipal notes the arrival of a messenger from a land which had not formerly communicated with Assyria: "The tongues of the East and of the West, which Assur had poured into my hand - there was no master of his language, and [his] tongue remained strange, so that they could not understand his speech."[1] The ability of Shulgi in responding to foreign ambassadors is certainly not normative: "I answered in those five languages while in my palace no one else could understand foreign tongues."[2]

---

[1] *AS* 5 17.9-13.

[2] Shulgi B 217-218. Note Wenamun's first words when he is cast ashore on Cyprus (*Wenamun* 2.76-78): "I greeted her (the princess) and I said to the people who were standing around her: 'Isn't there one among you who can understand Egyptian words?' And one of them said: 'I understand!' And I said to him: "Say to my lady that . . . ."

Interpreters[3] are already attested in the Sargonic period (*eme-bala*), with their office inscribed on seals and having their own supervisors.[4] Their presence among the Assyrian merchants in Cappadocia is not unexpected (*targumannum*),[5] and interpreters are known for foreigners in an Old Babylonian text.[6] From this point on, they are attested down through the Neo-Assyrian period.[7] Their relatively important status has been suggested in the light of some data.[8]

There is not an abundance of references to such individuals; nevertheless, they do appear in a few contexts where their role in translating messages is clear. In the Ur III period such figures are found receiving provisions as members of a foreign embassy.[9] Greater precision is possible in the later Amarna period where Burnaburiash sends his messenger along with an interpreter to Amenhotep IV (*EA* 11:5-6); the latter in turn does the same (*EA* 11:9-10). In each case, the messenger is named before the *targumannu*, and only the messenger is described by the possessive pronominal suffix "your." However, when Tushratta earlier wrote to Amenhotep III, he referred to pharaoh's interpreter as "the interpreter of my brother," again naming him

---

[3] The central study of interpreters in the ancient Near East is I. J. Gelb, "The Word for Dragoman in the Ancient Near East," *Glossa* 2 (1968) 93-104. In addition to further texts cited below, see also R. Labat, "Le rayonnement de la langue et de l'écriture akkadiennes au deuxième millenaire avant notre ère," *Syria* 39 (1962) 4 n.5.

[4] *UGULA* (I. J. Gelb, *Ibid.*, 94-95); such supervisors are also known in Ur III texts (*Ibid.*, 97) and Cappadocian sources (*Ibid.*, 97).

[5] I. J. Gelb, *Ibid.*, 97; K. Veenhof notes evidence for bilingualism in Anatolia, but citing the *rabi targumannī* attested there, also admits the necessity of translators "perhaps as a branch of the administration" ("The Old Assyrian Merchants and Their Relations with the Native Population of Anatolia," *Mesopotamien und seine Nachbarn* [XXVe Rencontre Assyriologique Internationale; ed. H.-J. Nissen and J. Renger; Berlin: Dietrich Reimer, 1982] 147-148).

[6] I. J. Gelb, *Ibid.*, 97-98.

[7] *Ibid.*, 98f.

[8] *Ibid.*, 102.

[9] *Ibid.*, 96.

after the messenger. Furthermore, both *mār šipri* and *targumannu* worked together and were honored together by Tushratta, "for their [plural!] report was pleasing" (*EA* 21:24-29).

The names are preserved of the two Egyptian interpreters sent abroad, Mihuni and Hane, providing an exception to Gelb's observation that the interpreters whose personal names are attested appear primarily in their native land.[10] However, the reason he cites for the generalization may also explain the exception: "the position of dragoman was of such a sensitive nature that only natives would be picked for that employment."[11] In general one is more likely to trust an interpreter from one's own land before trusting a foreign interpreter. It is likely that the Mitanni court had natives (e.g. former slaves or merchants) who could interpret Egyptian, but the Egyptian pharaoh would lose nothing by having a tuned set of Egyptian ears in the Mitanni court. In the same way that one messenger accompanied a foreign messenger on his trip home and provided a check on reportage, it is possible that interpreters representing the two nationalities similarly encouraged precision. In any case, the availability of translators makes it clear that linguistic prowess was not a prerequisite for messengers.

Gelb notes that the evidence for translators is most abundant in the earlier period and declines from the end of the second millennium onward; if this is not a result of the accident of discovery, he notes that the rise of Akkadian as a *lingua franca* may have diminished the need for translators. We might add, however, that even in the first millennium, when the Assyrian empire began to find Aramaic a desirable language of diplomacy, it was to their advantage to be able to address their vassals in their native language (2 Kgs 18:26-28).[12]

---

[10] *Ibid.*, 103.

[11] *Ibid.*

[12] Although the *rab-shāqēh* here may be using an interpreter himself (J. A. Montgomery, *The Books of Kings*, 489), it may be that he was chosen for the job precisely because of his linguistic and cultural knowledge of the Judahites (H. M. I. Gevaryahu, "The Speech of Rab-Shakeh to the People on the Wall of Jerusalem," *Studies in the Bible*

4.2 MEMORIZING THE MESSAGE?

Literary and poetic depictions of messengers may paint with sometimes wearying strokes the message being presented to the messenger which is then repeated *verbatim* to the recipient. One might conclude from this that the messenger's task was to replay *verbatim* his master's words. Indeed, it is a commonplace to speak of messengers who "memorize and recite texts"[13] which are given to them to communicate. However, this conclusion is not defensible in the light of the evidence.

If it were true, one would expect a good memory to figure high among the qualities required in an envoy. However, it was noted in section 1.1 that a good memory was normally not a criterion explicitly considered in the selection of a messenger, and the only times when recall was requisite were those occasions when no document was present (*ARM* I 76.20-29). The overwhelmed messenger in *Enmerkar and the Lord of Aratta* is not disqualified because he cannot retain the message in his head. There is no search for another envoy with more prodigious recall. The narrative instead assumes that he is doing his job by carrying the tablet, whose contents he is unable to repeat in their entirety. He remains a praiseworthy messenger.

One must not minimize the overwhelming impression made by the precise and extensive repetition of literary narratives. However, these texts must be analyzed with respect to genre, and immediately it becomes apparent that literary and poetic narratives enjoy repeating everything (not just messenger speech) twice and more.[14] An individual who is not a messenger may

---

Presented to Professor M. H. Segal [ed. J. M. Grintz and J. Liver; Jerusalem: Kiryat Sepher, 1964] 94-102 [Hebrew]).

[13] A. L. Oppenheim, "A Note on the Scribes in Mesopotamia," *Studies in Honor of Benno Landsberger on the Occasion of his Seventy-fifth Birthday* (*AS* 16; Chicago: University of Chicago, 1965) 254.

[14] The discussion in the chapter entitled "The Technique of Repetition" in R. Alter's *The Art of Biblical Narrative* (New York: Basic

repeat precisely dozens of lines of narrative which he has observed happening, this description again being repeated by the listener to his messenger who in turn repeats it (now the fourth occurrence of the description!) to another (*EE* I.128-161 II.15-48 III.19-52,77-110). It is inappropriate to suggest that the messenger was required to repeat this message *verbatim* anymore than Anshar in this episode was required to replay the message precisely as he received it from Ea. If we insist that such repetition portrays the necessary good memory required of a messenger, one must not neglect the equally good memory required of the king who gives him the message which he received from another.

Since messages are repeated *verbatim* by individuals who are not messengers in the formal sense, it is clear that such repetition is not a peculiar feature of messenger activity. A message may even recur a third time in the mouth of a god who prophesies what a message will be and what response should be made. Is one to assume that the latter response had to be diligently drilled into king Kirta by El until he could repeat it *verbatim* (*CTA* 14)?

We do not dispute that precise repetition may indicate complete fulfillment of a task, or total obedience in accomplishing what is commanded, or even faithfulness in relaying a message. But this genre-bound literary device can not be extricated from its home and then transplanted uncritically into the non-literary domain of actual messenger activity. The precise repetition of a message by a messenger is a literary device not confined to messenger speech, and as such it consequently tells us little about *verbatim* repetition as a necessary element in delivering a report. From other texts discussed, it is clear that eloquence and tact, diplomacy and faithfulness were paramount, not a good memory.

Books, 1981) 88-113 is now enhanced by George Savran's *Telling and Retelling: Quotation in Biblical Narrative* (Bloomington, IN: Indiana University, 1988). A fine synthesis of biblical data which includes both messengers and prophets, as well as any type of message designed to be relayed to another, is offered by Ann Vater in "Narrative Patterns for the Story of Commissioned Communication in the Old Testament," (*JBL* 99 [1980] 365-382).

4.3 DECEPTIVE MESSENGERS - WRITTEN AND ORAL COMMUNICATION

In an earlier chapter it was noted that one of the prominent qualities required of a successful messenger was that he be faithful and true. From the records it becomes clear that this trust placed in the messenger was often betrayed. The potential skepticism about a messenger's news is noted already in Sumerian literature, for Ninabgal replies to Enlil's envoy (*Sud* 64): "If there is truth in what you have told me - and may there be no falsehood . . . ." In biblical literature, Ahimaaz is a classic example of the messenger who tells the person to whom he speaks exactly what that person wants to hear, whether it be true or not (2 Sam 18:19-31). Joab initially declines Ahimaaz' request to relay the message to king David because it is bad news. This would have dissuaded most messengers, as Joab makes explicit, "Why will you run, my son, seeing that you will have no reward[15] for the tidings?" But Ahimaaz, the son of David's favorite priest, has no intention of telling David everything he knows, and he certainly does not intend to tell David the bad news, as the later course of the narrative makes clear. Ahimaaz' persistent motives are compelling, if never stated. One may assume that his close attachment to the king moved him to present good news to the king before the tragedy was revealed.[16] His deceit, motivated

---

[15] On the textual problem see P. K. McCarter, *II Samuel* (*AB* 9; Garden City, NY: Doubleday, 1984) 402.

[16] Any interpretation of this narrative requires going beyond the specific data given by the writer; some feel it is evident that Ahimaaz is lying (H. Smith, *I and II Samuel* [*ICC*; Edinburgh: T & T Clark, 1899] 360) while others claim that Ahimaaz does not know that Absalom is dead (P. K. McCarter, *II Samuel*, 408). The latter appears less likely: since the entire preceding section (v.9-18) deals with Absalom's death which climaxes the battle, followed immediately by Ahimaaz' urgent request to tell the news, some statement is necessary to indicate he is unaware of the death, the major concern of the narrator up to that

from compassion, is clear in the greeting "Peace!" (*šālôm*) which he, unlike the Cushite, is eager to call out (*wayyiqrā'*) in v.28.

Whatever the motive for Ahimaaz' deceit, the motive to please the sender, even to the point of obscuring the truth, surfaces elsewhere in the ancient Semitic world. The Egyptian pharaoh suspects that a breakdown in communication with the king of Babylon is to be attributed to such apple-polishing:[17]

> Your messengers don't speak truly to you . . . . Don't listen to your messengers whose mouths are false. . . . I swear they have not served you and so they told lies in order to escape your punishment.

In the same letter, the pharaoh again takes the Babylonian messengers to task, suggesting that their duplicity is the cause of their poor treatment in the Egyptian court (*EA* 1.66-77):

> I am angry at your messengers, for they say to you, "He gives nothing to us who go to Egypt." One of them comes and receives silver, gold, oil, garments, all fine things [more than in[18]] any other country and he speaks falsehood to the one who sent him. The first time messengers went off to your father, their mouths spoke falsehood. A second time they left and spoke falsehood to you. So I say (to myself), whether I give or don't give anything to them, they are going to speak thus falsely! So I laid down a rule: I didn't give!

The pharaoh's solution may have succeeded in keeping some luxuries out of the hands of the Babylonian messengers, but it would not endear him to them and it certainly would not cure their prevarication (if pharaoh's accusations are justified). But what could monarchs, or even the common person, do to

---

point. The ignorance of Ahimaaz would be a key narrative feature, yet up to the delivery of Ahimaaz' message, no clue to the reader of such ignorance ever occurs.

[17] *EA* 1.81-88, translation of W. Moran.

[18] Reading *eli ša ina* with a suggestion of W. Moran.

guarantee a faithfully delivered message? Certainly one wants to choose the truthful envoy, but guile by definition is difficult to perceive. If God himself cannot trust his own envoys (Job 4:18), how much more frustrating is the problem to a more gullible mankind.

In the first millennium, the lying messenger was still a problem,[19] and the monarchs of Assyria had a method by which (they thought) they could anticipate such deceit: they may have asked Shamash to give them an appropriate omen if the messenger was destined to cause problems.[20] A much craftier technique was employed in the second millennium by Shamshi-Adad I.[21] After receiving a messenger sent by the Gutians, he asks, "Who knows whether their words are trustworthy or treacherous?" Note that this query targets the validity not of the messenger's report but of the men who sent him. He proceeds to interrogate the messenger to determine the credibility of his message:[22]

> Who knows whether their words are true or false? I questioned him, and he explained to me indications (*ittātim*) concerning those (i.e., the entourage) of Warad-Sharrim. A *ḫullum*-ring which I had given to Mutushu, the messenger, he mentioned to me as an indication (*ana itti*). Further, Etellini, a colleague of Mutushu, has been taken ill at Arrapha, and the illness of this man he mentioned to me; and he explained all the indications (*ittātim kalāšina*) to me. On this basis, I trusted their word.

---

[19] *LAS* II 50 describes Sargonic (and other) courtiers who concealed bad news from their monarch.

[20] The exact petition about the messenger sent from Mugallu the Militan to Esarhaddon is lost from *AGS* 54, but note how the king asks elsewhere if the news which he had heard was in fact true or reliable (*PRT* 109).

[21] On the historical context, see Jesper Eidem, "News from the Eastern Front," *Iraq* 47 (1985) 83-107.

[22] *SH* 920.16-33. For *ittātim dabābum* to denote watchwords, see J. Laessøe, *The Shemsharra Tablets* (Copenhagen: Ejnar Munksgaard, 1959) 39.

The use of pronouns is curious in this letter; he seems to be trying to establish the messenger's credibility, but when he is satisfied he refers to the senders of the messenger as the ones who can be trusted. The prevalence of the problem is reflected further in an omen apodosis: "a messenger with treacherous messages will arrive."[23] Ramses II's interrogation of two reputed Shosu messengers uncovers their treachery, for upon his asking where the tribal leaders are who sent them, their reply is followed by the narrative note, "they spoke falsely."[24]

The most fool-proof system devised was precisely that which provides us with the most information about messengers to begin with, namely the clay tablet. In a treaty which the Hittite king, Muwatalli, made with a king of Kizzuwatna, this very issue of truthful messengers surfaces as an issue of major importance to the state. Muwatalli stipulates clearly (*PDK* 108,109.32-39):

> If the Sun sends you a tablet on which a message (*awatu*) is placed and the message from the messenger's mouth which he responds to you - if the word of the messenger agrees with the word of the tablet, trust that messenger, Shunashura. If the word from the mouth of the messenger does not agree with the word of the tablet, Shunashura, don't trust that messenger and don't take that word to heart for evil.

The actual practice of this safeguard appears in a Hittite letter to the Egyptian pharaoh: "I don't trust Kalbaya; he indeed spoke it, but it was not confirmed on the tablet."[25] And this is no doubt the reason for Zakar-Baal's ire when he asks Wenamun immediately after the initial greetings (*Wenamun* 1.51-54):

---

[23] *mār šipri sarrāti irruba* (A. Boissier, *Documents assyriens rélatifs aux présages* (Paris: Émile Bouillon, 1894) 7.16 (K7000).

[24] A. Gardiner, *The Ḳadesh Inscriptions of Ramesses II* (Oxford: Oxford University, 1960) 28-29.

[25] *CTH* 152.4-6.

> "Where is the edict of Amun, which should be in your hand? And where is the letter of the First High Priest of Amun, which should also be in your hand?" And I said to him: "I gave them to Smendes and Tanetamun!" He was really irate and said to me: "Indeed, edict or letter you have not . . . ."

It should be recalled that the absence of this written document was so significant that Wenamun was compelled to write back to Egypt for confirmation of his mission, delaying him from performing his task.

In the light of this perspective, namely that one function of the written document was to keep messengers accountable, certain comments in the letters can receive further clarification. For example, Tushratta informs pharaoh (*EA* 24.II.101-105) that

> The word that Mane will communicate to my brother is gracious and true. . . . It is not evil (and) not hostile towards my brother. Towards his affairs it is not hostile.

Such a written comment may be motivated as insurance, just in case Mane orally relates some items which intentionally or accidentally arouse pharaoh's anger. The letter confirms that there is no intention on Tushratta's part of being provocative. Any hostility which might appear is simply that - apparent, and no more.

It may be possible that a further safeguard guaranteeing truth among messengers was the custom of sending at least one messenger of a country with at least one messenger from another country. We find elsewhere the notion that two individuals are adequate as witnesses.[26] Unfortunately, the closest that the data come to this outlook with respect to messengers are the occasions on which an individual is advised to ask his own messengers for confirmation of a foreigner's report. The Babylonian king is incredulous of the Egyptian messenger's claim that the Egyptian king really lives so far away that he does not know when his

[26] Num 35:30; Deut 17:6; 19:15.

Babylonian counterpart is sick. The frustrated messenger says: "Ask your own messengers if the way isn't far!" When the response from them is equally affirmative, the issue is laid to rest.[27] Such counsel is an acceptable matter of course in international diplomacy.[28]

It is likely, however, that the silence of the data with regard to the notion of messengers functioning as witnesses is not accidental. We have already seen above how they could have a reputation for deceit. The tablets rather stress the notion of witness with regard to the tablet itself.[29] Thus, when a message is sent, the writer will often note that the receiver should keep the tablet as a witness to the fact that whatever instructions are in the tablet are authoritative: "keep this tablet (*ṭuppum*) as a witness to my words"[30] or "retain this tablet (*ṭuppum*) as my witness"[31] occur in the OB period. In the first millennium appears "let my document (*šipirtum*) be my witness,"[32] with the word "witness" often being marked (not unusually but in this case with a certain irony) with the logogram for a human being.[33]

The legal role of messenger and/or tablet as a witness may be extrapolated from an OB letter[34] where Tarish-Hattu reports how

---

[27] *EA* 7.8-32. See further discussion in section 5.1.

[28] Puduhepa advises the king of Alashiya when she writes: "Ask your messengers [whether it is so] or not so!" (*CTH* 176.24').

[29] In Egypt, letters could be used as testimony in court (*Lex. Aeg.* 859 *sub* "Briefe"). Note the statement, "keep this letter of mine, it will serve you (as) a testimony" (A. Bakir, *Egyptian Epistolography from the Eighteenth to the Twenty-first Dynasty* [Cairo: Institut Français d'Archéologie Orientale du Caire, 1970] 14).

[30] *TR* 295.11-13; *AbB* VI 189.33-34.

[31] *AbB* I 21.26; II 159.12'-13'; VI 124.30; VII 72.11-13. The same formula occurs also with the noun *ze'pu* (*AbB* VI 209.11-12; IX 164.6-8 172.15-16; XI 97.10-12). On the *ze'pu*, see now *YOS* XIII p.5-6.

[32] *NB* 84.23-24 104.17-18 119.12-13 176.18 211.22-23; *NBU* 63.27-28 129.15-16 135.200.

[33] E.g., *NBU* 63.27,28 129.15,16 135.20; *NB* 104.17,18.

[34] *ARM* X 114.14-20; for translation and discussion, K. Veenhof, "Observations on Some Letters from Mari (*ARM* 2,124; 10,4;43;84;114) with a Note on *tillatum*," *RA* 76 (1982) 138-140.

she is being maligned: a daughter of Kibri-Dagan claims that Tarish-Hattu sent a message to have her despoiled of her jewelry. Tarish-Hattu responds:

> Had I wished to do such a thing, I must have sent my instruction somewhere. Now then, let either my messenger come here or else (*ulūma*) let them give me my sealed order (proving) that it was in consequence of my writing that they stripped the girl of her jewels at my behest.

Even though this is not a strictly legal context, the minimal evidence which the maligned solicits is a single messenger or the tablet which she is reputed to have sent; either will suffice to lend credence to the accusation. She solicits the minimal evidence knowing it cannot be produced, as if to say, "My accuser has not one shred of evidence."

Although tablets were used as witnesses,[35] it should not be inferred that tablets or written documents never lied. In the text from Shemsharra discussed above, the receiver was incredulous of the news which he had heard. By quizzing the messenger, he at least was able to establish that the messenger was a bona fide representative of those who had sent him. But of course, the possibility always remained that even a written document could be written deliberately to deceive. Such a situation occurs in the first millennium when the king of Assyria is warned that the bearer of certain letters is not only a liar but the letters as well are untrue.[36] In the second millennium, a king sends his messenger with three tablets - two hostile and one conciliatory; the messenger deceitfully presents only those two which would provoke war and only three days later is the third produced,

---

[35] In addition, see *AbB* I 75.15-17; VII 9.13-16; IX 107.10,11; XI 71.6'-8'r. The personification of tablets in Old Assyrian is suggestive in this regard, for a document which becomes invalid is said to "die" (*CAD* M [1] 426).

[36] *SLA* 194; "When he brought letters to me (*šipirēti iššâ'a*) . . . . The king should not believe him (*lā iqâpšu*) . . . . these lying letters (*šipirēti aga ša sarrāti*)."

prompting considerable frustration.[37] The omen preserved on an OB liver model no doubt records such treachery in the use of messengers: "When the Subarians sent messages (*ištapparūma*) to Ishbi-Erra, and (then) the Subarians turned (*issaḫrūna*) to the side of the other," i.e., turned against Ishbi-Erra.[38]

Also in the second millennium, an astonished Shuppiluliuma sends his trusted court-official to Egypt, saying,

> "Go and bring thou the true word back to me! Maybe they deceive me! Maybe (in fact) they do have a son of their lord! Bring thou the true word back to me!"[39]

At issue here is deception on the part of the Egyptians and not the messenger. An offended queen replies, "You didn't believe me!"[40] Ultimately, the only way to insure veracity was to send a trusted member of one's own staff to investigate, as in the case just cited.[41] This was certainly a desirable benefit resulting from the custom of escorting a foreign messenger on his trip home.

Deceptive messages, designed to subvert social bonds which depend upon mutual trust, resulted in death and war more than once. Benaiah's case in I Kings 2 may be illustrative even though he is sent not so much as a messenger but as an assassin. Solomon's command makes this clear when he cries in v.29, "Go, strike him down!" But Benaiah passes himself off as an innocent messenger from the king when he remarks, "Thus says the king,

---

[37] S. Lackenbacher, "Nouveaux documents d'Ugarit," *RA* 76 (1982) 141-146 l.22f. (RS 34 165); the messenger is of course behaving according to his king's instructions in the timing of the presentation.

[38] FOIES in M. Rutten, "Trente-deux modèles de foies en argile inscrits," *RA* 35 (1938) 36-70. For the historical context of the inscription, see I. Gelb, *Hurrians and Subarians* (*SAOC* 22; Chicago: University of Chicago, 1944) 38-39.

[39] *DS* 28 A.iii.22-25.

[40] *DS* 28 A.iv.3.

[41] In the first millennium, a *qurbūtu* is sent on such a mission: "A *mār šipri* from GN^1 came saying, 'The people of GN^2 . . . .' Let the king my lord send a *qurbūtu* so he can hear the version of the people of GN^2" (*ABL* 165).

'Come out!'" (v.30). Joab knew from experience (2 Sam 11) how treacherous messages could be and declines to accept Benaiah's message from the king. He wisely saw through the false message, but ultimately to no avail.

Consequently, the oral message without authenticating documentation might be a less than desirable means of communication.[42] The confirmation of the high import of the written document comes remarkably from the oral message. By its very nature, we must remain largely in the dark about many aspects of the oral message which was not written down. We hear of the distinction between oral and written message, for example, "I have neither given an oral report (*ina pîya . . . ul ušašmû*) nor written (*lā alṭaru*), so now I send (*altapra*)" (*RMA* 268.1-2). Sufficient clues attest not only to the prevalence of the oral message, but also to the fact that such a message often did require a written document to authenticate the bearer of the oral message. For example, the following writer gives *carte blanche* authority to his messenger (*AbB* IX 16.9-15):

> Now I have despatched PN to you (*aṭṭardakki*); if he enters your presence, do what he says - if he does not enter your presence, act in accordance with this tablet (*ša pî ṭuppi annîm*).

Following this remark, instructions follow. Presumably, the directions which the messenger would give would be fuller, more precise and capable of adaptation should circumstances dictate. But letters are written in which the instructions are not written at all but are entrusted entirely to the messenger to relay orally (*TR* 146.7-16).

> I send you the plants you requested by the hands of Kani-azzu. As for my request, which Kani-azzu will tell

42 A document which requests that certain items be entrusted to a specific messenger (e.g. dates in *NB* 247) would likely be the authorization which the messenger would present in order to receive the shipment.

you (*iqabbêkkum*), if you have it available, send it to me, and do not delay.

Considerable trust is placed in a messenger such as Kani-Azzu.[43] The presence of the tablet, however, seems to function as a certification to the addressee that Kani-Azzu has the authority in this case to ask for anything (as far as the addressee is concerned).[44] This aspect of a written document certifying a messenger as credible, without actually giving his message, is known not only in the Old Babylonian and Old Assyrian[45] periods but in first millennium Assyria as well: "Adad-eresh I send to you on a secret mission (*ana puzurti ana muḫḫīka ašapparaššu*); send him back."[46] In his commentary to this text, Weidner notes that the Assyrian king might wish to conceal information from individuals along the path which the message must take to reach its destination. This meant of course, that a trusted man sent by the king had to traverse the entire route and could not relay the message. This particular text thus certifies that the messenger of the king will present no other written document. The messenger Bel-udu'a from this same period also bears a purely oral message. When the Assyrian administrator stops him *en route*, he is apparently not told what the message is, for Bel-udu'a speaks: "I

---

[43] Asmar 31.12-16 is similar. Compare also the following letter where, although he is not specified as a messenger, Yarim-Dagan is trusted to relay all the information: "Let Yarim-Dagan tell you everything (*awāti kalāšina PN lidbub*); may my lord pay attention to the matters" (*u bēlī ana awāti liqūl*; *ARM* X 35.5-9). The conclusion to *AbB* I 109 (edge) is suggestive as well, though unfortunately broken: "[ ]let the one whom I sent speak to you so that I may do what you send" [*ša aš*]*puraššu liqbīkumma* [*ša taš*]*apparam lūpuš*.

[44] Some have gone so far as to suggest that all Babylonian and Assyrian documents which we know as letters are in fact such certifications for the messengers (J. Friedrich, G. R. Meyer, A. Ungnad, E. F. Weidner, *Die Inschriften vom Tell Halaf* [*AfO Beiheft* 6 (1940)] 13).

[45] "Whatever our messengers te[ll you]" (*mala šiprūni iqa*[*bbi*]*'ū*[*nikkuni*]; *KTP* 6.r8'-9'). For reconstruction, see P. Garelli, *Les Assyriens en Cappadoce* (Paris: Adrien Maisonneuve, 1963) 339.

[46] Friedrich *et al.*, *Tell Halaf*, 13.

am sent to the palace" (*ina ekalli šaprāka*; CT LIII.68.14[47]), i.e. for the king's ears only, and the official does not note that he was apprised of the message destined for the palace. He simply observes that he sent the messenger on to the king, and "may the king my lord listen to what he has to say" (*šarru bēlī ša pîšu lišmi*; l.2-r3). Such treatment contrasts with the typical behavior of regional administrators noted in section 2.1, where under normal conditions the posts were empowered to elicit information as to a messenger's destination and purpose for travel, relaying this information on to the next post. Secret messages certainly required special documentation as noted above if they were to bypass successfully the rigorous network of official inquiry.

It stands to reason, in the light of what has been seen about the reputation of messengers for deceit, that correspondents would not employ an oral communication as their optimum means of communication. The only time it was preferred was in cases where a need for secrecy left them few options, as in the preceding case.[48] A clear case occurs where Yasmah-Addu had written to his father, king Shamshi-Addu, that he had something to say but did not feel comfortable putting it down in writing: "These matters are not suitable to inscribe on a tablet." Shamshi-Addu responded with typical eagerness for the forbidden (*ARM* I 76.20-29):

> "Why not? Have them inscribed on a tablet and sent to me! Otherwise, instruct a messenger (*kallûm*) who has a good memory; send him to me so he can lay these matters out before me.

---

[47] New fragments joining with *ABL* 1011, edited by F. Fales, "New Assyrian Letters from the Kuyunjik Collection," *AfO* 27 (1980) 147.

[48] Thus, although it is not stated, one may presume in the following letter that the message is oral: "About PN, the merchant, . . . I will send secretly" (*šapal qātā ašappara*; *SLA* 209.9-11r). Nevertheless, Sasson refers to an unpublished text which refers to a "secret tablet" *ṭuppum šū ṭuppi niṣirtim* (J. Sasson, *The Military Establishments at Mari*, 39).

It is curious that Shamshi-Adad continued to insist, in spite of Yasmah-Addu's counsel to the contrary, that the message be written down. We find here once again an overt preference for the written message, even in a possibly compromising situation. Not only is the issue of the reliability of messengers at stake (note his insistence on the selection of a good messenger), but there are clues elsewhere that oral messages simply cause problems. A lack of documentation spawns misunderstanding, as in the following letter (*TR* 121.5-13):

> You spoke to my maid, saying, "Take a maid from PN." But you wrote to me that he was not to give (me a maid) and you did not write (*ul tašpurī*) in your letter to me (to say that you had changed your mind); instead you are sending only an oral message with her (*ina pîšāma tašappar*). Must I have a fight with PN?

4.4 INTRODUCING THE MESSAGE

4.4.1 SELF-IDENTIFICATION

Self-identification statements made by messengers are frequently attested in Mesopotamia, although most of our evidence comes from incantation formulas. In these texts, the incantation priest identifies himself as a messenger from the gods, granted authority to speak and perform the appropriate rituals for the banishment of hostile and malevolent powers. The self-identification as a messenger takes two basic forms. The priest (who always speaks in the singular) may say, "I am the messenger of DN" (*mār šipri ša DN anāku*),[49] or secondly, "DN sent me."[50]

---

[49] See in general A. Falkenstein, *Die Haupttypen der sumerische Beschwörung* (*LSS* 1, 1931) 23-27. For further texts, see *STT* 73.52; E. Reiner, "*Lipšur* Litanies," *JNES* 15 (1956) 138 l.111; *Šurpu* V-VI 175). Note in later Mandaic incantation texts how the notion persists: "A messenger am I" (*'šg'nd' 'n'*; E. Yamauchi, *Mandaic Incantation Texts* [*AOS* 49; New Haven, Conn.: American Oriental Society, 1967] #22.119); cf. the Israelite priesthood in Mal 2:7.

However, in narratives and letters a substantial number of individuals also legitimate themselves with similar statements which identify them as messengers of another. At Mari, when questioned by a provincial governor, envoys may say, "We are sent (*šaprānu*) to our lord (i.e. Zimri-Lim)" (*ARM* XIV 110.17-18), or "We are sent (*šaprānu*) with regard to X" (*ARM* II 107.13-14). The self-identification also occurs in the context of the actual delivery of the message to its intended recipient. In Akkadian, one commonly says *PN išpuranni* in literary texts,[51] while a first millennium letter reflects again the use of the stative.[52] A Sumerian letter which became part of the Old Babylonian scribal curriculum reports how

> the messenger (*lú kin-gi$_4$-a*) of Ishbi-Erra [ ] fixed his eyes on me saying, "Ishbi-Erra my king has sent me as a messenger (*lú kin-gi$_4$-a*) to you saying: (message follows)."[53]

In the West Semitic sphere there is some evidence also that messengers employed such self-identification connecting them with their masters. One finds the Hyksos king's messenger so speaking in Egyptian literature when he replies to pharaoh Sekenenre's question, "Why are you sent?": "King Apophis sends me to you, saying (message follows)."[54] Another Egyptian account relates how two Shosu near Qadesh pass themselves off as messengers of tribal leaders, saying,[55]

---

[50] *Anim u Antum išpurūinni* (*Maqlu* I.52); *Asalluḫi bēl āšipūti išpuranni* (*Maqlu* I.62).

[51] See section 4.4.2 for references in literature and Sumerian counterparts.

[52] A messenger is reported to have spoken as follows: *mār šipri anāku šaprāk umma*, "A messenger am I, sent to say:" (after which his message is reproduced; *NBU* 200.18-19).

[53] F. Ali, *Sumerian Letters*, 49 l.4-6.

[54] M. Valloggia, *Recherche*, 183.

[55] A. Gardiner, *The Ḳadesh Inscriptions*, 28.

> Our brothers who are the headmen of the tribes of the Fallen One of Hatti have sent us to His Majesty to say that we will be his servants.

Furthermore, the statement by the one who brings word of Israel's defeat by the Philistines ("I am the one who comes from the battlefront," *'ānōkî habbā' min hamma'ărākāh*; 1 Sam 4:16) underscores that in such human encounters, self-identification is necessary for adequate communication. The clearest use by commissioned messengers in biblical literature occurs when David's messengers (1 Sam 25:42) address Abigail by noting, "David has sent us to you" (v.40). Therefore, although not common, the self-identification statement may be assumed in the West Semitic world also.

4.4.2 MESOPOTAMIAN LITERATURE

Apart from messengers who simply hand over a written document and at most give a greeting,[56] a ritual is often found introducing the actual delivery of a message by a messenger in literary texts. Often the messenger begins the dialogue (after an optional vocative[57]) with a statement taking the general form of "PN has sent me to you."[58] On occasion, the recipient of the

---

[56] As in *Lú-dingir-ra* 6-7.

[57] "My lady" (*nin-mu*; IE 2.1.9,43; 2.2.9,43 2.3.13,48).

[58] "My king has sent me to you (*za-a-šè lugal-mu mu-e-ši-in-gi$_4$-gi$_4$*), the Lord of Aratta, Ensuhkeshdanna, has sent me to you" (*EnEn* 53-54); "Your father, my king, has sent me to you (*a-a-zu lugal-mu mu-e-ši-in-gi$_4$-in-nam*), PN etc. . . . has sent me to you" (*ELA* 176, 177,378,379,515,516); same but omit *lugal-mu* and insert *za-a-šè* (*IE* 2.1.9-10,43-44; 2.2.9-10,43-44; 2.3.13-14,48-49), *PN išpuranni* (*BWL* 49.15 [see p.344],25-26 [no message is recorded for either reference] 51.42); "PN your father has sent me" (*PN abūki išpuranni maḫrīki*; *STT* 28 I.30' [cf. H. Hunger, *Spätbabylonische Texte aux Uruk*, 1.IV.5]); "Your daughter sent me" (*māratkunu išpuranni*; *STT* 28 V.17',45'); "PN your son sent me, the command of his heart he charged me to convey" (*PN*

message may respond to this announcement in various fashions, such as with a question of the form, "What does he say?"[59] Expansions of this qucry arc rarc.[60] However, no response from the recipient is not unusual and the messenger may begin his message immediately. When the messenger commences the message, he often starts with a statement introducing the message with the general form "PN[61] says."[62] If there are no initial comments about the message to follow,[63] the message then begins immediately with the messenger normally speaking as if he were

---

mārūkunu uma''iranni tēret libbīšu ušaṣbiranni iyāti; *EE* III.71-72); "Your father Anu, your counselor warrior Enlil, your chamberlain Ninurta, your sheriff Ennugi sent me (*išpuranni*; *Atra*.I.136-139; note how commanded in l.124-127; see *Atra*. 54).

[59] "What is it to me what your king has said; what is it to me he has added?" (*lugal-zu du$_{11}$-ga-ni nam-mu taḫ-a-ni nam-mu*; *ELA* 178,380,517); "What did my father say to you (*a-a-mu ta-am e-ra-an-du$_{11}$*), what did he charge you (*ta-am e-ra-an-dah*; *IE* 2.1.15,49; 2.2.15,49; 2.3.19,54). Although the rest of the passage relating the delivery is broken (l.49-59), when the messenger stands, Nanibgal immediately "asked him (about the message)" (*èn mu-mu-ni-ib-tar-tar-[re]* *Sud* 48). Note that no formalities precede in l.87.

[60] Inanna's elaboration "Why should his (Enki's) word not be changed?" (*IE* 2.1.16; 2.2.16,50; 2.3.20,55) is a direct response to Isimu's earlier elaboration.

[61] Strings of epithets describing the sender occur; see ELA 180-184,519-523 (broken).

[62] "My king has thus declared" (*lugal-mu na-ab-be-a*; *EnEn* 55); "My king, this is what he has said, this is what he has added (*lugal-mu a-na bí-in-du$_{11}$ a-na bí-in-taḫ-am*; *ELA* 179,381,518); in addition to the preceding, the epithets require a resumption: ". . . Enmerkar the son of Utu has sent me to you (*mu-e-ši-in-gi$_4$-nam*), my king this is what he says" (*lugal-mu na-ab-bé-a*; *ELA* 180-186); "My king said to me (*lugal-mu ga-a-ra ma-an-du$_{11}$*), PN charged me (*PN ga-a-ra ma-an-daḫ*; *IE* 2.1.17-18,51-52; 2.2.17-18,51-52; 2.3.22-23,56-57).

[63] Such as Isimu's reminder to Inanna that when Enki speaks one had better listen (*IE* 2.1.11-13,45-47; 2.2.11-13,45-47; 2.3.15-17,50-52).

the sender, that is, in the first person.[64] The message is delivered without interruptions until the messenger is finished, marked occasionally by the messenger's closing words "thus he said"[65] although such statements as "What shall I reply to my lord?"[66] occur.

In literary texts, it is exceptional for written documents to occur. On the few occasions where they appear, they are of the utmost importance for the discovery as to how the document related to the messenger. In *Enmerkar and the Lord of Aratta*, oral messages appear everywhere except on the one occasion when the message is too big for the messenger to remember. When he is given a tablet by the inventive Enmerkar, the messenger simply does not deliver an oral message but instead hands the tablet to the addressee with the words: "Enmerkar, the son of Utu, has given me a clay tablet. O lord of Aratta, after you will have examined the clay tablet, after you will have learned the heart of his word" (524-525). In this case, the messenger introduces and concludes his message with the same formulas noted above for his oral reports, but this time no oral report is given at all. The king simply takes the tablet (536-539).

4.4.3 UGARITIC LITERATURE

In Ugaritic literary texts, the messengers again have a formulaic tradition of introducing their messages. They simply begin by saying some form of the basic formula *tḥm PN hwt PN*

---

64 This is not universal. Ninshubur in the Sumerian Descent repeats Inanna's words which were given as if Ninshubur were pleading on behalf of the one who sent him! The same occurs when Adad repeats Ninurta's message in the *Anzu* myth (II.72f.). Note Marduk's envoy in *BWL* 51.41-44.

65 "He said unto me (*gá-a-ra ḫa-ma-an-dug$_{11}$*; *ELA* 388).

66 "After you will say whatever you may say to me for (epithets follow) . . . . Let me announce that message in the shrine Eanna as glad tidings, (and) in his Gipar, . . . to my king, the lord of Kullaba, let me repeat it" (*ELA* 208-217,526-535).

"Message of PN, word of PN,"[67] after which the message begins (the asterisk indicates commands to say the message[68]):

<u>*CTA*#</u>

2.1 *tḥm ym bʿlkm adnkm ṯ[pṭ nhr]**

2.1 *tḥm ym bʿlkm adnkm ṯpṭ nhr*

1.2 *tḥm [ṯr il abk hwt l]ṭpn ḥtkk*

1.3 *[tḥm ṯr il abh] hwt lṭpn [ḥtkk]**

6.4 *tḥm ṯr il abk hwt lṭpn ḥtkk*

3.3 *tḥm aliyn bʿl hwt aliy qrdm**

3.4 *tḥm aliyn bʿl hwt aliy qrdm*

3.6 *tḥm ali[yn bʿl] h[wt aliy qrdm]**

4.8 *tḥm aliyn bʿl [hw]t aliyn q[rdm]**

5.2 *tḥm aliyn bʿl hwt aliy qrdm**

5.2 *tḥm aliyn {bn} bʿl hwt aliy qrdm*

7.2 *[tḥm aliyn bʿl] hw[t aliy qrdm (*?)*

5.1 *tḥm bn ilm mt hwt ydd {bn} il ǵzr*

14.6 *tḥm krt ṯ[ʿ] hwt [n]ʿmn [ǵlm il]*

14.3 *tḥm pbl mlk*

14.5 *tḥm [pbl mlk]**

14.6 *tḥ[m pbl mlk]*

The erratic character of *CTA* 2.1 appears again. The only time messengers speak before this formula is the isolated case of Gapnu-wa-Ugaru sent to Anat; her trauma is eased by their opening words, "No foe rises to oppose Baal, no enemy against the Cloud-Rider" (*CTA* 3.4.5-6). Otherwise, no further additional

---

[67] That *tḥm PN* is to be understood as a construct phrase is evident from the interpretation of *umma PN* in Canaanite letters as a construct (L. Matouš, "Les textes accadiens d'Ugarit," [*ArOr* 24 (1956) 375-382] 381).

[68] Apart from broken passages, the only places where messengers use the following formula but are not commanded to do so is *CTA* 6.3-4 and 14.6.16,40. Compare also *CTA* 14.3.33 where El foretells what will happen in a dream: he omits the formula, just as Kirta will do even though the messengers will use it when reporting in 14.6.40. Those who bring tidings in general, of course, do not use the formula (*CTA* 19.2).

comments or expansions are made by any messenger who simply delivers the message exactly as he received it (i.e. in first person). A feature in common with the Mesopotamian material is the identification of El according to his familial position ("father").

Just as there was one exceptional case in Mesopotamian literature, so at Ugarit there is also a single reference to a written communication delivered by messengers. Whereas the Sumerian occurrence was generated by the narrative in which it occurred, the Ugaritic example is unobtrusive and is mentioned as if it were an off-hand remark (*CTA* 2.25-26).

aḥd ilm t'ny	The gods should reply as one[69]
lḥt mlak ym	to the tablets of Yam's messengers,
t'dt ṯpṭ nh[*r*]	of Judge River's embassy.

There is a general consensus that *lḥt* is here "tablets."[70] The "tablets" are mentioned by Baal while addressing the divine council before the messengers have even arrived, and the syntax of the lines affirms their close identification with the messengers as Yam's representatives. But there is no further reference to them, either in commissioning the messengers or when the messengers deliver their demands; as in other literature, the written document is simply ignored. At least this text makes explicit what was already known from the letters themselves.

It is important to draw attention also to cases where reports are relayed, although no one specifically sends those who give the report. Thus, two individuals inform Dan'il that Aqhat is dead with an initial summons to hear followed by a vocative: "Hear, O Dan'il, the hero Aqhat is dead" (*CTA* 19.2.90-91). Two others with a similarly dismal report simply begin, "We two have been

---

[69] The adverbial use of *aḥd* is preferable to emending the text *t'ny* > *a'ny*; it is El who replies to the messengers, not Baal. See J. San Martín, "Glossen zum Ugaritischen Lexikon," *UF* 9 (1977) 263.

[70] G. R. Driver (*Canaanite Myths and Legends*, 79) translates it as "harsh demands", while Gibson revises it to "message", stressing in a footnote literally "tablets" (J. C. L. Gibson, *Canaanite Myths and Legends* [Edinburgh: T & T Clark, 1978]).

travelling around (*sbn*) . . . and have arrived (*mǵny*) . . . Baal is dead" (*CTA* 5.6.3-9).

4.4.4 BIBLE

In biblical literature, one may assume from commands to messengers[71] and from actual performance[72] that they prefaced their message with the formula "Thus says PN". But even this is rarely noted, and few clues surface as to the actual delivery of the message beyond the fact that it is overwhelmingly presented as oral in form.[73] Several exceptional narratives, however, are found in the book of Samuel. Notable is the runner who reports the Philistine capture of the ark, for he reports to Eli in the following fashion:

> And the man said to Eli, "I am the one who comes from the camp[74] and I fled to day from the battle-

---

[71] Jacob commands his messengers, "Thus you shall say to my lord Esau, 'Thus says your servant Jacob'" (*kôh 'āmar 'abdĕkā ya'ăqob*), but the truncated narrative does not show us the messengers in action (Gen 32:4-6).

[72] *kôh 'āmar balaq bēn ṣippôr* (Num 22:16), *kôh 'āmar bēn hădad lē'mor* (1 Kgs 20:5 [cf.v.2 where the syntax is awkward]), *kôh 'āmar hammelek haggādôl melek aššūr* (2 Kgs 18:19; cf.v.29,31), *kôh 'āmar hammelek* (1 Kgs 2:30; 2 Kgs 9:18,19).

[73] Gen 32:4; Num 22:5,14,16; 1 Sam 4:16-18; 11:4,9; 18:22-26; 25:5-12,40; 2 Sam 11:7,18-25; 15:13; 17:21; 18:28-33; 1 Kgs 20:1-12; 2 Kgs 18:19-35; Jer 36:14. See in particular in messenger contexts the frequent expressions *wayyuggad* "it was told" (Gen 22:20; Exod 14:5; Josh 10:17; Judg 9:47; 1 Sam 19:19; 23:7; 27:4; 2 Sam 6:12; 10:17; 21:11; 1 Kgs 1:51; 2:29,41; 2 Kgs 6:13; Isa 7:2) and *wayyaggīdū* "and they told" (Judg 4:12; 9:42; 1 Sam 18:24,26; 19:21; 24:1; 25:12; 2 Sam 2:4; 10:5; 17:21; 2 Kgs 7:15).

[74] With LXX against repetitive MT.

field."[75] He (Eli) said, "What happened, my son?" The messenger (*mĕbaśśēr*) replied, saying, ". . . ."[76]

Two elements here precede the actual message, namely a self-identification followed by a query as to what the message is. However, the self-identification may not be of general significance, even though it bears an initial similarity to Mesopotamian examples, for it appears in this case to be motivated by Eli's blindness.[77] The query, though superficially like the Sumerian examples cited above, is also not of general significance. Eli's blindness is again the underlying focus of the narrative, for the message which is brought is clearly bad news of which even the blind Eli should be aware; after all, he has heard the lament (*z'q* and *ṣ'q*, v.13,14) of the people who have seen the

---

[75] The entire statement may be conflate, and as P. K. McCarter notes (*I Samuel*, 112), it is difficult to choose between the two alternatives.

[76] 1 Sam 4:16-17. We do not know how the message was delivered to the citizens of Shiloh. The narrative stresses Eli's blindness, hence he can not see that the messenger is running in mourning garb, the clue which prompts the city to cry out even though the city does not know the details. One may assume that the messenger makes his report first to Eli, who is not in the city but waiting for the news.

[77] In spite of careful argument, McCarter's decision to omit v.15 does not assist in the understanding of the passage (*1 Samuel*, 110-114). In the first place, the reference to Eli's blindness and age may be original, simply not stated twice in the conflate LXX due to overt redundancy; in both elements which make up the conflate text, there must be some explanation as to why Eli alone (the most eager for the news!) does not know what is going on. If the verse is (with McCarter) to be omitted, the narrative demands an interpretation echoing 3:2. Eli was in a position to receive the news first, the city gate was the place where public affairs were treated (why does McCarter insist on "the center of the city"?), and the man's torn garments are eloquent testimony to his message. Why should then Eli be the last to know? McCarter does not answer this most crucial question, which is clear from 3:2 or v.15 (if original).

runner's mourning garb[78] and the messenger himself has told Eli, "Today I fled (*nastî*) from battle" (v.16), hardly a neutral statement which could leave room for the possibility of good news. Eli's question, then, if it is a query for news, is simply a further reflection of his blindness. Otherwise, it may be simple interrogation of a messenger, which we will discuss later.

There is another narrative in Samuel where the receiver queries the messenger, namely the account of the defeat of Absalom (2 Sam 18:28-33). There the structure is of the type:

A) Greetings
B) Good news given by messenger
C) Question from listener
D) Response by messenger
E) Reaction of listener.

There is no self-identification in this otherwise very full account. Furthermore, the greetings and delivery are distinctive as given by first Ahimaaz and then the Cushite:

A) All is well. (*šālôm*)
A) Good tidings for my lord the king.[79]

B) Blessed be the Lord your God who has delivered up the men who raised their hand against my lord the king.
B) For the Lord has delivered you this day from the power of all who rose up against you.

C) Is it well with the young man Absalom?
C) Is it well with the young man Absalom?

---

[78] For the significance of the messenger's appearance in some cultures, see R. Numelin, *The Beginnings of Diplomacy*, 146; this note in Samuel suggests that the phenomenon was not unknown in the Semitic world.

[79] We have taken *yitbaśśēr* as formally parallel to *šālôm*, i.e. as some form of greeting. The *hithpa'el* of this root occurs only here in the Bible.

D) When Joab sent your servant,[80] I saw a great tumult, but I do not know what it was.

D) May the enemies of my lord the king, and all who rise up against you for evil, be like that young man.

E) And the king said, "Turn aside and stand here."

E) And the king was deeply moved. . . .

There is no stereotyped portrayal of the messenger here at all. Not only does Ahimaaz bow while the Cushite does not (see section 3.3), but there is no similarity in any of the speeches except for the crucial focus of the narrative - David's concern for his son. The narrator underscores this element by making David's words the only stereo feature in that they are repeated twice.[81]

But the books of Samuel provide more data in describing the messengers which David sent to Nabal (1 Sam 25:5-15,25). The actual performance of the mission is schematic and uninformative (v.9), but David's commissioning of the messengers provides the important clues. There we find an initial and very full greeting reminiscent of the greetings introducing the Amarna letters followed immediately by the message in the first person:

> So David sent ten young men; and David said to the young men, "Go up to Carmel, and go to Nabal, and greet him in my name. And thus you shall say to my brother:[82] 'Peace be to you, peace be to your house, peace to all that is yours. I hear . . . .'" (v.5-6)

Later in the same chapter, messengers sent by David introduce themselves with a self-identification, but deliver no first-person address: "David has sent us to you to take you to him as his wife"

---

[80] The impossible MT must be corrected with the LXX.

[81] The only difference is the occurrence of an initial interrogative *heh* in the second statement.

[82] Reading *l'ḥy* (with Vulgate) for MT *lḥy* (see S. R. Driver, *Samuel*, 196-197). For other alternatives see P. K. McCarter, *I Samuel*, 392.

(v.40). That these are messengers is clearly stated in v.42 (in spite of LXX B reading *tōn paidiōn*).

Outside of Samuel, only the Assyrian embassy to Hezekiah contains more than the superficial, for the *rab-shāqēh*'s opening words, "Thus says the king of Assyria," (2 Kgs 18:19) are not followed throughout with the words of the king. Beginning in v.23, the messenger departs from Sennacherib's words and speaks in his own right: "Come, now, make a wager with my master the king of Assyria." However, v.25 appears to resume the king's speech once again.

Of equal significance is the second address by the *rab--shāqēh* which he introduces as follows: "Hear the word of the great king! Thus says the king. . ." (v.28). The heraldic nature of this message's delivery is reinforced by this cry which may echo that of the herald, but we have already seen that messengers from hostile parties were traditionally compelled to deliver their commissions in this way. Further within the speech, the messenger again punctuates his message by reiterating, "Thus says the king of Assyria" (v.31).

4.4.5 SUMMARY OF LITERATURE

It can therefore be said that with regard to describing the messenger's presentation of his message, there is no pattern in biblical literature comparable to that found in the literature of Ugarit and Mesopotamia. The stereotyped Sumerian and Akkadian formulas provide much information, but their static nature and longevity over two millennia make one suspicious of their correspondence to reality. The Akkadian forms may be due to imitation of the canonical Sumerian literature, not a reflection of the actual performance of messengers. Furthermore, the actual information supplied about the delivery of messages decreases with time, for the Sumerian literature elaborates at length (see notes in section 4.4.2 where only here does the messenger speech close with a statement to that effect made by the messenger, only here does the messenger ask for a reply to the message, only here does the receiver ask for the message). Only in Sumerian and

Ugaritic (once) does one find a vocative. All the literatures employ self-identification statements, but it is particularly characteristic of Mesopotamia and rare in West Semitic. The high degree of regularity in Sumerian and Akkadian literature is, however, outclassed by Ugarit where a thoroughgoing leveling has occurred of all narratives about messengers (who are specifically sent) delivering their speeches.

The biblical literature, due to its variety, spontaneity and total lack of adherence to any consistent forms (even "Thus says PN" is more often than not omitted and on one occasion occurs twice), may provide the best insight into actual messenger performance. Only here is the messenger found giving greetings.

Three common denominators may be observed throughout all the literatures. Although employing different forms, messengers in some fashion tend to identify the individual who sent the message ("Thus says PN", "PN sent me saying", "PN says"). Secondly, the messenger while delivering the message speaks (although not always) as if he were the sender in first person.[83] Thirdly, references to written documents employed by messengers are conspicuous by their absence (noteworthy exceptions being (2 Kgs 19:14, *CTA* 2.1.26 and *ELA*).

4.5 THE MESSENGER AND THE DOCUMENT

One often finds that the common Akkadian epistolary introduction, *ana PN¹ qibīma umma PN²* "To PN¹ speak, thus PN²," is employed for insight into messenger behavior. Thus Munn-Rankin noted that "this was a command to the messenger who delivered the tablet,"[84] an opinion affirmed as well by Edel: "Der Imperativ 'sprich' gilt dem Boten, der den Brief

[83] In addition to texts cited above, note especially the OB letter A.649 (D. Charpin & J.-M. Durand, "Le Nom antique de Tell Rimah," *RA* 81 [1987] 125-146). But the Egyptian messenger (*DS* 28) speaks of his sender in the third person and himself in the first person (curiously plural!).

[84] J. M. Munn-Rankin, "Diplomacy in Western Asia," 98.

überbringt."[85] Speiser aligns himself with this perspective when he employs this Akkadian epistolary formula to modify the punctuation of the Hebrew text of Genesis 32, a text in which messengers are commissioned.[86]

However, there are some features which seem to point toward the ancillary nature of this epistolary formula for direct insight into messenger behavior. In the first place, the relevance of such a passage as Genesis 32:5 is questionable. Here, the messengers of Jacob are commissioned with the words, "Thus you shall say" (*kôh tô'mĕrûn*). The plural verb is appropriate, for as a group of messengers, they share the burden of the commission. It is strange, however, in the light of the numerous groups of messengers attested in Semitic culture that there is not a single occurrence of the plural form of the command *qibīma* in a letter. If this formula in fact echoes a commission to a messenger or was felt to reflect the direct commission of a messenger, one would expect somewhere a delegation of messengers to be addressed in the plural in the opening words of an Akkadian letter, just as Jacob spoke in the plural to his messengers. But the singular *qibīma* still occurs in documents where it is beyond question that more than one messenger carries the message, as in *EA* 23 (carried by Pirizzi and Tulubri), or in the letters borne by the large delegations travelling between Ramses II and Hattushili III.

It is further remarkable that in all of the cases which we have investigated of messengers being commissioned in Akkadian literature, never was a messenger commissioned with the phrase *ana* PN^1 *qibīma umma* PN^2. A variety of verbs and constructions sends messengers on their way, but never the formula found in the letters. This variety in the literature is in stark contrast to the static regularity of the letters.[87]

---

[85] E. Edel, *Ägyptische Ärzte und ägyptische Medezin am hethitischen Königshof*, (*Rheinisch-Westfälische Akademie der Wissenschaften* G 205; Göttingen: 1976) 41 n.95.

[86] E. Speiser, *Genesis* (Anchor Bible; Garden City, NY: Doubleday, 1964) 254.

[87] We are speaking of the second millennium B.C., and in particular the OB period. The imperative *qibīma* is characteristic only of the second millennium and diminishes in frequency in the first

millennium when a variety of forms appear. For the data, see Erkki Salonen, *Die Grüss- und Hoflichkeitsformeln in babylonisch-assyrischen Briefe* (*StOr* 38; 1967). A similar phenomenon appears in Sumerian, where a stereotyped epistolary style with a command, "speak" (*ù-na-du*$_{11}$) does not necessarily appear in the same form in the literature (it does appear in *ELA*) which also employs variety in its commissions. For Sumerian epistolary introductions, see E. Sollberger, *The Business and Administrative Correspondence Under the Kings of Ur* (*TCS* 1; Locust Valley, NY: J. J. Augustin, 1966). Early Hebrew letters tend to omit any form of a speaking verb in their preserved introductions, although a minority (and one Phoenician letter) are known with an imperative "speak" (*'mr*; see D. Pardee, *Handbook of Ancient Hebrew Letters* [Chico, CA: Scholars, 1982] 121,165-168; A. LeMaire, *Les Écoles et la formation de la Bible dans l'ancien Israel* [*Orbis Biblicus et Orientalis* 39; Vandenhoeck & Ruprecht, 1981] 26; D. Chase, "A Note on an Inscription from Kuntillet 'Ajrūd," *BASOR* 246 [1982] 63-67; Y. Beit-Arieh, "Ḥorvat-'Uzza - A Border Fortress in the Eastern Negev," *Qadmoniot* 19 [1986] 31-39; K. Yassine & J. Teixidor, "Ammonite Inscriptions from Tell El-Mazār in Jordan," *BASOR* 264 [1986] 45-50). Ugaritic formulas imitate Akkadian (*lPN*^{1} *rgm tḥm PN*^{2} to a superior or *tḥm PN*^{1} *lPN*^{2} *rgm* from a superior; for variations see O. Kaiser, "Zum Formular der in Ugarit gefundenen Briefe," *ZDPV* 86 [1970] 10-23), and do not precisely correspond to the forms used to commission messengers: a different word order is employed (the literature consistently employs *rgm lPN* and not verb final as the letters) and the same form is always used with no distinction between messages to superiors or subordinates:

CTA#			
1.3.4	*wrgm lkṯ[r wḫss*	*ṯny lhyn] dḥrš y[dm*	*tḥm...*
3.6.21	*wrgm lkṯr wḫss*	*ṯny lhyn dḥrš ydm*	*tḥm...*
3.3.8	*wrgm lbtlt 'nt*	*ṯny lymmt limm*	*tḥm...*
7.2.13	*]rgm lbtl[t 'nt*	*ṯny lybmt limm]*	*h[w]t...*
4.8.29	*wrgm lbn ilm mt*	*ṯny lydd il ǵzr*	*tḥm...*
5.2.8	*rgm lbn ilm mt*	*ṯny lydd il ǵzr*	*tḥm...*
6.3.24	*rgm lnrt il<m> špš*		
14.5.248	*wr[gm lkrt ṯ'*		*tḥm...*
2.1.16	*ṯny d'tkm wrgm lṯr abh [il ṯny lpḫr m'd*		*tḥm ...*

Others have suggested that the imperative *qibīma* in the Akkadian epistolary introduction was not addressed to the messenger at all but to the scribe who would read the letter to the addressee.[88] Oppenheim has most concisely documented how the scribe was often addressed by supplementary notes and comments in letters, confirming that he was the one responsible for the reading of the tablet on the receiving end.[89] In Egypt it is equally clear that when a letter arrives, the receiver calls a scribe to read it to him.[90] Such a custom seems to lie behind the protests of a Judahite soldier who insists that he is literate and never calls scribes to read his letters to him (*KAI* 193).[91] Regardless of the level of literacy at various locales at different times in the ancient Near East, it is evident that the scribe was normally the one who wrote the message and it was normally the scribe who read it. The messenger simply carried it. Nowhere did we find literacy as a prerequisite to function as a messenger,[92] and no messenger is ever known to read a tablet in our data.[93]

---

[88] M. Hutter, *Altorientalische Vorstellungen von der Unterwelt*, 78-79. J. Marty, "Les Formules de salutation," *Mélanges syriens offerts à Monsieur René Dussaud II* (Paris: Librairie Orientaliste Paul Geuthner, 1939; 844-855) 845.

[89] A. L. Oppenheim, "A Note on the Scribes in Mesopotamia," *Studies in Honor of Benno Landsberger on the Occasion of His Seventy-fifth Birthday* (*AS* 16; Chicago: University of Chicago, 1965) 253-256.

[90] A. Bakir, *Egyptian Epistolography*, 33.

[91] "You said, 'You didn't understand it - call a scribe (*qr' spr*)!' As Yahweh lives, no one has tried to read a letter to me ever and furthermore any scribe who might have come to me - I didn't summon him and further I would pay him nothing." (F. M. Cross, "A Literate Soldier: Lachish Letter III," *Biblical and Related Studies Presented to Samuel Iwry* [ed. A. Kort and S. Morschauser; Winona Lake, IN: Eisenbrauns, 1985] 41-47).

[92] It is true that some scribes functioned as *mārī šipri*, but these cases prove the rule. The fact that such individuals are identified as scribes implies that all messengers are not scribes.

[93] As Holmes claims (Y. L. Holmes, "The Messengers of the Amarna Letters," *JAOS* 75 [1975] 377), but the three texts cited prove nothing.

In most of our literary texts where documents are explicitly borne by messengers, it is beyond dispute that the messenger does not read the document. The messenger hands the tablet to the lord of Aratta (*ELA* 524-539), Lú-dingir-ra's letter will be delivered into the hands of the recipient without the messenger knowing its contents (*Lú-dingir-ra* 6-7), Hezekiah receives the letter from Sennacherib's messengers and then reads it (2 Kgs 19:14), while Uriah delivers his own death warrant to Joab, unaware of its contents (2 Sam 11:15,16). Uriah's experience is a replay of an earlier Sumerian account of the young Sargon before he became king of Sumer and Akkad: according to one tale, he also was sent by a king (Urzaba) with a letter ordering the messenger's (i.e. Sargon's) death, but in this case the letter was without an envelope and apparently Sargon learned its contents.[94] The narrative presumes that the messenger is not supposed to know the message he is delivering. The only narrative which mentions a document but the messengers still deliver an oral message is *CTA* 2.1. In that case, however, we do not know what is done with the document.

The clearest recital of the protocol for reception of messenger and tablet is to be found in Akkadian letters from the thirteenth century B.C. such as the following from Ramses II to Puduhepa:[95]

> My messengers reached me along with the messengers of my sister and they spoke the greetings (*iqtabûni šulmu*) of the Great King, the King of Hatti, my brother, and they spoke the greetings of my sister, and they spoke the greetings of my sister's sons, and they spoke the greeting of your land. My heart rejoiced

---

[94] J. Cooper and W. Hempel, "The Sumerian Sargon Legend," *JAOS* 103 (1983) 76-77. The fragmentary state of the text hinders clarity, but since Sargon in the larger fragment (3N T296) was sent on an earlier mission in a messenger capacity, it is likely that the messenger in TRS 73 rev. is Sargon himself.

[95] *CTH* 159.2.7-13. The same differentiation between the messenger speaking (*qabû*) and the subsequent seeing (*amāru*) of the tablet recurs in *CTH* 157.10-18, 158.11-25, 163.2.7-14.

> greatly when I heard. . . . And I saw (*ātamar*) the tablet which my sister sent me and I heard all the words which the Great Queen, the Queen of Hatti sent to me.

This text presents two distinct events: 1) reception and hearing of the messengers followed by 2) the display and hearing of the tablet. It is unlikely that the messengers are responsible for the reading of the tablet which they present, for it was noted in section 4.3 how a Hittite treaty stipulated that if the words of the messenger do not agree with the words of the tablet, the messenger is a liar. Clearly, someone beside the messenger must read or at least verify the letter if the liar is to be exposed. Such a situation seems to be presupposed in the letter just quoted.[96]

Other texts from the preceding century also make a distinction between the tablet and the words of the messenger. Rib-Addi's complaint echoes the notion that the presentation by the messenger is distinct from the reading of the tablet: "I sent my tablet and my m[essenger] to the king my lord, but the k[ing] did not listen to the words of my tablet or [my messeng]er" (*EA* 92.12-15). The distinction which is made in this comment between the written document and the oral message of the messenger reappears earlier in the Old Babylonian period when Shamshi-Adad I sends Shamash-naṣir with an oral message (*SH* 887.7-8): "Pay close attention to all that he presents before you (*mala maḫrīka*(!) *išakkanu*), and hear the words which I have sent to you (*mala ašpurakkum*)."

In the light of the forensic distinction maintained in the international treaty between the messenger's speech and the words of the tablet, the letters themselves are likely echoing the awareness of this same distinction. A further narrative which reinforces the notion that the messenger's report and the written tablet were treated as two distinct phenomena comes from Murshili's account of communications between his father and the queen of Egypt. When the Hittite envoy returns accompanied by

---

[96] In the tomb inscription of the Egyptian vizier Rekhmire, it is noted that proper decor for a vizier's messenger is to orally deliver the message and then leave to a waiting room (M. Valloggia, *Recherche*, 95).

the Egyptian messenger, it is narrated that "the queen of Egypt wrote back to my father in a letter thus" (*DS* 28 A.iii.51), after which the contents of the letter are given. The messenger does not speak to the king. However, after the contents of the letter are given and the Hittite king has a chance to react to its import, only then does the messenger engage in dialogue: "Thus spoke Hani to my father: 'Oh my lord! . . . .'" (*DS* 28 E.iv.13). What is most remarkable about the text of the messenger's words is that, though different, they sound just like the letter of the queen. We reproduce the entire text of both in parallel (queen's letter first) in order to underscore their similarity:

A) Why did you say, "They deceive me," in that way? Had I a son, would I have written about my own and my country's shame to a foreign land?

A) Oh my lord! This [is] our country's shame! If we had a son of the king at all, would we have come to a foreign country and kept asking for a lord for ourselves?

B) He who was my husband has died.

B) Nibhururiya, who was our lord, died;

C) A son I have not!

C) a son he has not.

D) Never shall I take a servant of mine and make him my husband! I have written to no other country, only to thee have I written!

E) Our lord's wife is solitary. We are seeking a son of our lord for the kingship in Egypt, and for the woman, our lady, we seek him as her husband!

E) They say your sons are many; so give me one son of yours! To me he will be husband, but in Egypt he will be king.

D) Furthermore, we went to no other country, only here did we come! Now, oh lord, give us a son of yours!

The correspondence of the messenger's words to the words of the letter is remarkable, occurring in the main in the same sequence (except at the end) and recapitulating all the main arguments. It is furthermore noteworthy that the messenger never speaks in the first person as if he were speaking the queen's words, unlike most messengers in literature. The lack of any stereotypical presentation argues for the reliability of this account of court protocol, an account which pictures the message of the written document distinct from the oral message of the messenger.

Insight into messenger protocol is enhanced by the letter found at Ugarit[97] which describes the Hittite messenger who upon arrival presented two tablets of war: *2 ṭuppāti ša nukurti ana pānīya uktallim* (l.24). One does not hear the messenger speak, nor does he read the tablets. He presents (*uktallim*) them, a presentation which is described with a term familiar from legal contexts.[98] Three days later, the same messenger raises eyebrows when he produces a third tablet, this time of peace: *ṭuppa ša šulmi ana pānīya uqtarrib* (l.29). Again the messenger is not described as speaking. Instead the receiver notes: "in his tablet was written . . ." (*ina libbi ṭuppīšu akanna šaṭir umma šūma*; l.30). No messenger is ever seen reading the letter which he carries. In this text, he surrenders it to the addressee as is done elsewhere: "my messenger who put the tablet before you."[99]

It is unfortunate in this regard that Wenamun's letter is missing when he presents himself before the prince of Byblos. When Wenamun arrives before his Egyptian lords in lower Egypt on his way north, the protocol appears to be similar to what has been seen so far. Wenamun does not read his own documents but surrenders them upon arrival (*Wenamun* 1.3-5):

> The day I arrived at Tanis at the place where Smendes and Tanetamun were, I gave to them the dispatches of Amun-Re', King of Gods, and they had them read before them.

---

[97] S. Lackenbacher, "Nouveaux documents d'Ugarit," *RA* 76 (1982) 141-156.

[98] *CAD* K 521,522.

[99] [*m*]*ār šip*[*rīya ša i*]*štak*[*an ṭuppa a*]*na muḫḫī*[*ka*] (*EA* 33.19-21).

Such protocol may also be reflected in the Egyptian tale of *Horus and Seth* as recorded on a papyrus from the reign of Ramses V. Although mythological in nature, presumably the narrative reflects features of contemporary culture when it describes the transfer of letters between the gods:

> The letter of Neith the Great, the divine mother, reached the Ennead as they sat in the hall, "Horned Horus," and the letter was placed in the hand of Thoth. Then Thoth read it aloud before the All-Lord and the whole Ennead.[100]

Thoth, as the scribe of the gods, not only wrote the letter sent to Neith (as described earlier in the story) but also receives the incoming correspondence which he reads to its intended addressees.

In conclusion, one may note the petition of a correspondent[101] to a courtier who may be the scribe Ili-milku: "The tablets which I sent to you, read (*šisi*) them to the queen and speak a reminder of my pleasing words to the queen" (*ḫissata ša amātīya damqāte*). It is not the messenger who is responsible for this presentation, but a literate individual (a scribe) on the receiving end.

It may be objected that one should expect many more references to scribes if one is to assume that a scribe is expected to be present on the receiving end of every letter. But scribes, or individuals trained in the scribal craft, must be assumed to have written every cuneiform letter which we possess, yet they remain anonymous and unmentioned in the documents. To compose such a document required a scribe, and therefore a documented correspondence is unthinkable without a scribe at the service of both correspondents.

---

[100] M. Lichtheim, *Ancient Egyptian Literature*, II 215-216.

[101] F. Thureau-Dangin, "Une lettre assyrienne à Ras Shamra," *Syria* 16 (1935) 188-193 (brought to my attention by W. Moran).

4.6 SUMMARY

The presence of translators throughout the Semitic world made it possible for one to be a messenger without necessarily being a polyglot. It is certain that linguistic ability could enhance a messenger's efficiency, and this may have been one motive for repeatedly sending international messengers to the same country. But messengers would travel with their own translators from their native land, knowing that in their host county one could also expect translators representing the host country. The custom of travelling with escorts also minimized the linguistic barriers which one might encounter along the way.

It may be true that great stress was placed upon memorization in the largely illiterate ancient world, but there is no reason in a world of letters composed and read by scribes to insist upon a messenger accurately memorizing the exact words of the one who sends him. Literary texts which seem to support this notion are in reality merely employing a stylistic feature which is characteristic of narrative and poetic genres. The only occasions in which precise recall may be necessary are those occasions when a specifically oral message is sent without written documentation. But as we shall see in the next chapter, the messenger even in such cases is less a tape-recorder and more a resource-person to whom one appeals for clarification and explication of the message which is sent.

When delivering a message, the messenger normally made some type of self-identification statement and tended to deliver the message itself in the first person as if he were the one who sent the message. In the analysis of the actual presentation of messages, there surfaced a significant difference in viewpoints. From the letters themselves, one may clearly see the high premium which was placed upon the written document as opposed to the oral message. Messengers often had strong motives for distorting their messages, and the tablet was the insurance that the messenger spoke truly. The tablet itself was likely to be read by a scribe in the receiving court, either before (e.g. *DS* 28) or after (e.g. *CTH* 159) the messenger had presented his oral message.

From the literary texts, however, one would be unaware of the existence of written messages without exceptional passages like *Enmerkar and the Lord of Aratta*, *CTA* 2.1, 2 Kings 19 and 2 Sam 11:15. The written message is largely an irrelevance to literature, which is more captivated by movement and action, not by mundane and legal realities.

5

AFTER THE MESSAGE IS DELIVERED

5.1. INTERROGATING THE MESSENGER

One particular type of interrogation has already been noted, namely where one seeks to discover whether or not the messenger is a genuine representative of his reputed sender (see section 4.3). However, the letters testify unanimously to the oral nature of the messenger's task in another very important regard. The messenger is represented as a resource person to whom one may pose questions which a letter is unable to answer. He can be interrogated as to details omitted in a written document, or he may be the person to ask for clarification of nuances that may be suggested by the letter itself.[1]

Some of the more familiar examples of this aspect of a messenger's delivery are known from biblical literature (2 Sam 11:7): "When Uriah came to him, David asked concerning the welfare (*wayyiš'al lišlôm*) of Joab and the welfare of the people and the state of the war." Later in the same chapter, David's barrage of irate questions for the messenger no doubt reflects a common response to bad news and the whipping horse that messengers often became in their senders' stead (v.20-21).

> Why did you go so near the city to fight? Did you not know that they would shoot from the wall? Who killed Abimelech the son of Jerubbesheth? Did not a

[1] Not included here is the interrogating of messengers *en route* to which reference has already been made (see sections 2.2.2, 2.3.1).

> woman cast an upper millstone upon him from the wall, so that he died at Thebez? Why did you go so near the wall?

The verbs throughout are addressed to the second person plural, affirming that David is specifically interrogating the single messenger as the representative of the actions of the army.[2] In one other place in Samuel, David also interrogates messengers. When a report is delivered by both the Cushite and Ahimaaz after the victory over Absalom, David asks both men the identical question (2 Sam 18:29,32): "Is it well with the young man Absalom?"

In many cases, there will be a similarity to the oral message discussed in the preceding chapter. For example, the sender of the following letter wishes to relay to the king some information but does not set it down in writing for reasons unknown. Instead, he authorizes those bearing his letter to answer for all details of the affair (*ARM* II 141.4-11).

> Let my lord interrogate (*lišt̄alšunūti*) the men carrying this my tablet (*awīlī wābil ṭuppīya*) who heard the word of PN's messengers. Let them give to my lord the decision of the matter.

This sounds very much like a simple oral message. But two features formally distinguish it. First, the individual who writes the letter is not giving a distinct message to the messengers. It is a report, but it does not originate with the sender. Secondly, the operative word is "interrogate" or "ask." That is, the initiative lies with the recipient of the message as to what degree he will be informed of the matter. The same situation appears again when Yatar-Addu had been sent by the king's bureaucrat, Yasim-Sumu, to investigate (at the king's request) the treatment of some Elamite

[2] The MT is in considerable disarray, with Joab precisely intuiting David's every word (v.20-21) while the latter remains silent and the messenger jumps the gun (v.24)! However, the words which Joab anticipates should be on the lips of David (so LXX); see P. K. McCarter, *1 Samuel*, 282.

guests. Yasim-Sumu then briefly relates the situation to the king in a letter, but closes by saying (*ARM* XIII 32.24-30):

> "They spoke of many things to Yatar-Addu. Now I send Yatar-Addu; he brings a complete report (*ṭēmam ga*[*mram*] *našī*). Let my lord interrogate him (*lištālšu*).

Now it may be that there was not felt to be any real difference between the oral message and the questioning of a messenger by a recipient of a message. However, there is a significant difference for our study in so far as it clarifies two very different functions of the messenger. If one delivers an oral message, the central feature of his task lies in a faithful reproduction of the sender's words and meaning. On the other hand, the task of responding to questions about a message moves the messenger into the realm of the diplomat, where his central task lies in responding to unanticipated issues in a manner which would please the sender. That the messenger was often put into very difficult situations over unanticipated issues is clear from the letter written by the formerly sick Babylonian king, which is presented here as a dialogue (*EA* 7.18-30; see discussion in section 2.1):

> King: "Why did not my brother send his messenger to me when I was sick?
>
> Messenger: "This is not a place close by that your brother can hear (you are sick) and send greetings. The country is far. Who can tell your brother so that he can write quickly? Would your brother hear you are sick and not send his messenger?"
>
> King: "Is there such a thing as a near or far land to my brother, the great king?"
>
> Messenger: "Ask your own messenger if the way is far! Your brother did not hear about you and therefore sent no greeting."

Upon taking the messenger's advice, he discovers that even his own messengers will vouch for the truth of this statement. The Babylonian king is not easy on this envoy who is forced to defend his own king before a sick king's wounded pride, an event which could have international repercussions. The second question which he put to the envoy is indeed a hard question: either way the messenger replies, he will have answered wrongly. If the envoy says the way is far, then he has admitted that his king must not be such a "great king" as he claims; if he answers that it is not all that far, then there is no excuse for not writing. But like a true diplomat, the envoy pursues a third alternative: instead of answering the question, he redirects the question to another.

The freedom to ask messengers for further clarification of messages or information is commonly granted in the letters.[3] Indeed, one finds that a writer will appeal in this regard to the messenger as a witness to the veracity of the contents of a letter. For example, Zer-ibni is accused of imprisoning a certain Marduk-erba; Zer-ibni writes to the king that this is slander, adding (*SLA* 200.20-3r):

> The king my lord should [ ] ask (*lišālšu*) the messenger through whom I am sending the letter whether he (Marduk-erba) is placed in fetters of iron or whether he is staying in his father's house.

In such cases, it is usually one messenger who is called upon to testify to the truth of the message. However, it is not that the words of the tablet itself are in doubt. It was seen above that the tablet was accorded the highest authority. Rather, what is being certified is the veracity of the sender. Consequently, the messenger stands as a resource person on trial so to speak; he can be interrogated to the satisfaction of the recipient that the events

---

[3] *b*[*ē*]*lī lišt*[*ā*]*lšunūt*[*ī*]*ma* (*ARM* XIII 148.6); *aḫū'a mār šiprīšu lišāl* (*EA* 27.58); *mār šiprīya ittīšunu šarru lišāl* (*ABL* 276.11-12); *šarru bēlī*(*ya*) *lišālšu* (*ABL* 1123.r7; 637.r4). One must distinguish these requests which originate with the sender from requests which originate along the route from individuals within the bureaucracy who forward messengers, saying, "let my lord ask him" (e.g. *SLA* 157.5-14).

which the sender has described are actually true. There is no doubt that the sender has actually said them; the doubt is whether the sender has spoken truly.

A particular type of encouragement to interrogate messengers results when one individual returns a messenger who had been sent to him. In sending him back, his lord is told to ask the messenger how he was treated (*EA* 20.66-67; 161.18-19).

The interplay of dialogue between a messenger and the one to whom he is sent is part of the royal protocol of international diplomacy. Indeed, one king is insulted when pharaoh failed to interrogate his messenger: "I sent my messenger to my lord but my lord did not interrogate him" (*lā išālšu*; *EA* 47.13). The failure to engage in inquiry expressed a lack of interest in the sender's message as well as the sender. But even the dialogue between messenger and hearer of the message could be used to insult the sender. When pharaoh writes to Babylon, he is compelled to exonerate himself of accusations that he spoke disdainfully with the monarch's envoys (*EA* 1.82):

> You wrote saying, "You spo[ke] to my messengers saying, 'Has [your] lord no troops?' and 'Ugly is the maid he gave me.' Those were your words." Not so. Your messengers do not speak truly to you.

As was discussed earlier with regard to lying messengers, this accusation is based solely upon the oral report given to their Babylonian lord; pharaoh clearly said no such thing in the tablet which he despatched to Babylon, and he reminds Kadashman-Enlil of that fact - trust the tablet and not the messengers. But the messengers may, in fact, be telling the truth! The report of any dialogue between messenger and receiver depends solely upon the messenger.[4]

There can be no doubt that messengers were often treated brutally in these interrogations and dialogues. Wenamun is

---

[4] Note the ethical problem this raised later: "And whence do we know that if one behaves insolently (*mitpĕqar*) toward the court's messenger (*bišĕlîḇā' dĕbêy dînā'*) and the latter comes and reports it, this is not deemed slander [on his part]?" (*Mo'ed Qatan* 16a).

abused by the prince of Byblos.[5] Hani feels the brunt of the unrestrained sarcasm and incredulity of Shuppiluliuma (*DS* 28 E.iv.1-12):

> "You suddenly did me evil. . . . You attacked. . . . You keep asking me for a son of mine (as if it were my) duty. He will in some way become a hostage, but king you will not make him!"

Yet it is to the credit of each of these men that they achieved their objective for which they were sent. To stand up and gainsay a monarch took no little self-confidence and courage. The simple delivery of a message need not exhaust the messenger's responsibility, for it could also include defending and explicating that message's claims and veracity before a reluctant or incredulous listener. David's orders to his messenger captured this perspective nicely: David instructed the messenger whom he sent to Joab - regardless of the words the messenger might use - that the objective of his mission was to convince Joab to subscribe to David's perspective: ". . . and so encourage him" (2 Sam 11:25).

5.2 TAKING COUNSEL

A feature found in ancient Near Eastern literature is the depiction of monarchs and deities taking counsel after the reception of a messenger. Thus, Ahab obligingly answers the threatening embassy of Ben-Hadad when first sent, but when they return with specific demands, Ahab seeks counsel (1 Kgs 20:5-9):

> The messengers came again and said, "Thus says Ben-Hadad, ..." Then the king of Israel called all the

[5] After the discovery of missing letters, there is a gambit focusing on the issue of boats and transportation, followed by bargaining as to who will pay for the lumber. This results in a perusal of past records and accounts, with each side vociferously arguing its case (*Wenamun* 1.57-2.34).

> elders of the land and said, "Mark, now, and see how this man is seeking trouble; for he sent to me for my wives and my children and for my silver and my gold, and I did not refuse him." And all the elders and all the people said to him, "Do not heed or consent." So he said to the messengers of Ben-Hadad . . . .

The narrative assumes that the messengers do not give their message to a gathered council, for the council is summoned only afterwards and the king must repeat to them the message which was delivered by the messengers. Furthermore, the message of the council must be repeated to the messengers by Ahab, implying that they were not privy to the deliberations.[6]

A similar crisis is handled in the same fashion when Agga also sends a messenger requesting that Gilgamesh and Uruk submit.[7] Gilgamesh turns to the council of the elders and then the young men, asking them for advice. The messenger is forgotten as the narrative continues with Gilgamesh's refusal to submit, as Ahab was so counselled.

The Hyksos Apophis challenges Sekenenre about a bellowing hippopotamus, and Sekenenre is speechless. Indicating that he will cooperate, Sekenenre sends the envoy on his way and only then gathers his council, which (as usual in Egyptian literature) is unable to give adequate advice to pharaoh.[8] Unlike the preceding cases, the episode serves as a foil to pharaoh's superior wisdom (which in this case must be presumed, as the text breaks off).

In a similar vein, the motif may be used in Mesopotamia to suggest the relative inferiority of an opponent. Enmerkar's challenges to the Lord of Aratta find the latter at one point turning to his *šatammu* with rhetorical questions of perplexity before giving a response to the messenger (*ELA* 438-456). A similar use

---

[6] Sumerian literature presents the possibility that a message could be presented to a gathered council. A foreign envoy (*sukkal*) is shouted down by a council of young men in assembly when he presents a declaration of war (Shulgi C 55-62).

[7] W. Römer, *Das Sumerische Kurzepos >Bilgameš und Akka<* (*AOAT* 290/1; Neukirchen-Vluyn: Neukirchener, 1980) 1.1-41.

[8] *ANET* 231-232.

may reappear with Enmerkar's opponent, Ensuhkeshdanna (*EnEn* 114-128):

> The messenger . . . approached. Ensuhkeshdanna asked for advice, searched for an answer. The . . . attendants who dwell in the *gipar* gathered together and took counsel. "What shall I say to him? What shall I say to him? To the lord of Uruk, what shall I say to him?" . . . . The convened assembly answered him straightforwardly.

Their advice is not to submit, counsel which in the remainder of the narrative proves to be folly. However, turning to receive counsel to answer a messenger in and of itself is not a sign of indecisiveness or weakness. The examples cited above make this clear, as does the Naram-Sin account in which he turns to his *sukkal* when a messenger brings a message of another's submission:[9]

> "You have no equal! . . . ." While the messenger repeated the message . . . the blazing fire in his heart was extinguished. Naram-Sin opened his mouth to speak to his *sukkal*: "Did you hear the message of Apishal? Does everything which he sent please you (*mimma išpuram īnka maḫra*)?"

The messenger then replies, but the text breaks off at this point. Here it is not a council but a single individual from whom the monarch solicits advice, and this person is present when the messenger speaks to the king.

The Hittite record of king Shuppiluliuma summoning his council after receipt of an Egyptian messenger provides a further perspective by its singularity. The Egyptian messenger is only mentioned once as he is sent by the Egyptian queen (*DS* 28 A iii.9). But the message is quoted and followed by this description:

---

[9] H. Güterbock, "Bruchstuck eines altbabylonischen Naram-Sin-Epos," *AfO* 13 (1939-41) 46-50, rII.8-17.

> When my father (i.e. Shuppiluliuma) heard this, he called forth the Great Ones for council saying, "Such a thing has never happened to me in my whole life!"

The stunning message provokes this royal disorientation, a crisis which can be resolved by summoning an advisory council. The council's deliberations and any response to the Egyptian messenger remain unresolved as the text continues by simply noting that the king despatched his own messenger to Egypt to confirm the veracity of the peculiar message which had been received (*DS* 28 A iii.20-25).

There is, therefore, a diversity of presentation of this common event. In three cases (Ahab and Ben-Hadad, Gilgamesh and Agga, Enmerkar and Ensuhkeshdanna), there was a summoning of a council to answer a messenger when the specific issue was submission before a foe, and all three councils advised resisting.[10] In two cases, this works out well, but Ensuhkeshdanna's solicitation of advice which is given by a misguided council is ultimately humiliating. In the case of Naram-Sin, counsel is received from a single ***sukkal*** who is present while the messenger speaks. But the council is not necessarily present at the messenger's speech, as the case of Ahab demonstrates. Only in the Egyptian account of the messenger from the Hyksos king does the council deliberate after the messenger departs.

It is difficult to assess the degree to which these stories accurately reflect court protocol. The popularizing format of many suggests that a generalized type-scene may structure the narratives, and propagandistic motives are obvious in utilizing these scenes to enhance the portrait (whether positive or negative) of the royal figures in view. At least one may observe that these cameo appearances by messengers in the environs of a royal council suggest how messengers were perceived to affect the palace decision-making process. It is likely that the royal council's function varied from palace to palace and from time to time, a

[10] That is, the counsel which the leader decided to follow was for rebellion. In the case of *Bilgamesh and Agga*, the first council summoned (of elders) counselled submission, but Gilgamesh convened the more volatile council of young men whose opinions he preferred.

variability contingent, for example, upon the waxing or waning of royal power *vis à vis* other social and political elements. The variety here displayed may accurately depict the potential responses which royal messengers might expect when their commission provoked perplexity on the receiving end.

5.3 CARING FOR THE MESSENGER

With respect to the message itself, the document or a memorandum of the messenger's report would be cycled into the palace's bureaucracy and filed. From the Amarna court, dockets written on the cuneiform tablets in hieratic record the date of the messengers' arrival and delivery of the messages, along with other relevant details.[11] It is the bureaucratic organization to which we are primarily indebted for the preservation of the letters which we possess, for they are found often in discrete archives where they were catalogued and kept on file.[12] Exceptionally, one may find a reference to do away with all traces of a correspondence after the

---

[11] *EA* 27: "Year 2, first month of winter; One (i.e. the king) was in the southern city (i.e. Thebes), in the palace of 'Rejoicing in the Horizon'; copy of the Naharain letter which the messenger Pirizzi and the messenger [Tulubri] brought." Compare *EA* 23: "Year 36, month 4 of winter; One (the king) was in the southern palace [ ] copy [of the letter of ...] which the messenger [ ] brought." For texts, see M. Valloggia, *Recherche*, 105-107.

[12] The maintenance of these files was of utmost import for international politics. One may cite the retrieval by Tukulti-Ninurta I of an old letter sent by Urhi-Teshub of Hatti to the former's father, Shalmaneser I; the copy was sent back to Hatti upon request when no copy was found in the Hittite archives (*CTH* 209.21; M. B. Rowton, "The Material from Western Asia and the Chronology of the Nineteenth Dynasty," *JNES* 25 [1966] 249-250). Note the frustration of Hattushili when the Assyrian archives do not contain a copy of his former correspondence which would confirm his benevolence to a Babylonian king when the latter was young (*CTH* 172.18-19; M.B. Rowton, *Ibid.*, 246).

message was delivered: "Hear my tablet and destroy it (*ḫipi*); any tablets I send you do not keep (*lā tanaṣṣar*)" (*TCL* XVII 58.36-38).

The concern of the present inquiry lies more with the messenger and his treatment after delivering his message. A characteristic response to a messenger is frequently found following epistolary introductions:

> [When Ma]nia, my brother's messenger [came and] I heard the greetings of my [brother], I rejoiced (*aḫtadu*) greatly. The gifts which my brother [sen]t I saw, and I rejoiced greatly. (*EA* 27:7-8)

> (The messengers) spoke the greeting . . . and I rejoiced (*aḫtadi*) exceedingly and my heart was greatly pleased (*libbī iṭṭibanni*) when I heard the greeting of my brother.[13]

The degree of joy is often exuberantly expressed with clusters of adverbs.[14] On occasion, these general affirmations of joy[15] are expanded with explicative details (*EA* 144.14-18):

> When he (my lord) wrote to his servant, my heart rejoiced (*yiḫdi libbīya*)[16] and my head was raised and my eyes brightened upon hearing the word of the king.

---

[13] *CTH* 157.14-15//*CTH* 158.16-18; *iṭṭib* is read in the parallel text. *CTH* 159.2.10 is the same but omits *aḫtadi danniš danniš*.

[14] Simple *danniš* (*EA* 16.7; 27.8; 147.27) or *mādiš* (*ARM* X 5.37; Apla. 10). Compounded adverbs are not infrequent: *danniš danniš* (*CTH* 157.15//*CTH* 158.18; 159.2.10; 169.14; *EA* 154.10; 164.7), *māda danniš* (*EA* 20.12).

[15] Similar statements appear in Hittite letters, e.g., *CTH* 176.1'-2'.

[16] Similar is *EA* 142.8-10: "I heard the words of the king my lord's tablet and my heart rejoiced (*yiḫdi libbī*) and my eyes considerably brightened."

The messenger may not always be mentioned, but the joy derives from hearing the words or tablets of another[17] or from the fact the the sender simply wrote: "I rejoiced (*aḫtadi*) very much that my father sent (*iltapra*) to inquire of my welfare" (*CTH* 169.13-16).

It is conceivable that this oft-repeated self-description is a vapid cliché. But at least three reasons argue the contrary. There is first of all the fact that the phrase does not always occur, and it actually appears in a minority of letters. Secondly, the variety of the forms of expression noted above indicates that there is some spontaneity involved in the formulation of the statement. Thirdly, and most important, is the fact that others apart from the letter-writer can actually observe this "joy". Zimri-Lim's envoy to the king of Carchemish relates how his news was received in Carchemish (Apla. 5-11):

> When I arrived in Carchemish, I met with Aplahanda. I gave him the order which my lord commissioned me - the matter pleased him (*awatum īnšu maḫrat*). He rejoiced greatly (*mādiš iḫdu*) when he heard my lord's word.

The fact that the hearer is favorable toward the message ("it pleased him") is expressed differently from another external response which the messenger is able to observe ("he rejoiced"). On another occasion, two women are addressed as follows (*ARM* X 141.7-9): "Why didn't you rejoice in the presence of my messenger?" The writer continues on, encouraging the women not to be sad. Joy (or lack of it) is therefore clearly observable, and in the latter case, an apparent breach of protocol which a messenger reports back to his lord. Another messenger writes back, "I met with the commander in Isin and he rejoiced (*iḫdâm*) at the mention of your name and provided me with companions (*muqerribī*)."[18] The enthusiastic reception of this envoy is

---

[17] Upon hearing the tablet: *ḫadi libbi ardīka* (*EA* 141.11), *aḫdu* (*AbB* VI 109.6).

[18] *TCL* XVII 34.6-8. The final vowel on the noun may be a case of sandhi, (*LÚ mu-qi-ri-bi iš-ku-nam*), presenting here, as normal elsewhere, only one escort for a messenger.

observable by this messenger in a tangible fashion: the host *en route* makes provision for the messenger's continued journey.[19]

This joy which is expressed and visible is often displayed with particular regard to the messengers themselves:[20]

> When I saw your messengers, I rejoiced greatly (*ḫadâ*[*k*]*u danniš*). Your messengers shall reside with me as objects of great solicitude.[21] A fine royal chariot . . . I have sent to you as a gift.

The joy here is focused not so much on the message as it is upon the arrival and care of the messengers themselves. The Assyrian king supplements this description by immediately specifying his provision for the messengers, including a gift for pharaoh. That this care extended to extensive festivities is made explicit by Tushratta when he notes (*EA* 20:8-13; 27.35-36):

> Mane, my brother's messenger, came again . . . and I read the tablet which he brought and heard his message. And my brother's message was very pleasing, as if I had seen my brother! So I rejoiced exceedingly on that day - that day and night I celebrated ([*ba*]*nâ ētepu*[*š*]).
>
> The day that I heard my brother's greeting, that very day I made a holiday (*banīta ētepussu*).

This joy may also be experienced by the whole population (*EA* 164.4-14):

---

[19] Even though in this particular case the commandant explains that the intended route is not passable (l.9-12).

[20] *EA* 16.6-12. Note the Sumerian hymn where the single element underscored which makes the messenger's task bearable or unbearable is whether or not one rejoices over him (D. Edzard and C. Wilcke, "Die Ḫendursanga-Hymne," *Kramer Anniversary Volume* [ed. B. Eichler; Neukirchen-Vluyn: Neukirchener, 1976] 155 l.215',226').

[21] Translation of W. Moran.

> Hatib came and brought the words of the king my lord, pleasing and refreshing, so I rejoiced (*hadi'āku*) exceedingly. And my land and my brothers, the servants of the king, my lord, and the servants of Dudu, my lord, rejoice (*hadûnim* [read tu_4]) exceedingly when the breath of the king my lord comes to me.

After noting how he rejoiced upon the message of another, Shamash-naṣir in turn closes his own letter with regard to an individual whom he sends: "Any loaf of bread which you might eat, don't eat without him!" (*AbB* VI 109.17-18). The object of the host's benevolence is the messenger: "I now send to you (*aštaprakkum*) PN the *rakbum* - be well-disposed toward him (*ḫudu*[*š*]*um*),[22] or "Be well-disposed (*ḫudê*, fem. sing.) toward the one who brings you the tablet" (*AbB* VI 2.16-18).

Expressions of personal joy occur in letters of both vassals and suzerains. However, these expressions tend to occur in letters where the writer has received some benefaction from the addressee. The messengers who bring the messages also bring brides, garments, furniture, precious stones and metals. The messenger who comes with hands full is more likely to spark congeniality: "When I saw the articles which my brother sent, I rejoiced greatly" (*EA* 27.8).[23] In fact, failure to give gifts is cause for grief (*EA* 29.145,163-164). It is in letters where the sender "rejoices" that he is most likely to send gifts to the one who prompted his joy.[24] When a spontaneous gift is sent, it is then that one looks forward to an answering gift which will bring joy in return.[25] This is not to say that one may still complain of not

---

[22] *TCL* XVII 68.5-7; reading with *CAD* Ḫ 26.

[23] As in *EA* 19.49-53,82-90. There is joy when messengers bring a bride in *EA* 29.28, joy which is expressed in festivity (*EA* 29.30).

[24] Joy with gifts sent in return in the same letter: *EA* 16:6-12; 19.26,80f.; 20.12,80f.; 27.8,110-114.

[25] Tushratta sends war booty and other items to Egypt (*EA* 17.36-45) and can not wait to "rejoice" when Egypt's messengers come to him (l.49-54). Perhaps anticipated "joy" is omitted in *EA* 15, even though a spontaneous gift is sent (l.11-15), since diplomatic relations

receiving enough,[26] nor do we mean to imply that gifts are sent only when one "rejoices".[27]

What we do wish to underscore, however, is that rejoicing in the contexts of messenger activity is not an abstract emotion but a visible and tangible expression of congeniality. In the ancient world, it is difficult to separate the notion "joy, delight" in an abstract sense from the very concrete physical manifestations by which joy is expressed. For example, in Israelite culture, one may find in cultic contexts the bare commands or cohortatives to "rejoice!" (e.g., *śmḫ* Deut 12:12, Ps 105:3; *ʿlz* Ps 68:5; *gyl* Ps 118:24), but it becomes clear from explicit statements elsewhere that rejoicing in these contexts was a communal (Deut 16:11,14), festive celebration. One wined and dined (Deut 14:26; 27:7)[28] in company with a host of others (Deut 12:7,18; 14:26), and the menu knew no bounds (Deut 14:26). The celebration of the moving of the ark in 2 Samuel 6 is certainly typical in its elements (although atypical in degree): food for all (v.19), with singing, dancing and merriment (*mĕśaḫăqîm* v.5) in a generally boisterous atmosphere (v.14-15).[29]

This rejoicing was not confined to specifically cultic activities but reappears in coronations (Judg 9:19 [cf. v.6]; 1 Sam 11:15; 2 Kgs 11:19-20) where again dining (I Kgs 1:41) along with

---

are not yet normalized. Note *EA* 28.28, where one anticipates joy upon hearing from another.

[26] Note joy and complaint in the same letter: (*EA* 16.7,27-31 20.12,46f.; 27.8,32). For the high frequency of complaints in such letters, see C. Zaccagnini, *Lo Scambio*, 83-89.

[27] No "joy" is mentioned yet the writer still sends gifts in *EA* 3.30-34; 5.16-33; 8.43; 9.36-38; 31.30-38.

[28] The Philistine cult shows a comparable emphasis (as seen through the eyes of an Israelite narrator), characterized by rejoicing which eventually results in "merry hearts", i.e. a considerable amount of wine is consumed (Judg 16:23,25).

[29] Joy is characteristically loud in such cultic observances (Neh 12:43): "the joy of Jerusalem was heard afar off." In this regard, the gaiety surrounding the golden calf of Exodus 32 is quite orthodox: eat, drink, merriment (*ṣḫq* as in 2 Sam 6, where the acceptable biform of *śḫq* occurs), singing, shouting heard from a great distance (v.6,17-19).

unrestrained (deafening!) music (1 Kgs 1:39-40) makes its appearance.[30] If one takes seriously the repeated testimony that wine is the single most effective catalyst for merriment (Zech 10:7; Judg 9:13; Ecc 10:19), then it becomes difficult to see joy expressed without this element. As Joseph dines with his brothers, "they drank and were merry with him" (Gen 43:34). One may cite Ps 104:15 as particularly instructive, for apart from gifts of garments and silver, the three elements most often given to messengers in our texts are wine, oil and food: "wine to gladden the heart of man, oil to make his face shine, and bread to strengthen man's heart" (cf. Jer 31:12).

Common hospitality reflects the notion that joy is concrete. Laban's words articulate the value system precisely: "Why did you flee secretly, and cheat me, so that I might have sent you away with mirth (*śimḥāh*) and songs, with tambourine and lyre?" (Gen 31:27). "Joy" (*śimḥāh*) is concrete to Koheleth[31] and it cannot be abstract in the eloquent parallelism of Proverbs 21:17:

He who loves *śimḥāh*	will	be a poor man,
He who loves wine and oil	will not	be rich.

A similar picture emerges from Akkadian sources. When royalty finds itself in good spirits, it is an occasion for the giving of gifts[32] and festal banqueting.[33] Such royal behavior in moments of triumph, accomplishment, and vindication is echoed by divine

---

[30] Note the semantic juxtapositions in the following passages: eat/drink/rejoice/sing (Isa 65:13-14), sing/rejoice/dance/satiate (Jer 31:11-13). If one will rejoice with Zion, it is no accident that the poet employs a metaphor of drinking to satiety from abundant breasts (Isa 66:10-11).

[31] Koheleth's investigation of *śimḥāh*'s dimensions includes laughter, wine, and song (Ecc 2:1-11); "I commended *śimḥāh*, for man has no good thing under the sun but to eat and to drink and to enjoy himself (*liśmoăḥ*, Ecc 8:10).

[32] The sequence joy - generosity is a natural one made explicit in texts such as BBSt VI.44, XXXVI iv 10-11,38ff.

[33] *Asb.* 63 vi 49-53; *OIP* II 116.65-76; E. Michel, "Die Assur-Texte Salmanassars III. (858-824)," *WO* 2/2 (1955) 148 l.70-71; *TCL* III 62-63.

activity, for when the gods rejoice, they also give gifts[34] and dine extravagantly.[35]

It is therefore difficult to escape the conclusion that expressions of joy upon the arrival of messengers were accompanied by the giving of gifts and extensive banqueting.[36] Several texts noted above explicitly made this connection, and it is likely that joy in these contexts (an expression of generosity toward the messenger and the one who sends him) can be assumed even where not explicit. After all, the messenger who returned to his master (as in *ARM* X 141) could easily confirm the truth as to how genuine any reputed joy might be. Threats are recorded in letters to the effect that should a host cause a messenger grief and the messenger reports back this mistreatment, dire consequences will follow (Emar 262.14-21). In the ancient Semitic world, communal joy without food, oil, wine, song, or the giving of gifts was not joy at all.

From other data and the evidence of the letters themselves, it is possible to flesh out these skeletal pieces of data. It is not simply true that the messenger was supplied with food which he could consume at his leisure. At least on the international level, the customs of diplomacy (no doubt arising in this case from the traditional regard for hospitality) called for the wining and dining of the messenger in the actual presence of the king.[37] Some Mari

---

[34] *Asb.* 5-6 vii 17-23.

[35] *EE* II.120-III.137 (cf. VI 71-78); *Lugal-e* I.18-19.

[36] The preceding discussion is largely a result of the inspiration of W. Moran and substantial input from Gary Anderson to whom I am indebted for references such as Y. Muffs, "Joy and Love as Metaphorical Expressions of Willingness and Spontaneity in Cuneiform, Ancient Hebrew and Related Literatures," *Christianity, Judaism and Other Greco-Roman Cults* [J. Neusner, ed.; Leiden: Brill, 1975) 1-36.

[37] Contrast Greece: "A state had little obligation to provide hospitality for visiting envoys. Normally they fended for themselves, staying at an inn or resorting to their *proxenos*. . . . When a conclusion was reached in the business upon which the envoys had been sent, by a formal resolution attached to the main proposal on the business an invitation was issued to the visiting envoys to dine at public expense on

receipts indicate the specific occasion for the use of the palace wine:

> When the *ḫadašu*-messengers of Sibkuna-Addu sat before the king in the Palm Court (*ARM* XXIV 65.15-20; cf. l.25-30).
>
> (When?) the messengers of Kahat, Kurda, Arrapha, Ilanṣura, and Talhayum sat before the king in the *É pa-pa-ḫi-im*" (*ARM* XXIV 72).
>
> When the messengers of Babylon, Yamhad, Hazor, and [ ] were before the king in *za-ka-nim* (*ARM* XXIV 75.5-11).
>
> When the messengers of Yamhad and Qatna and Byblos . . . sat before the king.[38]

At a later date, the Babylonian king feels that he must apologize for not so treating the Egyptian messenger: "Since my brother's messenger arrived, I have not been well and so his messenger could not eat food or drink beer before me" (*EA* 7.8-10). Similar is the case where Aziru claimed he was unaware of the arrival of the Egyptian messenger in his territory. Nevertheless, he insists that the messenger was well taken care of, for "my brothers and Batilu were at his service (*izzazzūnim ana pānišu*) . . . ; they supplied him with food and beer" (*EA* 161.11-22). One may also compare the reception of the Hyksos messenger by pharaoh Sekenenre, for the latter "took care of the messenger of Apophis and gave him all good things, food, cakes . . . ."[39]

Already in Sumerian literature this feature is found as the proper way to treat a messenger. Unfortunately, the sole literary text which narrates a banquet for the messenger is placed in the

---

the morrow or the day after that" (F. Adcock and D. J. Mosley, *Diplomacy*, 164).

[38] The last reference is an excerpt cited by G. Dossin without specifying the commodity in "Yamhad et Qatanum," *RA* 36 (1939) 46-54.

[39] M. Valloggia, *Recherche*, 184.

context of betrothal and marriage, and it is not entirely clear how much of the hospitality is due to the nuptial environment. In any case, after Nuska delivers his lord's proposal for marriage to Sud's mother, and she in turn gives him a message to take back, the narrative resumes (*Sud* 75-83):

> She set out the chair of honor and seated Nuska on it. [She set] a table of rejoicing, [ ]. Nanibgal called her daughter and gave her advice: ". . . go to his presence and pour him beer." [According to the instructions] of her mother, she washed (his) hands and placed a cup in his hands. The emissary opened his left hand, gave her the treasure.

The peculiar marriage context is underscored by the fact that Sud is summoned to wait on Nuska, and he rewards her handsomely with the gift which he had kept hidden until the proper moment (see discussion in section 1.3.4). But the chair of honor and the hand-washing may be elements of etiquette customary for any distinguished Sumerian messenger.

Often such banqueting could be used to insult the messenger. An Old Babylonian writer expressed disapproval of his messenger's treatment in contrast to other well-treated messengers (Asmar 35.14-22):

> Is my messenger supposed to take care of (providing) his own daily food ration? Please, indeed, it is good that messengers should receive a daily food ration, but my messenger should (also) receive food.

Similar discrimination seems to resurface when La'um writes from Babylon back to the king of Mari (*ARM* II 76):

> We went in for a meal with Hammurabi and went in to the courtyard of the palace, and they gave the three of us - Zimri-Addu, myself, and Yarim-Addu - clothes to wear, and the men of Yamhad who went in with us, all of them they (also) clothed. Since they had clothed all the men of Yamhad but they had provided no

> clothes for my lord's servants, the *ša sikkim*, I spoke up on their behalf to Sin-bel-aplim saying, "Why do you separate us as if we were sons of a sow?[40] Whose servants are we, and whose servants are the *ša-sikkim*? We are all [my lord's] servants."

Similar detail also surfaces in Ashurbanipal's first millennium account of Shamash-shum-ukin's rebellion. The latter deceptively sent a delegation to Nineveh (*ina šipir nikilti . . . išpuraššunūti*) which Ashurbanipal received grandly: he seated them at a tasty table (*ina paššūri taknê ulzizsunūti*), clothed them in linen garments with trim of many colors (*lubultī kitê birme ulabbissunūti*), and put gold rings on their fingers (*šemirē ḫurāṣi urakkis rittēšun*).[41] A later Aramaic text in Demotic script remarkably narrates the same scene with expansions:[42]

> The emissaries went out from Babylon until they brought into Nineveh - desiring first and foremost, rest and satiation - their letter from Sarmuge [Shamash-shum-ukin] to Sarbanabal [Ashurbanipal]. "I am the king of Babylon and you are the governor of Nineveh, my tributary city. Why should I pay homage to you?" The king sends down wine to the emissaries from the dining hall, and portions of bread and water . . . . He says to the king, "Lord of kings, hear! From the days of . . . your father's fathers, emissaries who have not eaten and portions of bread and water. Take out the emissaries from the dining hall. Let them be brought to the bathhouse. Dress them in embroidered garments. Go to its tables. Let their ointments be entrusted/apportioned to me."

---

[40] Translation of W. Moran.

[41] Streck II 30.85-95.

[42] R. Steiner and C. Nims, "Ashurbanipal and Shamash-shum-ukin: A Tale of Two Brothers from the Aramaic Text in Demotic Script," *RB* 92 (1985) 71-73. See the original edition for the many conjectural emendations and doubtful renderings which we have not reproduced in this difficult text.

This advice is pleasing to the king, and the text recounts how he performs all these activities in essentially the same words.

Uriah's inebriation suggests that excessive drinking was probably not uncommon at such affairs. Presumably David treated this envoy no different from other messengers whom the king sought to honor in a special way: "Now David called him and he ate and drank before him, and he made him drunk" (2 Sam 11:13). In the light of the custom of fêting messengers, David's treatment of Uriah in this regard is entirely above suspicion. It is true, of course, that David is using the custom to his advantage, hoping that Uriah will become so drunk that he does not remember if he slept with his wife or not.[43]

Reflections of the custom may be found in non-royal letters as well. One Old Babylonian woman requests that "they give [to] my [messeng]er rations (*epru*) according to my position as a lady of rank" (*AbB* VII 19.33-34). This comment reveals that the provisioning of messengers depended upon the status of the one who was sending them.

We have discussed elsewhere the accommodations of Wenamun in Byblos (namely, how he did not reside in the palace but was responsible for his own quarters), but we know nothing of his food provisions for the duration of his stay. It is only when he is ready to leave (and Wenamun's enemies are again close behind him) that the ruler Zakar-Baal softens his rough treatment of the Egyptian messenger. For the first time we read of food given to the messenger (2.67-70):

> The ruler was ready to cry because of the words which were quoted to him and which were sickening. And

---

[43] Y. Holmes does not support his observation that the wining and dining of a messenger was "possibly to interrogate him in a sly manner" ("The Messengers of the Amarna Letters," *JAOS* 75 [1975] 377). The only evidence of which I am aware is this biblical account, but David is not eliciting information from Joab. Because of the high prestige associated with the custom, it is unlikely to have been motivated by the attitude which Holmes suggests. Indeed, one would soon find kings requesting that their envoys *not* be banqueted!

> he let come out to me his letter-scribe bringing to me 2 flagons of wine and a sheep. And he sent to me Tanetna, a songstress from Egypt who was with him, saying, "Sing for him! Don't let him be desperate!" And he sent to me, saying: "Eat and drink! Do not despair! You shall hear what is to be said during the morning!"

This gesture is not part of the normal care for a messenger, but represents a special gift from the patron to the messenger at a time of particular crisis for the latter. It certainly shows that the palace held itself responsible for the messenger's welfare. The provision of a female companion from home (note her Egyptian name) remains a unique recorded benefaction toward messengers, although probably not uncommon.[44] As Goedicke notes (*Wenamun*, 120-121), "There were a considerable number of 'ladies' of Egyptian origin throughout the ancient Near East. Although called 'Songstress' . . . , there can be little doubt about the nature of their activities."

One way of expressing "joy" in a tangible fashion was to bestow gifts upon the messenger (*EA* 21.24-29).

> PN[1] the messenger of my brother and PN[2] the interpreter (*targuman*) of my brother I honored as gods (*kī ilī urte*[*bbīma*]) and many gifts (*qīšāti māda*) I gave them and treated them very well (*ubtinnīšunu*), for their message was excellent.

Two items in this reference must be underscored. First, the king of Mitanni feels it of sufficient import to remind pharaoh to whom he is writing that he has been very generous with the Egyptian messengers; the rewarding of messengers[45] is a barometer of

---

[44] The messenger Kubbutum receives a servant-girl from the palace at Mari (*ARM* XXII 73), but she is probably someone whom he is to escort to another.

[45] We are not speaking here of gifts between kings, which was itself such an indicator of international polity; see C. Zaccagnini, *Lo Scambio dei Doni.*

international good will. We find the bestowal of gifts upon messengers to be of such significance that the formal regulation of such gifts was on occasion found to be necessary. In a royal edict from the Hittite court regulating tribute, it is noted (*PRU* IV 83):

> If a prince or a noble from Hatti goes to Ugarit as (*ina*) a messenger and it pleases the king of Ugarit to give a gift, let him give. If he doesn't want to, he doesn't have to - there is no obligation.

This peculiar clause is designed to take pressure off of the vassal and restore a genuine sense of reward to any gifts which the vassal might give. The bestowal of gifts could easily become a burden when it became an expected part of every envoy's mission. It is likely that the Hittite king made explicit this policy in order to free himself of a similar obligation toward the messengers from Ugarit. The fact that gifts to envoys could easily get out of hand is made clear from the same period when the Babylonian messengers are reputed to have disdained the gifts given to them by pharaoh (*EA* 1.66-77; see note on this text in section 4.3):

> I am angry at your messengers, for they say in your presence, "He gives nothing to those of us who go to Egypt." Of those who come before me, one of them comes and receives silver, gold, oil, clothes, all fine things [more than in] any other country and he speaks falsehood to the one who sends him. . . . So I said (to myself), whether I give or don't give anything to them, they are going to speak thus falsely! So I laid down a rule: I didn't give anything!

Consequently, David's behavior toward Uriah (although not on an international level) is probably not unusual but quite proper, for when Uriah's message is complete, he is sent off and "there followed him a present from the king" (2 Sam 11:8).[46]

---

[46] Although this is the MT, it may not be the correct reading. As one variant, however, it suggests what some expected the text to read. See P. K. McCarter, *II Samuel,* 280 for discussion.

The second point to be noted from Tushratta's letter above is that he seems to imply that his generosity toward the messengers is to some extent dependent upon the quality of the message which they bring ("for their message was excellent," ***kī ṭēmšunu banû***). It was noted earlier that messengers had a reputation for coloring the truth; here may be a sufficient motive. It may have discouraged messengers from going on certain errands when they knew the information they carried was not going to be well received. Such an attitude may be reflected in the very difficult passage in which Joab tries to discourage Ahimaaz from taking the bad news of Absalom's death to David: "Why will you run, my son, seeing that you will have no reward for the tidings?" (2 Sam 18:22).[47] 2 Samuel 4:10 indicates that bad news[48] could result not only in no payment but the loss of one's life:

> The one who told me, "Behold, Saul is dead!" - thinking he was bringing me good news - I seized and slew him in Ziklag, which was the reward I gave him for his tidings (*'ăšer lĕtittî lô bĕśorāh*).[49]

---

[47] But this translation, if correct, may be interpreted to mean that he will receive no reward since that goes only to the messenger who first delivers the news (and Joab assumes that the Cushite who already departed will arrive first).

[48] The application of this passage to the issue of messenger payment is clear if one considers the verse only in its immediate context: David speaks of how he rewarded the one who brought the news. However, in the light of 2 Sam 1, David slew the "messenger" not simply because he brought tragic news but because he readily admitted to regicide.

[49] The Hebrew is awkward; see P. K. McCarter, *2 Samuel*, 128. Note in Sumerian culture how the treatment of embassies declaring war was not necessarily civil, if Shulgi's report is accurate: "A herald (*sukkal*) came with a message of the highlands that was about war, [the young men] from the assembly in the *IM.SAG.GA* (like) spirited oxen and dogs assailed [him]. The answer to his words [ ], the 'Intruder' with loud [shouts] they [chased(?)] from their presence" (Shulgi C 57-62).

How were good messengers reimbursed? Were they compelled to rely solely on these uncertain benefactions?[50] The Mitanni king, when complaining as usual of the paltry gifts he receives from his "brother" in Egypt, alludes to the fact that the pay of his messengers may come from the gifts which are sent from king to king: "The gold you send me is not enough for the wages of my messengers going and coming back" (*EA* 16.28-31).[51] But this statement should not be pressed too far, for he simply may be saying that the gifts are hardly worth the effort, without intending to indicate the source of the messengers' pay.

In the south in the Old Babylonian period, a glimpse into payment of messengers is afforded by one text where it is implied that the sender should have sent the messenger off with the payment and not waited until the message was delivered (*AbB* IV 145.36-39).

---

[50] Already in Ur III, silver rings were given as gifts to travellers, including messengers, perhaps as part of a greeting ceremony (P. Michalowski, "The Neo-Sumerian Silver Ring Texts," *Syro-Mesopotamian Studies* 2/3 [1978] 1-15). Contrast the Greek custom: "It was an old and chivalrous custom of the Greeks to exchange gifts, but it seems that envoys eschewed such practices and the reception of envoys by a state was not to be compared with reception by a personal host. In any case the risk of bribery or the appearance of bribery presented an obvious problem. That problem became the more acute when envoys encountered the hospitality of a ruler such as the king of Macedon or Persia" (F. Adcock and D. J. Mosley, *Diplomacy in Ancient Greece*, 164). Adcock and Mosley further note that one envoy to Persia in 367 B.C. was so lavishly endowed with gifts that he was executed on his return to Greece. However, when Athens honored King Strato of Sidon (c.367 B.C.), they provided the envoys with tokens to present as gifts and instructed them on the protocol for receiving gifts in return (*Ibid.*, 165). In general, a Greek envoy sought the position as an honor, assuming expenses for any attendants who accompanied him, and receiving only a subsistence allowance for himself (*Ibid.*, 155-156).

[51] For *idī* "wages" see A. Sachs, "Two Notes on the Taanach and Amarna Letters," *AfO* 12 (1937-1939) 371-373.

> Whoever brings this tablet to you (*ša kunukkam ubbalakkum*), give him 1/6 shekel of silver; I have no silver with me and so can not give him anything (*kaspam ula naši'ākūma ula anaddin*).

Exceptionally, then, payment could be made at the receiving end of the message. No doubt, the payment would still be charged to the sender's account.

In many Mari texts, variable quantities of silver are recorded as given to messengers.[52] Where it is possible to identify messengers by name and the specific quantity of silver which they receive, one discovers that quantities of either one[53] or two shekels[54] most frequently appear. However, frequent gifts of 5 shekels[55] and even 10 shekels[56] also appear, with a variety of other amounts.[57] Evidence of this nature for the first millennium is minimal, but at least one text is known (*TCAE* 337-342) which records gifts of silver to envoys (*ṣīrāni* - *LÚ.MAḪ*) who had brought tribute to the Assyrian king probably toward the beginning of the seventh century.[58]

---

[52] J.-R. Kupper, "L'usage de l'argent à Mari," *Zikir Šumim - Assyriological Studies Presented to F. R. Kraus on his Seventieth Birthday* (Ed. G. Van Driel, Th. J. H. Krispijn, M. Stol, K. R. Veenhof; Leiden: Brill, 1982) 164-165.

[53] Even though an individual in the following citations may not be explicitly identified as a *mār šipri,* he is known to be one on the basis of other texts. *ARM* VII 110.1' 112.7,8,10 113.4 133.6 159.3,14 165.11,13 169.10,11,12 208.1,2 212.17 219.45.

[54] *ARM* VII 112.5 113.2,3,16 133.2 164.9 168.5 169.4 173.6 209.5,10 210.7,9 211.18 219.35 XXIII 560.3.

[55] *ARM* VII 112.1 113.14,17 159.1 165.15 169.3,7,9 173.2,4 208.4 XXIII 560.1.

[56] *ARM* VII 113.1,6 168.1 169.2 209.1,2,4.

[57] 4 shekels (*ARM* VII 211.11 [probably the same person found in *ARM* XXII 151.11] XXII 241.19); 3.5 shekels (*ARM* VII 208.6); 3 shekels (*ARM* VII 133.1); 2.5 shekels (*ARM* VII 112.3); 1.5 shekels (*ARM* VII 169.5,6 173.8 209.6 XXIII 560.5).

[58] R. Zadok, "Historical and Onomastic Notes," (*WO* 9 [1977-1978] 35-56) 35.

A considerable amount of evidence from the second millennium makes it clear that the provisioning of messengers by their hosts was an essential part of international diplomacy. One finds that the messenger upon delivering his message was given provisions to meet his needs. Provision lists are preserved from the courts of several palaces, some of which assigned to messengers quantities of wine (from Ugarit[59] and Rimah[60]), while provision for both wine and honey is known from Mari.[61] Quantities of oil for anointing were supplied at Mari for Ishme-Dagan's messengers,[62] in addition to oil for unspecified use given to other visiting messengers (*ARM* XXII 274). Food allotments at Mari are known for a messenger who arrived from Qatna (*ARM* XII 10) and for other unspecified messengers.[63] In Egypt, a list[64] of messengers who came from Megiddo, Kinnereth, Achshaph, Samaria, Ta'anach, Mishal, T-n-n, Sharon, Ashkelon, and Hazor (in that order) are each given one jar of beer and 1 1/2 sacks of grain,

---

[59] "2 jars wine for the sheikhs (*abbū*) of Ura, 1 jar wine (*karpat karānu*) for the messenger of Amurru" (*Ugar.* V p.193 #100).

[60] The format of the tablets relates three pieces of information in addition to the date and place of issue: number of jars of wine, person(s) to whom given, and the individual in charge (*gìr*).

[61] *ARM* IX 56 (a fragmentary tablet devoted entirely to this disbursement). The editors of the text note that since other texts make it clear that honey was brought in to Mari, text 56 must be of a similar nature with regard to wine, i.e. "remis à des messagers du roi de Mari pour leur maître" (p.271). But it is only one jar of wine which is given to the messengers, a provision which is best understood in terms of the evidence noted above.

[62] *ana pašāš awīlī ša ṭuppātim . . . ublūnim* ("for anointing the men who brought the tablets"; *ARM* VII 21). *ana pašāš mubassirī* ("for anointing the messengers"; *ARM* VII 75).

[63] *ARM* XII 299,300,617. After 4 lines listing items for the royal meal (*naptan šarrim*) in text 299, the tablet notes provisions for the messengers whose fare seems to be included in the *naptan šarri*. Special note should be made of *ARM* XII 747.

[64] M. Valloggia, *Recherche*, 101. The rubric which begins the list identifies the contents as "Provisions(?) for the *mariannu* of Djahy", but each *mariannu* is identified as a messenger.

while a separate account notes that the messenger from Lachish received for 15 days "10 sacks making (a total?) of 20 sacks of grain."[65] Provisions of shoes[66] and garments[67] are attested, with one writer specifically requesting that the addressee clothe his messenger (*šipru*) with a garment (Asmar 20.35-36).

The maintenance of messengers at a foreign court could become an attractive lure to messengers to over-stay their welcome. It could also be a costly enterprise for the host, entertaining delegations from many countries. How long did messengers stay before returning home? We now turn to the issue of the homeward trip.

5.4 RETURNING THE MESSENGER

There is a curious tension which becomes apparent in the issue of the return of the messenger. Two values are in conflict: on the one hand, there is a high premium placed upon receiving news quickly and accurately, while on the other hand there is the need for the expression of hospitality, both received and given. Do the messengers "eat and run," so to speak? It was seen in the previous section how the provisions provided for messengers by the host country were an important part of international protocol. Nevertheless, it will be seen that the ancient Semitic world unanimously came down in favor of maximizing speed of communication in this context.[68]

It is first of all important to underscore that the messenger's task was not complete when he had delivered his lord's message to its intended addressee. Rather, the messenger's task was finished when the messenger had returned safely back to the

---

[65] *Ibid.*, 100.

[66] *ARM* XIX 288, XXII 151.11.

[67] *ARM* VII 210,221; XXII 151; XXIII 21,37.

[68] We might note that delay tends to lead to unfortunate consequences in biblical literature in similar contexts - cf. Judg 18, 1 Kgs 13.

point of despatch.[69] This perspective becomes clear from several converging lines of evidence. One may first note the discussion earlier on the escort, a concept which assumes great respect and concern for the returning messenger. He is not left to his own resources once a communication has been delivered. The one who receives a message shoulders a responsibility to safely return the messenger.

Secondly, one may point to many narratives where the presupposition of a round-trip is often made explicit. As early as *Enmerkar and the Lord of Aratta*, one sees this in the first message delivered: upon completing the message, the messenger asks for a response which he might return to Enmerkar (l.208-217). This passage clarifies that the despatch of a message was not an end in itself; the one who sends has sent the message for a response: if he wants something done, he wants to hear that he has been obeyed; if he sends a challenge, he wants to hear that it has been accepted; if he sends a request, he wants to hear it granted; if he sends information, he wants to know that it is being acted on. Wherever one does not find the notion of the escort, one finds nevertheless the round-trip messenger relaying message and response in Sumerian, biblical,[70] Akkadian[71] and Ugaritic[72]

---

[69] Some cultures document that a messenger who fails to return with a response was rewarded with death (R. Numelin, *Beginnings of Diplomacy*, 151).

[70] Jacob's messengers returned by Esau (Gen 32:3-6), Balak's by Balaam (Num 22:4-14), David's by Nabal (1 Sam 25:14), Joab's by David (2 Sam 11:18-25), Ben-Hadad's by Ahab (1 Kgs 20:1-12), the dialogue between Jepthah and the king of Ammon (Judg 11:12-14). The query of Ahaziah to his messengers (so *RSV*), "Why did you return?" *mah zeh šabtem* (2 Kgs 1:5) does not imply that they were not to return - after all, they were supposed to bring back the oracle from Ashdod. A better translation would be, "What, back so soon?" Note the dismay in the two reports about Joram's two messengers: "He did not return" (2 Kgs 9:18,20).

[71] Nuska in *Atr.* I.70-166, Namtar in *Nergal and Ereshkigal* (*STT* 28), Adad in the *Anzu* myth (tab. II). For the sake of the narrative in *EE*, the gathering of the gods is sufficient to indicate that Kakka's message was heeded.

literature. The sender may make this explicit when the messenger is sent: "Bring back her answer speedily" (*Sud* 43). When Ashur-uballit speaks of his messengers' wages, it is in terms of "their going and returning" (*alāki u târ*[*imm*]*a*; *EA* 16.29).[73]

A messenger, therefore, typified not only the mouth of the one who sent him but his eyes and ears as well. His task was not only output in dispensing information from his master but also input in collecting data for the benefit of the one who sent him. Indeed, the descriptive title "king's eye" or "king's ear" became a graphic designation in the Persian period for the royal messenger who reported to the king after making inspection tours of the provinces.[74] The messenger as a fact-finder, inspector or investigator is a widely attested phenomenon.[75]

In literary texts, one finds a mounted messenger despatched in order to discover an approaching rider's intentions (2 Kgs 9:17-20). Elsewhere, when Ishtar hears of Ṣaltu's clamor for war, she sends her *sukkal* Ninshubur to investigate and discover what is taking place: "find out all about her - her haunts, wherever they are(?); bring word of her signs, recount to me her ways."[76]

---

[72] Clearest cases are Baal's messengers (Gapnu-wa-Ugaru), returned by Mot (*CTA* 5.1) and king Pabil's messengers returned by Kirta (*CTA* 14.6).

[73] Compare the words of an accomplished mission (a grain delivery) spoken by the *mār šipri*: "To Dayyan-ahhe-iddina, son of Gimillu, and Nadin, son of Bel-ahhe-iqisha, I have given it" (*TCL* XIII 231.6-8). A receipt such as *GCCI* II 86, specifying that the *mār šipri* delivered the stated goods, might serve as a confirmation to the messenger's master that the commission was fulfilled.

[74] A. Olmstead, *History of the Persian Empire* (Chicago: University of Chicago, 1948) 59.

[75] In other cultures, Numelin notes (*The Beginnings of Diplomacy*, 139) that Rhodesian messengers "go from one court to another to inquire after family matters." Another African tribe sends messengers "to other villages to make sure or check that everything is in order" in times of crisis such as transfer of power.

[76] Translation by B. Foster, "Ea and Ṣaltu," *Essays on the Ancient Near East in Memory of Jacob Joel Finkelstein* (Memoirs of the Connecticut Association of the Arts and Sciences; ed. M. de Jong Ellis;

Ninshubur obeys and brings back a description to his mistress of all that he has seen.

In the OB period one hears of messengers making inspection,[77] already an old aspect of messenger activity if one considers Shulgi's envoy sent "to learn the state of your country,"[78] "to learn the words of their leaders."[79] Kings naturally expected their subjects to use discretion in the presence of such visiting messengers. Zimri-Lim throws one of his subjects into prison(?)[80] for indiscriminately talking of confidential matters with an Eshnunna messenger.[81] A Hittite named Benteshina in the Hittite court curses the king of Babylon and is overheard by the Babylonian king's messenger who reports the offense back to Babylon (*CTH* 172.26-33).

We have already described the custom typified by Shuppiluliuma of sending one's own messenger to confirm the truth of a report from another source (*DS* 28). The messenger is sent not with the primary task to relay but rather to discover information. Shuppiluliuma's contemporaries on occasion make this intention explicit (*EA* 15.7-19):

> I send my messenger to you to see you and to see your land. . . . The messenger whom I send to you I send to investigate (*ana amāri*). Let him see and be on his way!

Hamden, CN: Archon Books, 1977) 79-88. For the text, see B. Gröneberg, "Philologische Bearbeitung des Agushayahymnus," *RA* 75 (1981) 107-134.

[77] "After the messenger of PN had inspected (*īmuru*)" (*AbB* IX 227.16-19)

[78] F. Ali, *Sumerian Letters*, 31.

[79] *Ibid.*, 39.

[80] *Nepārim* - see *CAD* N (2) 341-342.

[81] Itur-Asdu sends on Iṣi-Nabu in *ARM* II 128, who is specifically said to be sent by Shallurum of Eshnunna to Zimri-Lim. This is probably the same Iṣi-Nabu in A.2801, a letter addressed to Itur-Asdu (in G. Dossin, "*Adaššum* et *kirḫum* dans des textes de Mari," *RA* 66 [1972] 111-130).

The messenger in this context is hardly a spy since his purpose is not covert or clandestine. Tushratta freely employs the Egyptian messenger's inspection as a confirmation of the beauty of his daughter, the future bride of pharaoh: "The one whom my brother requested, I showed to Mane, and he saw her; when he saw her, he praised her a great deal" (*EA* 19:21-22). Mane is here functioning as pharaoh's eyes at a thousand miles removed, and Tushratta exploits this fact to his own advantage: there is no room for complaint on pharaoh's part when his highest ranking envoy finds the woman attractive.[82] Of course, the ploy could backfire if the goods were not delivered, as happened when pharaoh showed wonderful gifts to Tushratta's messengers but never sent them (*EA* 27:29-32).

> He (Amenhotep III) said to my messengers, "Behold the statues . . . which I am about to send to my brother, and look upon it with your own eyes." And my messengers saw it with their own eyes. And now, my brother (Amenhotep IV), you have not sent the statues."

In the later Assyrian empire, one finds a request that the king send his messenger to question individuals (*SLA* 66.r3-4) or to investigate and report back his findings to the king (*ABL* 925.8-9; 995). When astrologers are foiled because of a cloud-cover, messengers may be sent to other cities to gather the needed information about the astral phenomena which occurred (*LAS* 323).

From the Neo-Babylonian period, similar requests appear: "let your messenger come and see" (*līmur*; *NBU* 200.42-43). The role of the messenger as one who seeks and finds is described in detail with respect to a water ordeal where the body of the guilty party fails to surface. The royal guard despairs and the king's (Nebuchadnezzar) anger rises. At this point,

---

[82] Amenhotep III advises the Babylonian king to send men of rank to investigate (*ana amāra* assuming scribal error) his sister's living conditions as pharaoh's wife (*EA* 1.32-36).

> a messenger (*mār šipri*) went to and fro (*illak u iturru*), but they did not . . . the man. He crossed the ford of the river and moved (?) into the desert; since no one had ever seen him, they could not answer. The keeper (?) of the bridge and some scouts went along the river, watching the banks from ford to ford. When midday arrived his corpse came up from the river.[83]

In addition to this material, there is the testimony of the letters themselves which testify overwhelmingly to the urgency of speedily returning one's messengers. The persistence of the reminder, "please don't detain my messenger, send him quickly back to me!" echoes in all periods in Mesopotamia. In the first millennium, the common idiom which frequently closes letters is basically of the form, "Quickly put the road at his feet,"[84] referring to the messenger or those who seem to be functioning in this capacity. Occasionally the additional reminder, "Don't let him spend the night!"[85] is joined with the preceding, among other expressions.[86] In the Old and Middle Babylonian periods, on the other hand, it is not possible to speak of a standard form, although the request is made on the order of "let him come" (*ARM* X 114.16), "don't hold him back,"[87] "send him on,"[88] or combinations of these.[89]

---

[83] W. Lambert, "Nebuchadnezzar King of Justice," *Iraq* 27 (1965) 6,9.

[84] *NB* 19.27-29 31.12-14 119.14-15 171.10-11,20-22 214.21-23; *NBU* 136.11-13 147.30-31 178.14-16 193.28 216.11-13 221.20-22 227.32 242.25-26 247.18-19 252.15 359.20-22 *et passim*.

[85] *NBU* 28.12-16,21-24 40.40-41 167.10-14 257.29-33.

[86] E.g. "my messenger must not stay before you" (*mār šiprīya ina pānīka lā izzazu*; *NBU* 79.33).

[87] *TCL* XVII 22.15; XVIII 142.12-13; *AbB* II 94.19 182.10; VI 11.10 57.10).

[88] *ARM* II 36.16-17 95.10-15; *AbB* V 82.9,10; VI 128.16; *EA* 17.47-49 18.6r 157.34.

[89] *ARM* II 141.24-26; *EA* 8.44-47 19.72 33.21-26.

To be a messenger who is not allowed to return to his homeland was more than a simple fear, it was a veritable nightmare of reality. Records show a Cypriote messenger held in Egypt for two years (*EA* 36:18), an Egyptian messenger detained for three years in Cyprus (*EA* 35.35-36), an Assyrian messenger held three years in Hatti,[90] a Babylonian messenger held six years in Egypt (*EA* 3.14), Egyptian messengers held for 17 years in Byblos (*Wenamun* 2.51-52) and messengers from Tunip staying in Egypt for 20 years (*EA* 59.13-14). An Assyrian messenger is taken out of circulation by the Hittite king for an undetermined period of time (*CTH* 173), but apparently long enough to have fathered a scribe bearing a Hittite name.[91] Death in a foreign land as a messenger may thus have not been an uncommon event. The seventeen year stay of one group of messengers noted above was so concluded (*Wenamun* 2.51-53):

> "Truly, I have not done to you what was done to the messengers of Kha'emwase after they spent 17 years in this country and they (actually) died in their positions!" And he said to his servant: "Take him! Let him see their tomb in which they lie!"

This statement made by the ruler of Byblos to Wenamun is part of an argument by which he wishes to convince Wenamun that staying in Byblos for the winter is not the worst thing that could happen. He wants Wenamun to count his blessings and be glad that he isn't being held for years on end![92] Such logic recurs when the Hittite king comforts his Assyrian counterpart regarding a messenger he is holding:

---

[90] "[The messenger] of the land of Assyria who went to Hatti and was detained for 3 years, they have released him and he has returned to Ashur and the messenger of Hatti with him" (O. R. Gurney, "Texts from Dūr-Kurigalzu," 139.17).

[91] *KUB* XXXVII 210; for this individual and other Assyrians who settled in Hatti, see G. Beckman, "Mesopotamians and Mesopotamian Learning at Hattusha," *JCS* 35 (1983) 111.

[92] Goedicke, *Wenamun*, 106.

> That's why [I have detained] him. The messengers whom you regularly sent here in the days of the king Urhi-Teshub usually had sad experiences. Today . . . you must by [no] means say: "Just as in those days he will have sad experiences." You will not even need to ask Bel-qarrad upon his return whether [ ] treated him well.[93]

This type of behavior is nostalgically contrasted by one king with the "good old days" when messengers weren't so treated (*EA* 3.9-15):

> Previously, my father would send you a messenger and you wouldn't detain him many days. Quickly you sent him off, and you sent fine gifts. Now when I sent you my messenger and you held him for 6 years, you sent (only) 30 minas gold.

It is therefore clear that messengers can not in any sense be pictured as having diplomatic immunity, even among those to whom they are sent. Indeed, the messenger is a pawn whom one may dispose of as one wishes. This is nowhere more clearly stated than in Ashur-uballiṭ's note to pharaoh:[94]

> Surely my messengers are not to be delayed in reaching me. Why should messengers stay constantly in the sun and so die in the sun? If they remain in the sun and the king profits then let them remain and die there. The king profits! If he doesn't, why should they die there? As to the messengers which we send, do they keep my messengers alive? They are made to die in the sun.

Among hostile powers in the MB period, it was seen earlier how it could be a policy not to allow the messenger to make a

---

[93] *CTH* 173.14-19r.; A. Goetze, *Kizzuwatna and the Problem of Hittite Geography* (*YOS* 22; New Haven: Yale University, 1940) 30-31.

[94] *EA* 16.41-55; W. Moran's translation.

round trip: "If PN sends you a message, seize the messenger and send him to the Sun's father. . . . Do not send the messenger back to PN without authorization" (see discussion in section 2.1). If messengers did travel between foes, such messengers could be delayed from returning in order to allow time to maneuver troops before the opponent received an official declaration of war.[95] But even among otherwise amicable allies, messengers were detained. What motivated this behavior among friends?

One must first of all recall that in the ancient Semitic world, the seizure of persons dependent on an individual was a common means of compelling that individual to accountability (particularly in the payment of debts).[96] Thus, the retention of a monarch's envoys may be simply an extension of this cultural phenomenon. Some support for this notion is found on the few occasions when a reason for detention of messengers is mentioned. Wenamun is detained in Byblos for approximately a month for this very reason: the prince of Byblos will not grant the Egyptian request for lumber until he sees cash on the table. Consequently, another messenger must return to Egypt and then come back to Byblos with the goods while Wenamun waits.[97] In another example, Tushratta explains to pharaoh in two separate letters why he will not return the Egyptian messenger: he will hold the messenger until pharaoh lets his own messengers go free.[98]

A similar motive may be assumed for an Assyrian messenger's detention in the Hittite court, for the Hittite king complains that no gifts were sent to him when he assumed kingship. Following this plaint he immediately notes:

---

[95] Thus Tukulti-Ninurta I sent a declaration of war to Kashtiliash who delayed his response in order to surreptitiously gather his troops: "he deceitfully delayed the message until he had his warriors deployed" (*adi uterriṣ qurādīšu kīma šupruṣi šipirta urrik*; so *CAD* A [2] 225 and cf. Kuk Won Chang, *Dichtungen der Zeit Tukulti-Ninurta I. von Assyrien* [Frankfurt am Main: Peter Lang, 1979] 104).

[96] G. R. Driver & J. C. Miles, *The Babylonian Laws*, (Oxford: Clarendon, 1952) I 208-221.

[97] *Wenamun* 2.3-43.

[98] *EA* 28.17-19; 29.149-150 (see reconstruction in C. Kühne, *Chronologie*, n.199).

Now I have detained here my ambassador (*mār
šiprīya*) whom I sent to you and Bel-qarrad. And for
the following reason I have detained him: all the
wishes you wrote me about, I [   ] sent to you. That's
why I have detained him.[99]

If the verb tenses in this letter can be trusted, the letter is sent by
the hand of new envoys, for the detention of both the Hittite and
the Assyrian messenger continues (*aktala*); the Hittite king does
not send his own messenger which he had earlier sent (*ša
ašpurakkuni*), waiting for the Assyrian king to send his presents.
In such cases, the messenger is employed as leverage to compel
fulfillment of what is perceived as an obligation.[100]

Consequently there is significant despair when one's
messengers are detained. It may have been a common complaint
to write, "You are holding my messengers!"[101] or to inquire, "Why
is my man whom I sent to the palace detained?" (*EA* 138.80-81; cf.
Asmar 30.10-15). It is for this reason also that if a messenger is
legitimately delayed for reasons beyond the notion of leverage, a
ruler will take pains to explain that the distraint is not intended as
a coercive move.[102] The ruler of Cyprus tells pharaoh not to be
upset that he has retained his messenger for three years, for there

---

[99] *CTH* 173.11-14r; A. Goetze, *Kizzuwatna*, 30-31.

[100] Note how caravans could be detained to pressure a foreign
kingdom to make good on damages (A. Malamat, "Silver, Gold and
Precious Stones From Hazor," 71-79).

[101] *mār šiprīya taktala* (*EA* 7.50); "you do not let my messenger
depart" (*mār šipr[īya] lā tušaṣṣuna; EA* 126.41-42).

[102] This may be true of private parties as well as potentates if
Waschow's restoration is correct: "Weil du so weit fortgereist bist,
schicke ich dir deinen Boten nicht" *attā ma'da kī terīqani mār šiprīka
ul a-[šap-pa-ra]* (*BE* 17/1 92.5-6; H. Waschow, "Babylonische Briefe aus
der Kassitenzeit" [*MAOG* 10/1; 1936] 11-12). However, this raises the
question as to how this present letter was delivered. More likely one
should read, "I haven't seen your messenger" *ul a-[mu]-u[r]*, for the tops
of two vertical wedges (which Waschow may have understood as *šap*)
are apparent in the copy.

is a plague raging on the island which has even claimed the life of one of the king's own sons (EA 35.35-39). Or Ashur-uballiṭ I claims that the distraint was benevolent and for the protection of the messengers, keeping them until the Sutu nomads could be controlled.[103] Tushratta also explains that part of the delay is attributable to the extensive preparations of merchandise which he intends to send to the Egyptian pharaoh; he promises to send the messengers quickly.[104] The delay of a messenger is not always intentional or avoidable, for an OB messenger writes back to his lord that he is being detained pending further information (Apla. 11-23):

> As soon as he heard my lord's message (i.e from me), he sent that very same day with regard to the troops to Yamhad, Qatna and the land of Zalmaqum. But his messengers have not yet brought back word. For this reason I am detained (*aššum kêm kalêku*). He said, "As soon as my messengers whom I sent bring back word, you shall bear a complete report to your lord."

The accusation of detaining messengers is an opprobrium which all seek to avoid (*EA* 24.IV.40-46):

> And may my brother not detain my envoys. . . and my envoys may my brother let go as fast as possible. . . . And I would like to hear about the well-being and the situation of my brother, and I will rejoice very much over the well-being of my brother. My brother may say, "You yourself have also detained my envoys." No, on the contrary, I have not detained them.

---

103 "The ones who detained your messengers are the Sutu. They were in mortal danger. I detained them until the Sutu could be captured." (*EA* 16.37-42; translation of W. Moran).

104 "For this reason, Mane has been detained. I was going to send Keliya and Mane quickly but I had not finished. . . . Within six months I'll send Keliya and Mane." (*EA* 20.23).

The detention of messengers was such a sensitive issue because it could reflect potential or present hostility.[105] Sargon II in the first millennium complains that his friendly overtures are met with such expressions of animosity (*SLA* 28.5-15):

> From the beginning I have done good unto Elam, and although they did not repay my kind acts, I have protected their fugitives, kings and princes alike. I did give them food and drink and sent them back to their country. But they bound (*iktesū*) my messengers whom I sent to bring greetings to them.

The messengers are not simply detained but in this text actually treated like prisoners and put in fetters.[106] Ashurbanipal, of course, later reciprocates toward the Elamites:[107]

> The two nobles whom Teumman sent with an insolent message - I held them before me in great wrath toward their lord.

The emphasis in letters upon quickly returning the messenger finds unanimous assent as well in literature and royal inscriptions. For example, no signs of hospitality are ever shown toward messengers in the Ugaritic literature. They deliver their message, turn around and return on their way, without even spending the night. And it is no wonder, since part of their commission may include the note of urgency, "Don't stay!"[108]

---

[105] Perhaps Asmar 15.11 is appropriate as well, if the restorations are accurate: "Your messenger (*šipir*[*ka*]) got sick."

[106] The torture of two Shosu by Ramses II at Qadesh to elicit information is not comparable since these two pretended to be sent as messengers by Shosu tribal leaders when in fact they were spies sent by Muwatalli (A. Gardiner, *The Ḳadesh Inscriptions of Ramesses II*, [Oxford: Oxford University, 1960] 28,36).

[107] E. F. Weidner, "Assyrische Beschreibungen der Kriegs-Reliefs Assurbanaplis" (*AfO* 8 [1932] 175-203) 181 l.12.

[108] The commission "Don't stay!" is actually a part of the command in telling the messengers to hurry on their way to deliver

Tuthmosis III boasts that his authority is so extensive that no one in Asia dares detain his messengers.[109]

Biblical literature also echoes the need for messengers to return quickly, although in a different fashion. Only three accounts in the Bible provide precise information about elapsed time before messengers are returned. Balak's messengers spend only one night before returning (Num 22:8-14,19-21), while Uriah stays three nights in Jerusalem. In this latter case, it is clear[110] that one night would have been normal (2 Sam 11:7-14); mischief results due to Uriah's lingering.

The tension between hospitality and speed is clearly depicted when Abraham's servant[111] spends only one night with Laban after a several hundred mile journey (Gen 24:54-61). He can not graciously return to his master without his hosts' explicit consent, and so in the morning he requests, "Send me back (*šallĕḇûnî*) to my master." Although his hosts ask him to remain longer for Rebekah's sake, he insists firmly: "Do not delay me (*'al tĕ'aḫărû*) . . . , send me back (*šallĕḇûnî*) so that I may go to my master." The issue is finally arbitrated by Rebekah who expresses her desire to depart immediately. When the servant and entourage finally leave, they do not simply leave but are explicitly

---

their message (*CTA* 2.1.13,19; cf. 5.2.8-14). However, Baal's messengers return to him with Mot's response and do so explicitly without delay and in the same words (*tb' wl yṯb*; *CTA* 5.1.9). When Pabil sends messengers to Kirta, the command is broken, but the return trip when they bring Kirta's response is explicit (*ttb' mlakm lyṯb*; *CTA* 14.6.35,36).

[109] M. Valloggia, *Recherche*, 93.

[110] It is only when David learns that Uriah has not spent the night with his wife that he encourages him to stay longer (v.10-12). Although David promises to send him back after the second night (v.12), he does not keep his promise but detains him a third night in which he gets him drunk. The present MT division is awkward, and the final word of v.12 must be construed with v.13.

[111] This individual is not explicitly identified as a *mal'āk*, but the mission on which he is sent (escorting a bride) is a common one for the *mārī šipri* on the international level. If he is not a *mal'āk*, the narrative nevertheless provides a rare illustration of protocol which messengers might have expected, as the parallels cited below indicate.

"sent" (v.59), underscoring again the lack of independence which a messenger had while under the jurisdiction of his hosts.

This latter text dealing with the treatment of a private messenger finds a close analogy in an OB text of a royal messenger (TEXT).[112] An envoy (Yaqqim-Addu, otherwise known as the governor of Sagaratum) sent by Zimri-Lim arrives in Babylon and delivers his message to Hammurabi. Two days later (*ina šalšim ūmim*), the envoy personally requests Hammurabi that he be allowed to return to his lord (*wu''urtam īriš*), upon which Hammurabi replies, "I send you off - go!" (*luwa''erka alik*; l.22-25). The request for permission to leave again underscores the dependent posture of an envoy in a foreign court.[113]

As with Abraham's servant, it is the messenger who initiates discussion of the return trip by asking permission to depart. After his 300 mile trip to Babylon, Yaqqim-Addu's almost immediate desire (after only two nights) to return to Mari is striking, but in this case understandable since he is supposed to return with troop reinforcements. However, it is Hammurabi's reply which is unusual and so underscored by the letter-writer, Ibal-piel: "Thus he (Hammurabi) replied, 'I send you off - go!' Hammurabi said this to him" (l.23-25). In contrast to Laban, there is no feigned obsequy to lure the envoy to enjoy further hospitality, no doubt an otherwise common social gesture for guests in general (cf. Judg 19:4-9[114]). Hammurabi's unorthodox reply becomes clear later when it is revealed that he is not intending to send with the envoy the troops which were requested. A protest by fellow Marians prompts Hammurabi to suggest that the envoy wait five more days

---

[112] F. Thureau-Dangin, "Textes de Mari," *RA* 33 (1936) 169-179.

[113] See also the OB envoys of Rim-Sin, unduly detained in the Eshnunna court and counselled by Rim-Sin to speak to the king as follows: "You have detained us a long time [five months according to l.20], and you have not granted us the water (rights). But our master has written us to leave, (so) give us our instructions (*wu''ianniāti*), that we may leave." (M. Rowton, "Watercourses and Water Rights," *JCS* 21 (1967) 269 l.31-34).

[114] The contrast is significant also: where the messenger requests permission to depart, a simple guest may leave when he desires, having fulfilled, of course, any customary demands required of a guest.

and then the envoy will see for himself that the troops are unnecessary (l.26-45).

In general, then, a royal messenger's stay of a fortnight or so may not have been unusual in the light of normal protocol and hospitality. Ramses II recommends that his messengers be returned by the Hittite king and cites as an example his own (what he considers exemplary) treatment of the Hittite envoys who were allowed to return after "the fourteen days which Kulaziti spent here in Egypt, the twenty days which Zitwalla spent in Egypt" (*CTH* 165.1.r4-7). If this is true in the large sphere of Mediterranean politics, it is likely in the smaller world of northern Mesopotamia that the messenger from Kurda (Gimil-Shamash) who received silver in Mari in one month and at least 18 days later (and perhaps as many as 45 days later) received another disbursement of silver is probably here representing Kurda on two separate embassies (*ARM* VII 164.1 168.2). This is certainly the case with Asdi-Nihim, a messenger of Ishme-Dagan, who receives silver in Mari on two separate occasions four months apart (*ARM* VII 159.6 173.6) and Niluk from Suna who also receives silver at an interval of four months (*ARM* VII 113.17 281.2).

5.5 SUMMARY

The ***mal'āk*** and the ***mār šipri*** were not neutral figures, but could stand as defendants of those who sent them, explicating their messages, arguing on their behalf. They could be resources available for questioning in order to clarify written documents or confirm the veracity of reports. The questioning of a messenger was even a necessary aspect of long distance communication, and it required a substantial amount of tact and diplomatic acumen to endure the sometimes rigorous encounters between potentate and messenger representing his absent master.

Before responding to the messenger, a monarch occasionally turned to a trusted confidant or a council in order to elicit advice. This action was a motif in several narrative accounts, all of which were in the context of relationships between vassals and suzerains (or potential), where the decision focused on whether or not to submit as a vassal to the demands of another, or to accept the submission of another.

Expressions of joy upon hearing the message are probably to be understood as encompassing the generous care for the needs of the messenger: banqueting and gift-giving is the appropriate response to express appreciation for the news which a royal envoy brings. Dining in the presence of the royal host himself marked the highest expression of hospitality, accompanied by the meeting of all of the envoy's needs. Provisions of commodities included garments and shoes, in addition to food, wine, and oil. Gifts of silver, varying from envoy to envoy even within the same delegation, are attested from the third to the first millennium B.C.

Expressions of hospitality had to compete with the necessity of returning the messenger quickly to the one who sent him. Normally, the messenger's errand can be assumed to be a round-trip, for he not only dispenses but also collects information: at the least, the one who sent the messenger wishes to know how the message was received. Those who send messengers reiterate persistently that they wish the messenger to be returned quickly. Detaining a messenger is a sign of an uncomfortable relationship between correspondents, for such detention often was used as a means of coercion. Indeed, among enemies, messengers may not be returned at all. An acceptable length of stay for messengers in a normal international embassy may have been about a fortnight, but crises or emergencies could shorten such a stay, while special festivities could no doubt lengthen it. The stay was terminated when the envoy requested permission to depart, amidst polite protestations by the host under normal circumstances.

CONCLUSION

In this final section, the highlights of the preceding pages will be recapitulated, painting a composite summary portrait of the *mār šipri* and *mal'āk*. Behavior and customs relating to such individuals were certainly variable with time and place and we do not wish to appear to paint a misleading picture. However, the following observations seem to capture the essential elements regarding the role of the messenger (*mār šipri* and *mal'āk*) in the ancient Semitic World, based upon the fragmentary evidence presently available.

When one sent a messenger, one's primary expectations centered upon the messenger's truthfulness and speed. In addition to general reliability, it was also explicitly desirable that he be articulate. A messenger's independent social status could play a significant role in his selection, particularly when the sender was of royal status. In such a case, nobles and merchants figured prominently as royal envoys. Presumably individuals of greater age prompted more respect as envoys, and those with an established reputation as envoys were in constant demand. Indeed, some individual royal messengers acted as international envoys over an extended period of time. One might even send one's own son as an authoritative representative.

Experience and family connections might play a role in obtaining royal commissions, but the ability to read and write, a good memory, or ability in foreign languages was not necessary (although desirable) to obtain such a commission. The type of message which one sent also determined the selection of the messenger, for good news seems to have been associated with one's best envoys, while less appealing tidings could presumably be sent through expendable individuals. Messengers who travelled between hostile powers certainly could have no expectations of hospitable receptions. The selection of a messenger could also be left up to the palace bureaucracy when the message to be carried could be effectively transmitted by any individual.

Messengers could be conscripted into service by the palace. In such cases, it is unlikely that the messenger had any choice in accepting or declining the commission. However, in other contexts it may be possible that messengers could decline a commission. The only known case of a messenger actually depicted as volunteering for a commission is the biblical Ahimaaz.

It is not possible to exhaustively detail all occasions on which messengers were despatched. However, frequent protestations of innocence or accusations of neglect underscore certain occasions on which messengers were expected to appear. In particular, these moments tended to be the crucial moments of life (whether positive or negative): illness, death, accession to the throne, marriage and celebrations.

Once the messenger was selected, the actual commissioning was described differently in two distinct genres. In literary descriptions, the stress was upon the oral commissioning of the messenger, described with vocatives of address, imperatives of speech or movement or bowing. Characteristic of West Semitic literature was the phrase, "Thus says PN", while characteristic of Akkadian was the statement, "I will send you". On the other hand, the evidence of the letters emphasized less the verbal commissioning of the messenger and more the written document entrusted to the envoy. The envoy could be ignorant of the contents of the written document which he delivered.

Before departing, one would ascertain the propitious days on which to depart, seeking to guarantee a safe journey through omens, ritual and prayers. Finally, provided with authenticating documents where necessary and rations for an extended journey, the messenger would be ready to depart at any time of day or night deemed appropriate.

The actual journey of the messenger was not an enviable enterprise, for he was compelled to travel over difficult terrain with less than desirable road conditions. Travelling as a solitary messenger was quite normal, but travelling in groups somewhat minimized danger from brigands. Escorts provided assistance in travelling through foreign territory, for which passports were a necessary element in guaranteeing a relatively unhindered passage. But in spite of all precautions, abuse of messengers on the road was not an uncommon experience. Attempts to stabilize information transfer by the establishment of posts at regular intervals are already apparent in the third millennium B.C. and reappear in the centuries which follow. But more often than not messengers found lodging and food at taverns and in the private dwellings of any who would offer hospitality.

All types of transportation were utilized. In addition to one's own feet, the messenger employed boats on the Mesopotamian waterways and ships on the Mediterranean, supplemented on land by the ass and horse (often with chariot).

Literary descriptions of arriving messengers in West Semitic literature depict the event as one fraught with emotion, a phenomenon echoed in the omen literature of Mesopotamia. A significant literary topos attested in the West was the depiction of scenes where an individual fails to discern accurately the news which was about to be delivered by the arriving messenger, the individual in question behaving in a manner inappropriate to the import of the actual message.

Messengers might arrive at all hours of the day or night, depending on the urgency of the despatch or other factors such as a need for cover of darkness in clandestine activities. Where a messenger was sent to an individual otherwise unknown to the messenger, he would be provided with a description of the person to whom he was sent and other details which would assist him in locating the addressee.

International and governmental messengers would have their arrivals announced in advance of their coming, if a sophisticated post system was present. Hospitality would greet the ambassador who was welcome, while the unwelcome messenger would find his way blocked by bureaucratic impasse or even deliberate abuse. The messengers of hostile parties were not even allowed to enter the city gates. If well-received, appropriate signs of respect were exchanged between messenger and the recipient of the message, prostration being performed to whichever of the two represented the socially more elevated individual. If the messenger bowed, he nevertheless resumed the upright position in the actual delivery of his message.

A messenger could bring along his own translator in international contexts, but he could generally expect foreign courts to have available adequate interpreters as well. When delivering his message, the messenger began by identifying himself and then usually proceeded to deliver his message as it was spoken by the one who sent him. To insure that the messenger accurately relayed the message which had been entrusted to him, the written document which he carried would be read and confirmed by a scribe on the receiving end.

But the messenger's task was not the *verbatim* delivery of a message. Rather, he was commissioned as a defendant of the one who sent him, empowered to argue, reason and answer questions on his sender's behalf. The messenger was thus required to be a diplomat in often tense and unanticipated circumstances, representing his sender's interests with tact, truth and firmness.

Before responding to a messenger, a monarch would often turn to a council to obtain advice in the light of the message which had been delivered. If the message was a favorable one, expressions of appreciation would be accompanied by the wining and dining of the messenger. The generous giving of gifts and banqueting in the king's presence was the highest mark of hospitality.

But such hospitality had to compete with the necessity of quickly returning the messenger to his sender. A messenger's task was not complete until he had returned to his sender with the response to the message. The detention of messengers was an accusation which was ardently avoided by amicable allies. The messenger's stay was brought to an end when he requested permission to leave, a request which was granted usually after polite protestations by the host.

BIBLIOGRAPHY

This bibliography is severely truncated for two reasons. 1) Reproducing the bibliography of all texts in Akkadian in which messengers appear would result in a list of most text editions which have been published in the field, thus indefensibly lengthening this section. More helpful in this regard is the appended index of texts cited in this work. 2) Not all secondary works cited in this book have been included below, particularly if cited only once and not of general relevance to the larger subject.

Adcock, F. and Mosley, D. J. *Diplomacy in Ancient Greece*. London: Thames and Hudson, 1975.

Albright, W. F. "The Lachish Cosmetic Burner and Esther 2:12," *A Light Unto My Path: Old Testament Studies in Honor of Jacob M. Myers*. Eds. H. N. Bream, R. D. Heim, & Cary A. Moore. Philadelphia: Temple University, 1974, 25-32.

_____. "Cuneiform Material for Egyptian Prosopography 1500-1200 B.C.," *JNES* 5 (1946) 7-25.

Ali, F. A. *Sumerian Letters: Two Collections from the Old Babylonian Schools*. Ph.D. dissertation, University of Pennsylvania, 1964. (University Microfilms 64-10,343)

Arnaud, D. *Emar - Textes sumériens et accadiens*. 3 Volumes. Paris: Recherche sur les Civilisations, 1985-1986.

Aro, J. and Nougayrol, J. "Trois nouveaux receuils d'haruspicine ancienne," *RA* 67 (1973) 41-56.

Artzi, P. "El Amarna Document #30," *Actes du XXIXe Congrès Internationale des Orientalistes - Assyriologie*. Paris: L'Asiathèque, 1975.

Bakir, 'Abd El-Moḥsen. *Egyptian Epistolography from the Eighteenth to the Twenty-first Dynasty*. Cairo: Institut Français d'Archéologie Orientale du Caire, 1970.

Beckman, G. "Mesopotamians and Mesopotamian Learning at Hattusha," *JCS* 35 (1983) 97-114.

Beit-Arieh, Y. "A Border Fortress in the Eastern Negev," *Qadmoniot* 19 (1986) 31-39. (Hebrew)

Berlin, A. *Enmerkar and Ensuhkešdanna.* Philadelphia: University Museum, 1979.

Boissier, A. *Documents assyriens rélatifs aux présages.* Paris: Émile Bouillon, 1894.

Boneschi, P. "Is '*malak*' an Arabic Word?" *JAOS* 65 (1945) 107-111.

Bordreuil, P. "Quatre documents en cunéiformes alphabétiques mal connus ou inédits," *Semitica* 32 (1982) 5-14.

Borger, R. *Die Inschriften Asarhaddons Königs von Assyrien. AfO Beiheft* 9. Graz: 1956.

Caminos, R. *Late Egyptian Miscellanies.* London: Oxford University, 1954.

Casson, L. *Travel in the Ancient World.* London: George Allen & Unwin, 1974.

Castellino, G. R. *Two Shulgi Hymns. Studi Semitici* 42. Rome: Istituto di Studi del Vicino Oriente, 1972.

Chang, Kuk Won. *Dichtungen der Zeit Tukulti-Ninurtas I. von Assyrien.* Europäische Hochschulschriften 5.27, Asiatische und Africanische Studien 27. Frankfurt am Main: Peter D. Lang, 1979.

Chase, D. "A Note on an Inscription from Kuntillet 'Ajrūd," *BASOR* 246 (1982) 63-67.

Civil, M. "Enlil and Ninlil: The Marriage of Sud," *JAOS* 103 (1983) 43-66.

_____. "The 'Message of Lú-dingir-ra to His Mother' and a Group of Akkado-Hittite Proverbs," *JNES* 23 (1964) 1-11.

Cohen, S. *Enmerkar and the Lord of Aratta.* Ph.D. disseration, University of Pennsylvania, 1973. (University Microfilms 73-24,127)

Cooper, J. S. *The Curse of Agade.* Baltimore & London: Johns Hopkins University, 1983.

Cooper, J. S. and Hempel, W. "The Sumerian Sargon Legend," *JAOS* 103 (1983) 67-82.

Cross, F. M. "A Literate Soldier: Lachish Letter III," *Biblical and Related Studies Presented to Samuel Iwry*. Ed. A. Kort and S. Morschauser. Winona Lake, IN.: Eisenbrauns, 1985, 41-47.

____. "Two Notes on Palestinian Inscriptions of the Persian Age," *BASOR* 193 (1969) 21-24.

Crown, Alan D. "Tidings and Instructions: How News Travelled in the Ancient Near East," *JESHO* 17 (1974) 244-271.

Cunchillos, J.-L. "*La'ika*, *mal'āk* et *mĕlā'kāh* en sémitique nord-occidental," *Rivista di Studi Fenici* 10 (1982) 153-162.

Dalley, S. *Mari and Karana*. London & New York: Longman, 1984.

Dalley, S. and Postgate, J. N. *The Tablets from Fort Shalmaneser*. Oxford: Alden, 1984.

Dalley, S., Walker, C. B. F., and Hawkins, J. D. *The Old Babylonian Tablets from Tell Al Rimah*. London: British School of Archaeology in Iraq, 1976.

Dietrich, M. and Loretz, O. "Ug. *BŚR* 'Botschaft bringen, senden" und die Nomina *BŚRT TBŚR* 'Froh-Botschaft'," *UF* 14 (1982) 303-306.

Dietrich, M., Loretz, O., and SanMartín, J. *Die Keilalphabetischen Texte aus Ugarit*. AOAT 24/1. Neukirchen-Vluyn: Neukirchener, 1976.

van Dijk, J. *LUGAL UD ME-LÁM-BI NIR-GÁL*. Vol.1. Leiden: E. J. Brill, 1983.

Donner, H. and Röllig, W. *Kanaanäisch und aramäische Inschriften*. Wiesbaden: Harrassowitz, 1962-4.

Dossin, G. "Adaššum et Kirḫum dans des textes de Mari," *RA* 66 (1972) 111-130.

____. "Aplahanda, roi de Carkemish," *RA* 35 (1938) 115-121.

Driver, G. R. *Canaanite Myths and Legends*. Edinburgh: T & T Clark, 1956.

Driver, S. R. *Notes on the Hebrew Text and the Topography of the Books of Samuel*. Second Edition. Oxford: Oxford University, 1912.

Ebeling, E. "Kultische Texte aus Assur," *Or* 22 (1953) 25-46.

____. *Neubabylonische Briefe*. *ABAW* 30; 1949.

_____. *Neubabylonische Briefe aus Uruk.* Beiträge zur Keilschriftforschung und Religionsgeschichte des Vorderen Orients 3. Berlin: 1930-1934.

Edel, E. *Ägyptische Ärzte und ägyptische Medezin am hethitischen Königshof.* Rheinisch-Westfälische Akademie der Wissenschaften G 205. Göttingen; 1976.

_____. "KUB III 63, Ein Brief aus der Heiratskorrespondenz Ramses' II.," *JKF* 2 (1953) 263-273.

_____. "Neue keilschriftliche Umschreibungen ägyptischer Namen aus den Boğazköytexten," *JNES* 7 (1948) 11-24.

_____. "Die Stelen Amenophis' II. aus Karnak und Memphis," *ZDPV* 69 (1953) 97-176.

_____. "Die Abfassungszeit des Briefes KBo I 10 (Hattušil - Kadašman-Ellil) und seine Bedeutung für die Chronologie Ramses' II," *JCS* 12 (1958) 131-133.

_____. "Die Teilnehmer der ägyptisch-hethitischen Friedensgesandschaft im 21. Jahr Ramses' II," *Or* 38 (1969) 177-186.

_____. "Weitere Briefe aus der Hieratskorrespondenz Ramses' II.," *Geschichte und Altes Testament.* Tübingen: J. C. B. Mohr, 1953.

Edzard, D. O. and Wilcke, C. "Die Hendursanga-Hymne," *Kramer Anniversary Volume. AOAT* 25. Ed. B. L. Eichler. Neukirchen: Neukirchener, 1976, 139-176.

Eidem, Jesper. "News from the Eastern Front: The Evidence from Tell Shemshara," *Iraq* 47 (1985) 83-107.

Fales, F. "New Assyrian Letters from the Kuyunjik Collection," *AfO* 27 (1980) 136-153.

Falkenstein, A. *Die Haupttypen der sumerischen Beschwörung literarisch untersucht. LSS* 1. Leipzig; 1931.

Farber-Flügge, G. *Der Mythos "Inanna und Enki" unter besonderer Berücksichtigung der Liste der* ME. Studia Pohl 10. Rome: Biblical Insititute, 1973.

Finet, A. "Le *ṣuḫārum* à Mari," *ABAW* 75 (1972) 65-72.

Fitzmyer, J. A. *The Aramaic Inscriptions of Sefîre. BibOr* 19. Rome: Pontifical Bible Institute, 1967.

Follet, R. "Deuxième bureau et information diplomatique dans l'Assyrie des Sargonides - quelques notes," *RSO* 32 (1957) 61-81.

Forbes, R. J. "Land Transport and Road-Building," *Studies in Ancient Technology*. Vol.2 (second edition). Leiden: E. J. Brill, 1965, 131-192.

Foster, B. "Ea and Ṣaltu," *Essays on the Ancient Near East in Memory of Jacob Joel Finkelstein*. Ed. M. de Jong Ellis. Memoirs of the Connecticut Association of the Arts and Sciences 19; Hamden, CN: Archon Books, 1977, 79-84.

Freedman, D. N. and Willoughby, B. E. *"Mal'āk,"* *Theologisches Wörterbuch zum Alten Testament*. Vol. 4. Ed. G. J. Botterweck, H. Ringgren, and Fabry, H.-J. Stuttgart: W. Kohlhammer, 1984, 887-904.

Friedrich, J. *Staatsverträge des Hatti-Reiches in hethitischer Sprache. MVAG* 31 (1926), 34 (1934).

_____. "Briefwechsel zwischen Chatti und Babylon," *AO* 24 (1925) 1-32.

Friedrich, J.; Meyer, G. R.; Ungnad, A.; Weidner, E. F. *Die Inschriften vom Tell Halaf. AfO Beiheft* 6. Berlin: 1940.

Gadd, C. J. "Inscribed Prisms of Sargon II from Nimrud," *Iraq* 16 (1954) 173-201.

Gardiner, A. H. *Egyptian Hieratic Texts*. Vol. I/1. Hildesheim: George Olms, 1911.

_____. *The Ḳadesh Inscriptions of Ramesses II*. Oxford: Oxford University, 1960.

Gelb, I. J. "The Word for Dragoman in the Ancient Near East," *Glossa* 2 (1968) 93-104.

Gevaryahu, H. M. I. "The Speech of Rab-Shakeh to the People on the Wall of Jerusalem," *Studies in the Bible Presented to Professor M. H. Segal*. Ed. J. M. Grintz and J. Liver. Jerusalem: Kiryat Sepher, 1964, 94-102. (Hebrew)

Gibson, J. C. L. *Canaanite Myths and Legends*. Edinburgh: T & T Clark, 1978.

Ginsberg, H. L. "Baal's Two Messengers," *BASOR* 95 (1944) 25-30.

Goedicke, H. *The Report of Wenamun*. Baltimore and London: Johns Hopkins University, 1975.

Goetze, A. "A New Letter from Ramesses to Hattusilis," *JCS* 1 (1947) 241-251.

_____. *Kizzuwatna and the Problem of Hittite Geography*. *YOS* 22. New Haven: Yale, 1940.

_____. *Madduwattaš*. *MVAG* 32. Leipzig: 1927.

_____. *Old Babylonian Omen Texts*. *YOS* 10. New Haven and London: Yale University, 1947.

Greene, J. T. *The Old Testament Prophet as Messenger in the Light of Ancient Near Eastern Messengers and Messages*. Unpublished Ph.D. dissertation, Boston University, 1980. (University Microfilms 8024188)

Greengus, S. *Old Babylonian Tablets from Ischali and Vicinity*. Nederlands Historisch-Archaeologisch Instituut te Istanbul, 1979.

_____. *Studies in Old Babylonian Texts from Ischali and Vicinity*. *Bibliotheca Mesopotamica* 19; Malibu: Undena, 1986.

Greenstein, E. "Trans-Semitic Idiomatic Equivalency and the Derivation of Hebrew *ml'kh*," *UF* 11 (1979) 329-336.

Gruber, Mayer I. *Aspects of Nonverbal Communication in the Ancient Near East*. *Studia Pohl* 12/I-II. Rome: Biblical Institute, 1980.

Gurney, O. R. *The Middle Babylonian Legal and Economic Texts from Ur*. Oxford: Alden, 1983.

_____. "Texts from Dūr-Kurigalzu," *Iraq* 11 (1949) 131-142.

_____. "The Sultantepe Tablets," *AnSt* 10 (1960) 105-131.

Güterbock, H. "Bruchstück eines altababylonischen Naram-Sin-Epos," *AfO* 13 (1939-1941) 46-50.

_____. "The Deeds of Šuppiluliuma as Told by His Son, Muršili II," *JCS* 10 (1956) 75-130.

Helck, W. "Ägypten - Die Mythologie der alten Ägypter," *Wörterbuch der Mythologie*. Vol. 1. Ed. H.W. Haussig. Stuttgart: Ernst Klett, 1965, 313-406.

Herdner, A. *Corpus des tablettes en cunéiformes alphabétiques*. *MRS* 10. Paris: Imprimerie Nationale, 1963.

Herman, A. "Jübel bei der Audienz," *ZAS* 90 (1963) 49-66.

Holmes, Y. L. "The Messengers of the Amarna Letters," *JAOS* 75 (1975) 376-381.

Hruška, B. *Der Mythenadler Anzu in Literatur und Vorstellung des alten Mesopotamien*. Budapest: 1975.

Hunger, H. *Spätbabylonische Texte aus Uruk*. Teil I. *ADFU* 9. Berlin: Gebr. Mann, 1976.

Hutter, M. *Altorientalische Vorstellungen von der Unterwelt. Orbis Biblicus et Orientalis* 63. Göttingen: Vandenhoeck & Ruprecht, 1985.

Irvin, D. *Mytharion*. *AOAT* 32. Neukirchen-Vluyn: Neukirchener, 1978.

Jacobsen, T. *The Harps That Once . . .: Sumerian Poetry in Translation*. New Haven: Yale, 1987.

Kaiser, O. "Zum Formular der in Ugarit gefundenen Briefe," *ZDPV* 86 (1970) 10-23.

Keel, O. *Vogel als Bote*. *Orbis Biblicus et Orientalis* 14. Göttingen: Vandenhoeck and Ruprecht, 1977.

Kempinski, A. and Košac, S. "Der Išmeriga-Vertrag," *WO* 5/2 (1970) 191-217.

Klauber, E. G. *Politisch-religiöse Texte aus der Sargonidenzeit*. Leipzig: 1913.

Klein, J. *Three Shulgi Hymns*. Ramat-Gan, Israel: Bar-Ilan University, 1981.

_____. "Shulgi and Ishmedagan," *Beer-Sheva II*. Ed. Michael Cogan. Jerusalem: Magnes, 1985, 7*-38*.

Klengel, H. "Zum Brief eines Königs von Hanigalbat," *Or* 32 (1963) 280-291.

Knudtzon, J. A. *Assyrische Gebete an den Sonnengott*. Leipzig: Eduard Pfeiffer, 1893.

_____. *Die El-Amarna-Tafeln*. *VAB* 2. Leipzig: J.C. Hinrichs, 1915.

Komoróczy, G. "Die Beziehungen zwischen Mesopotamien und dem iranischen Hochland in der sumerischen Dichtung," *Mesopotamien und seine Nachbarn*, 87-96. XXVe Rencontre Assyriologique Internationale. Berlin: Dietrich Reimer, 1978.

Korošec, V. "Relations internationales d'après les lettres de Mari," *La Civilization de Mari*. XVe Rencontre Assyriologique Internationale. Paris: Sociéte d'Édition "Belles Lettres," 15 (1967), 114-149.

Kramer, S. N. "Poets and Psalmists: Goddesses and Theologians," *The Legacy of Sumer*. ed. Denise Schmandt-Besserat. Malibu: Undena, 1976, 3-22.

Kraus, F. R., ed. *Altbabylonische Briefe*. 11 Volumes. Leiden: E. J. Brill, 1964-1986.

Kühne, C. *Die Chronologie der internationalen Korrespondenz von El-Amarna*. *AOAT* 17. Neukirchen-Vluyn: Neukirchener, 1973.

Kümmel, H. M. *Nichtliterarische Texte in Akkadische Sprache*. *KBo* XXVIII. Berlin: Gebr. Mann, 1985.

Kupper, J.-R. *Documents administratifs de la salle 135 du palais de Mari*. *ARM* XXII. Paris: Éditions Recherche sur les Civilisations, 1983.

____. "L'usage de l'argent à Mari," *Zikir Šumim - Assyriological Studies Presented to F.R. Kraus on his Seventieth Birthday*. Ed. G. Van Driel, Th.J.H. Krispijn, M. Stol, K.R. Veenhof. Leiden: E.J. Brill, 1982, 163-172.

Kutscher, R. and Wilcke, C. "Eine Ziegel-Inschrift des Königs Takil-ilišśu von Malgium, gefunden in Isin und Yale," *ZA* 68 (1978) 95-128.

Labat, R. *Traité akkadien de diagnostics et pronostics médicaux*. Leiden: E.J. Brill, 1951.

____. "Un almanach babylonien," *RA* 38 (1941) 13-40.

____. *Hémérologies et ménologies d'Assur*. Paris: Librairie d'Amérique et d'Orient, 1939.

Lackenbacher, S. "Nouveaux documents d'Ugarit," *RA* 76 (1982) 141-156.

Laessøe, J. "IM 62100: A Letter from Tell Shemshara," *Studies in Honor of Benno Landsberger on his Seventy-fifth Birthday April 21,1965*. *AS* 16. Chicago: University of Chicago, 1965, 189-196.

____. *The Shemshara Tablets*. Copenhagen: i kommission hos Ejnar Munksgaard, 1959.

Lambert, W. G. *Babylonian Wisdom Literature*. Oxford: Clarendon, 1960.

____. "Nebuchadnezzar, King of Justice," *Iraq* 27 (1965) 1-11.

Lambert, W. G. and Millard, A. R. *Atrahasīs - The Babylonian Story of the Flood*. Oxford: Clarendon, 1969.

Landsberger, B. and Jacobsen, T. "An Old Babylonian Charm Against Merḫu," *JNES* 14 (1955) 14-21.

Langdon, S. *Babylonian Menologies and the Semitic Calendars*. Oxford: Oxford University, 1935.

_____. *Die neubabylonische Königsinschriften*. *VAB* IV. Leipzig: J. C. Hinrichs, 1912.

Langdon, S. & Gardiner, A. H. "The Treaty of Alliance between Hattušili, King of the Hittites, and the Pharaoh Ramesses II of Egypt," *JEA* 6 (1920) 179-205.

Laroche, E. *Catalogue des textes hittites*. *Études et Commentaires* 75. Paris: Éditions Klincksieck, 1971.

Larsen, M.T. *Old Assyrian Caravan Procedures*. Istanbul: Nederlands Historisch-Archaeologisch Instituut in het Nabije Oosten, 1967.

Leemans, W. F. "The *Asīru*," *RA* 55 (1961) 57-76.

_____. *Foreign Trade in the Old Babylonian Period*. Leiden: E. J. Brill, 1960.

_____. *The Old Babylonian Merchant*. Studia et Documenta 3. Leiden: E. J. Brill, 1950.

Lewy, H. "Notes on the Political Organization of Asia Minor at the Time of the Old Assyrian Texts," *Or* 33 (1964) 181-198.

_____. "On the Historical Background of the Correspondence of Bahdi-Lim," *Or* 25 (1956) 324-352.

Lewy, J. "On Some Institutions of the Old Assyrian Empire," *HUCA* 27 (1956) 1-79.

Lichtheim, M. *Ancient Egyptian Literature*. 3 Volumes. Berkeley and Los Angeles: University of California, 1973-1980.

Littauer, M. A. and Crouwel, J. H. *Wheeled Vehicles and Ridden Animals in the Ancient Near East*. *Handbuch der Orientalistik*, VII.1.B1; Lieden: E. J. Brill, 1979.

Loewenstamm, S. "Prostration from Afar in Ugaritic, Akkadian and Hebrew," *BASOR* 188 (1967) 41-43.

Luckenbill, D.D. *The Annals of Sennacherib*. *OIP* 2. Chicago: University of Chicago, 1924.

_____. "Hittite Treaties and Letters," *AJSLL* 37 (1921) 161-211.

MacDonald, John "The Identification of *Bazahātu* in the Mari Letters," *RA* 69 (1975) 137-145.

_____. "The Role and Status of the *Ṣubāru* in the Mari Correspondence," *JAOS* 96 (1976) 57-68.

_____. "The Supreme Warrior Caste in the Ancient Near East," *Oriental Studies Presented to Benedikt S. J. Isserlin*. Ed. R. Y. Ebied and M. J. L. Young. Leiden: Brill, 1980, 39-71.

Malamat, A. "Silver, Gold and Precious Stones from Hazor - Trade and Trouble in a New Mari Document," *Essays in Honor of Yigael Yadin*. Ed. G. Vermes and J. Neusner. New Jersey: Allanheld, Osmun and Co., 1983, 71-79.

Margalit, B. "The Messengers of Woe to Danʾel: A Reconstruction and Interpretation of KTU 1.19:II:27-48," *UF* 15 (1983) 105-117.

Marty, J. "Les Formules de salutation," *Mélanges syriens offerts à Monsieur René Dussaud*. Vol. II. Paris: Librairie Orientaliste Paul Geuthner, 1939, 844-855.

Mayer, Walter *Nuzi Studien I*. *AOAT* 205/1. Neukirchen-Vluyn: Neukirchener, 1978.

McCarter, P. K. *I Samuel*. *AB* 8. Garden City, N.Y.: Doubleday, 1980.

_____. *II Samuel*. *AB* 9. Garden City, N.Y.: Doubleday, 1984.

McEwen, G. J. P. *The Late Babylonian Tablets in the Royal Ontario Museum*. *ROM Cuneiform Texts* II. Toronto: Royal Ontario Museum, 1982.

McNeil, R. *The 'Messenger Texts' of the Third Ur Dynasty*. Ph.D. dissertation, University of Pennsylvania, 1970.

Meier, G. *Maqlû*. *AfO Beiheft* 2 (1937).

Meissner, B. "Die Beziehungen Ägyptens zum Hattireiche nach hattischen Quellen," *ZDMG* 72 (1918) 32-64.

Meyer, G. R. "Zwei neue Kizzuwatna-Verträge," *MIO* 1 (1953) 108-124.

Michalowski, P. "The Neo-Sumerian Silver Ring Texts," *Syro-Mesopotamian Studies* 2/3 (1978) 1-15.

Michel, E. "Die Assur-Texte Salmanassars III. (858-824)," WO 2/2 (1955) 137-157.

Montgomery, J. A. *The Books of Kings*. *ICC*. Edinburgh: T & T Clark, 1951.

Moorey, P. R. S. "Pictorial Evidence for the History of Horse-Riding in Iraq before the Kassite Period," *Iraq* 32 (1972) 36-50.

Moran, W. "Additions to the Amarna Lexicon," *Or* 53 (1984) 297-302.

_____. "The Ancient Near Eastern Background of the Love of God in Deuteronomy," *CBQ* 25 (1963) 77-87.

Mosley, D. *Envoys and Diplomacy in Ancient Greece*. Wiesbaden: Franz Steiner, 1973.

Munn-Rankin, J. M. "Diplomacy in Western Asia in the Early Second Millennium B.C.," *Iraq* 18 (1956) 68-110.

Na'aman, N. "East-West Diplomatic Relations in the Days of Zimri-Lim," *RA* 75 (1981) 171-172.

Nougayrol, J. "Une amulette de Syrie et un nouvel 'oeil'," *RA* 64 (1970) 67-68.

_____. "'Oiseau' ou oiseau?" *RA* 61 (1967) 23-38.

_____. *Palais royal d'Ugarit*. Volumes III-IV, VI. Paris: Imprimerie Nationale, 1935, 1956, 1970.

_____. "Textes et documents figurés," *RA* 41 (1947) 23-51.

_____. "Textes hépatoscopiques d'époque ancienne," *RA* 44 (1950) 1-40.

Numelin, R. *The Beginnings of Diplomacy*. Copenhagen: Ejnar Munksgaard, 1950.

Oppenheim, A. L. *Ancient Mesopotamia - Portrait of a Dead Civilization*. Revised by E. Reiner. Chicago: University of Chicago, 1977.

_____. "The Archives of the Palace of Mari," *JNES* 11 (1952) 129-139.

_____. "The Archives of the Palace of Mari II," *JNES* 13 (1954) 141-148.

_____. *Letters from Mesopotamia*. Chicago: University of Chicago, 1967.

_____. "A Note on the Scribes in Mesopotamia," *Studies in Honor of Benno Landsberger on his Seventy-fifth Birthday*. *AS* 16. Chicago: University of Chicago, 1965, 253-256.

Pardee, D. "Further Studies in Ugaritic Epistolography," *AfO* 31 (1984) 213-230.

_____. *Handbook of Ancient Hebrew Letters*. Chico, CA: Scholars, 1982.

Parker, B. "Administrative Tablets from the North-west Palace, Nimrud," *Iraq* 23 (1961) 15-67.

Parpola, S. *Letters from Assyrian Scholars to the Kings Esarhaddon and Assurbanipal*. *AOAT* 5 (Part 1: Texts; Part 2: Commentary and Appendices). Neukirchen-Vluyn: Neukirchener, 1970, 1983.

Parrot, A. and Dossin, G. ed. *Archives royales de Mari*. Volumes 1-19. Paris: Imprimerie Nationale, 1950-1979.

Petschow, H. *Mittelbabylonische Rechts- und Wirtschaftsurkunden der Hilprecht-Sammlung Jena*. *ASAW* 64/4. Leipzig: 1974.

Pfeiffer, R. H. *State Letters of Assyria*. *AOS* 6. New Haven, CN: American Oriental Society, 1935.

Pfeiffer, R. H. and Speiser, E.A. *One Hundred New Selected Nuzi Texts*. *AASOR* 16. New Haven: 1936.

Piepkorn, A.C. *Historical Prism Inscriptions of Ashurbanipal I*. *AS* 5. Chicago: University of Chicago, 1933.

Pohl, P. A. *Neubabylonische Rechtsurkunden*. *AnOr* 8-9. Rome: Pontifical Bible Institute, 1933, 1934.

Postgate, J. N. *Taxation and Conscription in the Assyrian Empire*. *Studia Pohl Series Maior* 3. Rome: Biblical Institute, 1974.

Radau, H. *Letters to Cassite Kings from the Temple Archives of Nippur*. *BE* 17/I. Philadelphia: 1908.

Reiner, E. "Fortune-Telling in Mesopotamia," *JNES* 19 (1960) 23-35.

_____. "Lipšur Litanies," *JNES* 15 (1956) 129-149.

_____. *Šurpu*. *AfO Beiheft* 11. Graz: 1958.

Römer, W. *Das sumerische Kurzepos >Bilgameš und Akka<*. *AOAT* 209/1. Neukirchen-Vluyn: Neukirchener, 1980.

Rowton, M. "The Material from Western Asia and the Chronology of the Nineteenth Dynasty," *JNES* 25 (1966) 240-258.

_____. "Watercourses and Water Rights in the Official Correspondence from Larsa and Isin," *JCS* 21 (1967) 267-274.

Sachs, A. "Two Notes on the Taanach and Amarna Letters," *AfO* 12 (1937-1939) 371-373.

Saggs, H. W. F. "The Nimrud Letters," *Iraq* 17 (1955) 21-50; 126-154; 18 (1956) 40-50; 20 (1958) 182-212; 21 (1959) 158-179; 25 (1963) 70-80; 27 (1965) 17-32; 28 (1966) 177-191; 36 (1974) 199-221.

Salonen, E. *Die Grüss- und Hoflichkeitsformeln in babylonisch-assyrischen Briefe*. *StOr* 38; 1967.

Sauren, H. "Der Weg nach Aratta," *Wirtschaft und Gesellschaft im alten Vorderasien*. Ed. J. Harmatta and G. Komoróczy. Budapest: Akadémiai Kiadó, 1976, 137-144.

Schaeffer, C. F. A. *Ugaritica V*. Paris: Imprimerie Nationale, 1968

Scheil, V. *Actes juridiques susiens*. MDP 22 & 23. Paris: Librairie Ernest Leroux, 1930 and 1932.

von Soden, W. "Zu den politischen Korrespondenz des Archivs von Mari," *Or* 21 (1952) 75-86.

Sollberger, E. *The Business and Administrative Correspondence under the Kings of Ur*. *TCS* 1. Locust Valley, N.Y.: J. J. Augustin, 1966.

Speiser, E. A. *Genesis*. *AB* 1. Garden City, N.Y.: Doubleday, 1964.

Steiner, R. and Nims, C. F. "Ashurbanipal and Shamash-shum-ukin: A Tale of Two Brothers from the Aramaic Text in Demotic Script," *RB* 92 (1985) 60-81.

Steinkeller, P. "The Mesopotamian God Kakka," *JNES* 41 (1982) 289-294.

Stowers, S. *Letter Writing in Greco-Roman Antiquity*. Philadelphia: Westminster, 1986.

Streck, M. *Assurbanipal und die letzten assyrischen Könige*. *VAB* 7. Leipzig: J.C. Hinrichs'sche, 1916.

Talon, P. *Textes administratifs des salles "Y" et "Z" du palais de Mari*. *ARM* XXIV.1. Paris: Éditions Recherche sur les Civilisations, 1985.

Thompson, R. C. *The Devils and Evil Spirits of Babylonia*. London: Luzac & Co., 1903-4.

_____. *The Reports of the Magicians and Astrologers of Nineveh and Babylon*. London: Luzac, 1900.

Thureau-Dangin, F. "Les fêtes d'Akītu d'après un texte divinatoire," *RA* 19 (1922) 141-148.

_____. "Une lettre assyrienne à Ras Shamra," *Syria* 16 (1935) 188-193.

_____. "Le rituel pour l'expédition en char," *RA* 21 (1924) 126-137.

Valloggia, M. *Recherche sur les "messagers" (*wpwtyw*) dans les sources égyptiennes profanes*. II Hautes Études Orientales 6. Genève-Paris: Librairie Droz, 1976.

Vanstiphout, H. L. J. "Problems in the Matter of Aratta," *Iraq* 45 (1983) 35-42.

Vater, A. "Narrative Patterns for the Story of Commissioned Communication in the Old Testament," *JBL* 99 (1980) 365-382.

Veenhof, K. R. *Aspects of Old Assyrian Trade and Its Terminology*. Leiden: E. J. Brill, 1972.

_____. "Observations on Some Letters from Mari (ARM 2,124;10,4;43;84;114) with a Note on *tillatum*," *RA* 76 (1982) 119-140.

Weidner, E. F. "Assyrische Beschreibungen der Kriegs-Reliefs Assurbanaplis," *AfO* 8 (1932) 175-203.

_____. "Hof- und Harems-Erlasse assyrischer Könige aus dem 2. Jahrtausend v. Chr.," *AfO* 17 (1954-1956) 257-293.

_____. *Politische Dokumente aus Kleinasien*. *Boghazkoi Studien* 8,9. Leipzig: J. C. Hinrichs, 1923.

White, J. *Light from Ancient Letters*. Philadelphia: Fortress, 1986.

Whiting, R. *Old Babylonian Letters from Tell Asmar*. *AS* 22. Chicago: Oriental Institute, 1987.

Wiseman, D. J. "A New Stela of Aššur-naṣir-pal II," *Iraq* 14 (1952) 24-39.

Zaccagnini, C. *Lo Scambio dei Doni nel Vicino Oriente Durante i Secoli XV-XIII*. Orientis Antiqui Collectio 11. Rome: Centro per le Antichità e la Storia dell'Arte del Vicino Oriente, 1973.

_____. "The Merchant at Nuzi," *Iraq* 39 (1977) 171-189.

Bible

Hebrew

Ugaritic

Aramaic

Akkadian

Sumerian

Hittite

Egyptian